Reading Images

Edited by Julia Thomas

palgrave

First published 2001 by
PALGRAVE
Houndmills, Basingstoke, Hampshire RG21 6XS and
175 Fifth Avenue, New York, N.Y.10010
Companies and representatives throughout the world

PALGRAVE is the new global academic imprint of St. Martin's Press LLC
Scholarly and Reference Division and Palgrave Publishers Ltd (formerly
Macmillan Press Ltd).

ISBN 0–333–76540–0 hardback
ISBN 0–333–76539–7 paperback

This book is printed on paper suitable for recycling and
made from fully managed and sustained forest sources.

A catalogue record for this book is available
from the British Library.

Library of Congress Cataloging-in-Publication Data
Reading Images/edited by Julia Thomas.
    p. cm.—(Readers in cultural criticism)
    Includes bibliographical references and index.
    ISBN 0–333–76540–0 (cloth)—ISBN 0–333–76539–7 (pbk.)
    1. Image (Philosophy). 2. Vision. 3. Gaze. I. Thomas, Julia, 1971–
II. Series.

B105 .I47 R43 2000
12F .35—dc21   00–041492

10   9   8   7   6   5   4   3   2   1
09 08 07 06 05 04 03 02 01 00

Printed and bound in Great Britain by
Creative Print & Design (Wales),
Ebbw Vale

Contents

vi   *Contents*

List of Illustrations

List of Illustrations

General Editor's Preface

Culture is the element we inhabit as subjects.

Culture embraces the whole range of practices, customs and representations of a society. In their rituals, stories and images, societies identify what they perceive as good and evil, proper, sexually acceptable, racially other. Culture is the location of values, and the study of cultures shows how values vary from one society to another, or from one historical moment to the next.

But culture does not exist in the abstract. On the contrary, it is in the broadest sense of the term textual, inscribed in the paintings, operas, sculptures, furnishings, fashions, bus tickets and shopping lists which are the currency of both aesthetic and everyday exchange. Societies invest these artefacts with meanings, until in many cases the meanings are so 'obvious' that they pass for nature. Cultural criticism denaturalises and defamiliarises these meanings, isolating them for inspection and analysis.

The subject is what speaks, or, more precisely, what signifies, and subjects learn in culture to reproduce or to challenge the meanings and values inscribed in the signifying practices of the society that shapes them.

If culture is pervasive and constitutive for us, if it resides in the documents, objects and practices that surround us, if it circulates as the meanings and values we learn and reproduce as good citizens, how in these circumstances can we practise cultural *criticism*, where criticism implies a certain distance between the critic and the culture? The answer is that cultures are not homogeneous; they are not even necessarily coherent. There are always other perspectives, so that cultures offer alternative positions for the subjects they also recruit. Moreover, we have a degree of power over the messages we reproduce. A minor modification changes the script, and may alter the meaning; the introduction of a negative constructs a resistance.

The present moment in our own culture is one of intense debate. Sexual alignments, family values, racial politics, the implications of economic differences are all hotly contested. And positions are taken up not only in explicit discussions at political meetings, on television and in the pub. They are often reaffirmed or challenged implicitly in films and advertisements, horoscopes and lonely-hearts columns. Cultural criticism analyses all these forms in order to assess their hold on our consciousness.

There is no interpretative practice without theory, and the more sophisticated the theory, the more precise and perceptive the reading it makes
possible. Cultural theory is as well defined now as it has ever been, and
as strongly contested as our social values. There could not, in consequence, be a more exciting time to engage in the theory and practice of
Cultural Criticism.

Catherine Belsey
Cardiff University

Acknowledgements

In compiling this anthology I have had the advice and friendship of staff at the Centre for Critical and Cultural Theory, Cardiff University. In particular, I would like to thank Neil Badmington, whose help has been unwavering and invaluable, and Catherine Belsey, who remains a constant source of encouragement and inspiration. Diane Elam led me to Derrida and architecture, while Christa Knellwolf discussed this and other projects over countless cups of coffee. My gratitude also goes to the Leverhulme Trust for financial support that made this project possible, and to my friends and family for their emotional support. As always, I am indebted to Stuart, not only for his incisive comments, but for helping me unwind over late suppers and *Babylon 5*.

The editor and publishers wish to thank the following for permission to use copyright material:

Roland Barthes, 'Ariadne', 'The Family, the Mother', 'The Little Girl', 'The Luminous Rays, Color', 'The Pose', 'That has Been' and 'The Winter Garden Photograph' from *Camera Lucida: Reflections on Photography* by Roland Barthes, trans. Richard Howard, Jonathan Cape. Translation copyright © 1981 by Farrar, Straus & Giroux, Inc., by permission of Random House Group Ltd and Hill and Wang, a division of Farrar, Straus & Giroux, LLC; Jean Baudrillard, for 'Aesthetic Illusion and Virtual Reality', in *Jean Baudrillard Art and Artefact*, ed. N. Zurbrugg (1997), pp. 19–27, by permission of Sage Publications Ltd; Walter Benjamin, 'The Work of Art in the Age of Mechanical Reproduction' from *Illuminations: Essays and Reflections* by Walter Benjamin, Jonathan Cape, and forthcoming, *Selected Writings of Walter Benjamin*, Harvard University Press. Copyright © 1955 by Suhrkamp Verlag, English translation by Harry Zohn, copyright © 1968, renewed 1996 by Harcourt, Inc., by permission of Random House UK, Harcourt, Inc, and Harvard University Press; Norman Bryson, for 'Semiology and Visual Interpretation' in *Visual Theory: Painting and Interpretation* by Norman Bryson, Michael Ann Holly and Keith Moxley, Polity Press (1981), pp. 61–73, by permission of Blackwell Publishers; Rosalind Coward, for material from *Female Desire* by Rosalind Coward, Paladin (1984), pp. 75–82, by permission of HarperCollins Publishers Ltd; Jacques Derrida, for 'Why Peter Eisenman Writes Such Good Books', *Architecture and Urbanism*, August 1988, extra edition, pp. 95–101, by permission of the author; Michel Foucault, 'Las

Meninas' from *The Order of Things* by Michel Foucault, trans. Alan Sheridan-Smith, Tavistock (1970), pp. 3–17. Copyright © 1970 by Random House, Inc., by permission of Routledge and Pantheon Books, a division of Random House, Inc.; and material from *Discipline and Punish: The Birth of the Prison* by Michel Foucault, trans. Alan Sheridan-Smith, Penguin Books (1977), pp. 195–209, Pantheon Books, first published as *Surveiller et punir: Naissance de la Prison* by Editions Gallimard (1975). Copyright © Alan Sheridan, 1977, by permission of Penguin Books Ltd and Georges Borchardt, Inc. on behalf of the author; Richard L. Gregory, for material from *Eye and Brain* by Richard L. Gregory, Weidenfeld & Nicolson (1966), pp. 136–7, 160–76, by permission of The Orion Publishing Group Ltd; bell hooks, for material from *Black Looks: Race and Representation* (1992), pp. 115–31, by permission of South End Press; Julia Kristeva, for material from *Desire in Language: A Semiotic Approach to Literature and Art* by Julia Kristeva (ed.), Leon S. Roudiez, trans. Thomas Gore, Alice Jardine and Leon S. Roudiez, pp. 237–50, 266–9, first published in *Peinture*, 10–11 (1975). Copyright © 1980 by Columbia University Press, by permission of Columbia University Press; Jacques Lacan, material from *Four Fundamental Concepts of Psycho-Analysis* by Jacques Lacan, trans. Alan Sheridan, Hogarth Press, pp. 80–90. Copyright © 1973 by Editions du Seuil. English translation copyright © 1977 by Alan Sheridan, by permission of Random House Group Ltd and W. W. Norton & Company, Inc.; Teresa de Lauretis, for material from *Alice Doesn't: Feminism, Semiotics, Cinema* by Teresa de Lauretis (1984), pp. 37–9, 53–8, by permission of Macmillan Ltd and Indiana University Press; Kobena Mercer, for 'Monster Metaphors: Notes on Michael Jackson's *Thriller*', Screen, 27:1 (1986), 26–43, by permission of *Screen*; Jackie Stacey, for 'Desperately Seeking Difference', *Screen*, 28:1 (1987), 48–61, by permission of *Screen*; Susan Sontag, for 'In Plato's Cave' from *On Photography* by Susan Sontag, Penguin Books (1978), pp. 3–24. Copyright © 1977 by Susan Sontag, by permission of Penguin Books Ltd and Farrar, Straus and Giroux, LLC; Slavoj Žižek, for material from *Looking Awry: An Introduction to Jacques Lacan Through Popular Culture* by Slavoj Žižek (1991), pp. 109–19, by permission of MIT Press.

Every effort has been made to trace the copyright holders but if any have been inadvertently overlooked the publishers will be pleased to make the necessary arrangement at the first opportunity.

1

Introduction

Julia Thomas

When the anthropologist James L. Watson stepped out of his taxi on a trip around Hong Kong in 1989 he was confronted not with the sights of the Anglo-Chinese market town that he had pleasantly anticipated but by a sparkling new American fast-food outlet. His reaction to this encounter Watson describes as 'sensory disorientation', a curious feeling of geographical insecurity and displacement. At first, he is not quite sure where he is, although this is not because what he sees is unfamiliar. Rather, it is the very familiarity of the spectacle, albeit its familiarity in an unusual location, that makes it strange. Turning to his friend, Watson mutters gloomily, 'I didn't fly all the way from Boston to eat at McDonald's!'[1]

The omnipresent golden arches of McDonald's, shining like beacons over the most foreign landscapes, are an apt signifier of what has come to be known (and, ironically, through a sound-bite) as 'visual culture'. We live in a visualised world, a world in which we are bombarded everyday and everywhere with images that appear transglobal, capable of crossing geographical and racial divides, or, as one famous advertisement implied, of 'uniting', hand in virtual hand, people of different age, sex and ethnicity. Such a global community is manifest in Internet technology, which offers world-wide the new experiences and pleasures of cyberspace, an arena where images do not reflect but constitute reality. The image, however, is only one aspect of visual culture, for it also relies on an activity prior to it that both determines and is determined by it: the process of looking itself. Thus, Watson's 'sensory disorientation' is not only caused by a confusion inherent in the visual world but is the effect of an *interaction* with it, a product of the 'senses', of sight. For a split second, seeing itself becomes strange and alien, no longer recording a truth that is anterior to it; the anthropologist has to look twice: he cannot believe his eyes.

Another confrontation with the problems of seeing and the trappings of processed food is described by the French psychoanalyst Jacques Lacan, and bears an uncanny (or perhaps too 'can-ny') relation to Watson's experience. In a rare autobiographical moment, Lacan recounts how, while he was out at sea with a group of fishermen in Brittany, one of them pointed to a small sardine can that glittered in the sun's rays.

'You see that can? Do you see it?' the man taunted, 'Well, it doesn't see you!'[2] The psychoanalyst's distinct lack of amusement at this joke is described in terms reminiscent of Watson's 'sensory disorientation', a feeling of unease with one's surroundings, of being out of place. Here it is the young intellectual himself, who stands out from, and seems strange to, the uneducated and poor fishermen that accompany him. But there is also a way, Lacan argues, in which the fisherman is not funny because he is wrong: the sardine tin *does* look back, in that the very light that enables it to be viewed also positions the viewer as something seen and objectified.

This reciprocal nature of seeing is what Lacan calls the gaze (in French, *le regard*, the look). Conventionally, the word 'gaze' is used to describe a fixed or intent observation performed and controlled by the viewer through the eyes, but Lacan's gaze undermines the very notion of a powerful and controlling spectator. Here is no simple dichotomy between seeing and being seen but unstable roles that conflict and overlap. The subject's place in the specular order is like that of the viewer of Velázquez' painting, *Las Meninas* (Plate 3), who looks at the image but is also placed as its spectacle, the figure that the artist seems to be painting. Indeed, according to Lacan, the gaze is not even dependent on, but split from, the eye because, as opposed to the subjective associations of the anatomical organ, the gaze is on the side of the object – the golden arches or the sardine can – which exposes the very conditions of visuality, the fact that, as we see, we are also positioned as objects, spectacles, and consumers.

While the gaze is distinct from the eye, however, it is not necessarily distinct from the 'I', the person who looks and is looked at. Seeing is, after all, a way of negotiating the relation between the self and the things that surround it, and Lacan contends that it is in this relation that the idea of selfhood is created. This formation occurs when the baby recognises its image in the mirror.[3] The child is seduced by this reflection, which seems to suggest its mastery, autonomy, and difference, but the recognition is also a misrecognition: not only does the baby identify with an external counterpart, an image that is not the same as, or coincidental with, itself, but the reflection gives a misleading impression of its autonomy: the actual baby, Lacan points out, is unable as yet even to stand without support. The child's relation with the image at the mirror stage reveals some important aspects of the politics and psychology of seeing that shape the visual world and offers a direct challenge to the conventional Cartesian notion of a subject who is unified and authoritative. Here, far from mastering what he or she sees, the viewer is mastered by it, placed in a pre-existing specular order over which he or she has no control. Spectatorship, then, is more about how the subject is positioned by the visual than about how it has any agency to position itself. But, despite this relative powerlessness, the mirror stage marks the moment when the subject is first deluded into thinking of itself as the source and centre of vision, able to own what it sees, or obliterate it in the blink of an eye. It is because of this illusory power that Lacan refers to this phase as taking place within the realm of the 'Imaginary', a term that stresses the connection between the image and deception.

It is a delusion, however, that does not end with the baby but is engrained in the mechanisms and practices of Western society. Michel Foucault has described how at different historical moments it is the apparent power of the spectator that allows discipline and control to be regulated and enforced. A hierarchical relation of authority and subordination is established between the surveyor and surveyed because those who look can gain knowledge of, and thereby command, what they see. The power and prestige of the viewer is also at the forefront of the European tradition of oil painting, which, according to John Berger, cements the link between seeing and ownership, with the picture not only representing material possessions but standing itself as a commodity that augments the position of the spectator-owner.[4] Today the genre of oil painting has all but disappeared but a 'universal' image like the golden arches has a surprisingly similar effect, offering another assurance of the viewer's autonomy, a way of mastering and mapping the environment, of recuperating and thereby repressing difference and otherness. The sight of a McDonald's restaurant is ultimately reassuring because it makes familiar the strange, giving reign to the idea that things are the same the world over. And if the viewer and the image alone are incapable of controlling what lies within the field of vision, then there is always the camera which, Susan Sontag argues in her essay here, provides a barrier and distance between spectator and situation, containing whatever is visually remarkable, while also disabling participation or intervention in the circumstances pictured.

The power and autonomy that go along with looking in Western culture serve to differentiate this activity from being looked at, to separate the conditions of visuality that are united under Lacan's idea of the gaze. And this is important not only for the meanings of what we see and the relations that it establishes but for the actual process of seeing itself. If there is no innate distinction between viewing and being viewed, if, in other words, the position of the spectator is culturally constituted, then looking might also be something conventional and acquired. Is it possible, then, that we learn to see? The question might seem strange because the traditional conflation of perception with the biological means that this activity is often overlooked, regarded as natural or instinctual. But it is more than biology that dictates how one sees. Seeing is bound up in value judgements (one assesses things by their appearance) and, because it is spatially and temporally limited (one cannot see everything simultaneously but only a certain amount and at any one moment), it involves an element of choice. Deciding where to look is highly political because it involves deciding where *not* to look, what to exclude from sight, and these choices are as much influenced by what culture has on offer as by any decisions made by the individual. Moreover, not everyone in society has the right or opportunity to look, and at the same things.

Our eyes are not simple recorders or receptacles of information: they do not simply mirror a world that exists unproblematically outside them. For a start, the retinal image is inverted and of a different size from the thing itself. According to the psychologist Richard L. Gregory, it is actually the brain that does the 'seeing' by compensating for retinal distortion and converting random dots and shapes into objects familiar from a knowledge and experience of the world. Perception involves not just the act of looking but decision-making too: the brain searches for the best possible interpretation of the available data. And this idea of 'interpretation' is of more than passing significance because in order for the brain to transform what is seen into something recognisable, to create meanings through sight, it relies on learnt assumptions about the characteristics of, and differences between, things. Such distinctions, however natural they seem, are not inherent in sight or even in the visualised world. There is no such thing as a pure or unmediated vision: our eyes alone are unable to inform us that a tree is a tree rather than a bush or a flower. Indeed, some people see differently to others. A bricklayer might look at a house and recognise the various types of brick and stone that constitute it but to a non-expert these remain invisible. Not even the divisions of colour are universal: the Welsh blue, or *glas* is not the same as the English idea of blue but contains elements that overlap with green and grey. But if these distinctions are not inherent to vision or the visual then where do they come from? Why do we see things differently and as separate entities?

Perhaps an answer lies in the realm of language. Language and vision, it seems, are intimately connected, an idea promoted by the Swiss linguist Ferdinand de Saussure, who argued that the process of differentiation at work in the act of looking occurs with the emergence of language itself. Language is not a mould into which pre-existing ideas or concepts fit but a system of signs that actually constructs these ideas, dividing them up and attributing a sound to them. There are, then, no values outside language but only those that are constituted by the system itself, in a sign's negative difference from every other sign. Thus, we recognise a dog as a dog because it is not a cat, a bird, a jellyfish, and so on. Without language, Saussure asserts, ideas as well as sounds would be an indistinguishable continuum.[5] And so with vision. Biologically, one might have the capacity to look, just as one has the ability to make noises, but this is different from the ability to make things intelligible, to make meanings. We have to learn to see because otherwise we could not make sense of the visual; the specular field would be the undifferentiated continuum described by Saussure.

There is a sense, therefore, in which looking is always a type of reading because it involves interpreting what is seen. Even when we seem to absorb or passively consume what we look at we continue to differentiate between things and thereby rely on a linguistic and cultural knowledge of them. Such methods of interpreting the visual world were brought to the fore by critics like Roland Barthes, who drew on the structuralist ideas of Saussure to formulate a science of signs known as semiotics or semiology. Barthes 'read' social rituals like eating meals, or visual signs such as clothes or architecture, while Michel Foucault employed similar critical methods but emphasised the importance of 'discourse', the inscription of a specific knowledge in a language usage that is bound up with power. His discussion of visual representations in terms of their historical and discursive networks is significant both for an analysis of the image and the relations of looking and being looked at that it propagates. The reading of the specular world is not only a theoretical exercise, however, nor is it an activity that is undertaken independently by a viewer and imposed on a pure realm of visuality. Rather, it is in this process that the surveyor and the surveyed come together in the way implied by Lacan. The image here is not separate from the meanings attributed by the spectator but is a product of these meanings that always contains their possibility. Indeed, this 'readability' is frequently exploited in contemporary visual culture that offers the image for interpretation and challenges spectators to uncover its strategies, perhaps with the less than liberating purpose of flattering them into believing that they are removed from and immune to these conventions. The Wonderbra advertisement, launched in Britain on 14 February 1994, depends on such a potential for plural meanings. With its scantily-clad model, accompanied by the captions 'Hello, Boys', 'Or are you just pleased to see me?' and 'Look me in the eyes and tell me that you love me', the poster instigates an active call to interpretation that the media were quick to respond to. The effectiveness of this image lies in the fact that it manipulates its explicit imagery and the viewer's familiarity with feminist discourses to question its own representation and the relations of seeing that it enables. Thus it plays with questions of whether the model is a sex object or in charge of her sexuality, whether it is empowering to incite the male gaze, or whether the image is exploitative because it implies that this gaze can be elicited only if women give the impression of having bigger breasts.

The confrontation between visuality and textuality involved in 'reading' such images is at the forefront of the essays in this anthology, but is taken to its farthest limits in the work of the poststructuralist philosopher Jacques Derrida. In the essay reprinted here Derrida alludes to the architect Peter Eisenman as a 'writer', a status, he argues, that does not come simply from the fact that Eisenman often accompanies his work with theoretical commentaries, but is inherent in the architecture itself, in the buildings and structures, where the 'two writings' of the textual and architectural coincide 'outside the traditional hierarchies'.[6] 'I did not understand,' writes Derrida, 'to what extent, and above all in what way, his architecture confronted the very conditions of discourse, grammar, and semantics.'[7] But although Derrida contends that writing is a graphic mark which undermines the seemingly full presence of speech, it is arguable whether this is equivalent to a visual representation. His discussion begs the question whether the visual *can* be accounted for in linguistic and discursive terms, to what extent the two systems *are* interchangeable. For some critics, indeed, the convergence of the textual and visual is far from 'outside traditional hierarchies'. They argue that such 'linguistics-based' theories establish a textual model of the world that is hierarchical and even 'imperialist'.[8]

It is easy to see why the ideas of structuralism and poststructuralism are so contentious, for they undermine conventional ways of looking at visual representations. The goal of art, for example, can no longer be seen as mimesis, the mirroring of an anterior world: first, because the reality we know is itself constituted by language and is not, therefore, an unmediated presence that can be re-presented; and, second, because art actually participates in the construction of what is traditionally regarded as outside it, forming part of the practices and ideologies that determine difference. Even the notion of perspective, which has dominated Western art since the Renaissance, is challenged by such theories, exposed as a vehicle for ordering the world that has come to seem inevitable rather than the way we necessarily see things. As Richard L. Gregory argues in the essay which opens this collection, perspective is not natural precisely because it is Western: other cultures do not see distance and space in the same way. Perspective relies on a monocular rather than binocular view that works to enforce the illusory power of the spectator, placing him or her in an impossible position: at the centre of the visual experience, the point at which the lines of the painting converge. Not only is the viewer here all-seeing, but he or she is the source rather than the receptacle of the effects of light, distance and space.

The issues raised by the practice of reading images come to the fore in the anthology *Visual Theory*, a book that represents what its editors describe as 'two distinct approaches': one which argues that visual representation is a matter of convention and defined by historical context, and another that identifies an essence or truth of art, a positive difference that is transhistorical and universal.[9] The conflict between these two views, concerned primarily with the relevance of the artefact's cultural setting, frequently comes down to a contest between those theories 'borrowed' from language and those that emphasise visual specificity. Richard Wollheim, a critic who is firmly of the latter school, sets his analysis of the mental processes of the artist 'against all those schools of contemporary thinking which propose to explain pictorial meanings in terms like rule, convention, symbol system, or which in effect assimilate pictorial meaning to something very different, which is linguistic meaning'.[10] Wollheim's blacklisting of 'linguistic theories', including structuralism, iconography, hermeneutics and semiotics, is followed in the same volume by David Summers, who argues that visual and textual media are 'absolutely different from one another' and that the significance of art is to be found in an area of 'prelinguistic certainty'.[11] However, while it is true that the theories which emphasise the interaction of language and the visual are themselves cultural products, and therefore never free from the hierarchical distinctions that their labelling as 'imperialist' implies, they cannot be easily dismissed as 'linguistic'. Derrida's deconstructive project undermines the idea that there is ever a pure realm of language or visuality. Because a signifier relies for its value on its negative relation with the rest of the sign system, it always already contains the trace of its other, and this also applies to the meanings of 'visuality' and 'language', which are interdependent rather than distinct.

The specular, then, is not a self-evident or self-constituting arena, but the site of political and theoretical struggles for meanings, the space where conflicting ideologies are articulated and played out. Indeed, ideology has always been enmeshed in visuality: Karl Marx used the metaphor of the *camera obscura* to describe the 'distorted' effects of false consciousness, where abstract ideas, stemming from the economic base, are absorbed by the subject. This notion of ideology was modified by the French structuralist Marxist Louis Althusser, who argued that ideology permeates everywhere and everything and is inherent in material practices and institutions themselves.[12] In his account the image can be seen as the inscription of those values and beliefs which are also evident in thoughts and actions and which hierarchise, differentiate and exclude. The visual is not the tool of an anterior society or ideology, but a mechanism that *produces* as well as represents culture to itself, constituting its relations of power and difference. This production comes to the fore in contemporary visual representations, which serve to perpetuate and determine social values. Queer theory has been instrumental in identifying not only how heterosexual relations are presented as the norm in visual media, but how it is the circulation and repetition of such images that actually define sexual categories as fixed and natural. And if heterosexuality is established as a visual rule, then so is whiteness. bell hooks has drawn on Foucault's ideas that vision is complicit with power and discipline to argue that the subordination of blacks has been achieved by refusing them the right to look and by constructing whiteness as the ideal. Even when black people are visualised, it is most frequently in terms of what Edward Said calls 'Orientalism',[13] a stereotypical and hierarchical construction of the East as savage, mysterious and exotic that serves to define the West as rational and superior. One might consider the representation of blacks in advertising today, of the way that 'oriental' women are used to market products from perfume to chocolate, or that black men are defined in terms of an uncontrollable and threatening sexuality.

The gaze, then, is far from democratic, but the idea that images and spectatorial positions are ideologically and historically constituted can also be liberating because it allows the possibility that meanings can be changed and challenged. hooks points not only to the case of black women film-makers, who intervene critically in this genre to produce a space in which a black female subjectivity can be articulated, but to an 'oppositional' or critical gaze, developed by marginalised spectators, who have not fallen into the trap of identification with, and absorption of, the image. Indeed, the fact that difference is constituted by, rather than inherent in, the visual also has radical implications for sexual difference, implying that it too is a matter of convention: it is not nature but culture that defines the anatomical as the primary method of classification.

Sexual difference is intimately connected with vision because it is something that is seen. According to Freud, it is the *sight* of the genitalia that precipitates the castration complex and the differentiation that it sets in motion, the boy believing that his penis will be cut off by the father, and the girl that she has already been castrated. For the feminist critic Luce Irigaray, Freud's discussion is complicit with the oppositions that it describes. She argues that woman's lack of a penis, her 'nothing to see' is potentially disruptive because it cannot be mastered visually; it is an absence, lack or flaw which suggests the points at which signification and representation fail, a 'nothing' that is 'not subject to the rule of visibility or of specula(risa)tion'.[14] But, while this disruption is evoked, it is simultaneously neutralised. Culture imbues vision and the visualised with a primacy that, Irigaray argues, is bound up with patriarchy and Freudian psychoanalysis itself, and equates the woman's having nothing to see with her having nothing. She is thus placed in a sexual void in which she exists only in terms of a negative absence as opposed to the visual presence of a penis. For Irigaray, the otherness that might have challenged oculocentrism is ultimately rendered invisible and powerless by it.

But it is also the very visibility of woman in contemporary culture that covers over her danger. John Berger argues that in Western society the female is repeatedly positioned as an object to be looked at, and in a famous article Laura Mulvey analyses this in terms of the cinema, where the spectacle of the beautiful woman serves to enforce 'proper' patri-

archal relations and mask the threat of castration.[15] For a female spectator, however, the confrontation with such representations is not so positive. Rosalind Coward suggests in her essay here that a woman's
appearance determines her value and dictates whether or not she will be
loved. The visual encounter is therefore riddled with anxieties as the
spectator recognises her failure to match up to the ideal and feels dissa-
tisfied with herself and the way she looks. It is a negative effect that is
seemingly rebutted in the Wonderbra advert and its ironic Valentine's Day
launch. The female depicted here teases with the salutation of love and
romance, 'Look me in the eyes and tell me that you love me', as if she
relishes the fact that this shift of gaze is an impossibility. But this woman's
value still seems to reside in her body and the man's view of it. In such a
relation the male spectator holds the balance of power. Indeed, it is revealing that, although the sexi(st)ness of this advert was defended on the
grounds that the product was not male-oriented, the gender specificity
of its captions, along with the eroticised image of the woman that it
depicts, means that it does directly address a male viewer. She is there
for him to see. Paradoxically, the image attempts to capture the female
market by presenting the spectatorship of women as marginal and transgressive; the potential buyers come to the picture surreptitiously, looking
voyeuristically at a representation that declares itself as not for them.

But are there any alternative positions for the female spectator in a
visual culture which so often places her as spectacle? For Jackie Stacey the
answer is yes, at least in cinematic representations. She asserts that
female viewers do not simply identify with, or look with dissatisfaction
at, the images of other women that they see on screen. Rather, they often
recognise, and find pleasure in, the differences between them. And this is
assuming that gender and visual relations are ever as fixed as they
appear. In *Sexuality in the Field of Vision* Jacqueline Rose argues that
because sexual difference depends on how visuality is itself perceived
in culture (that is, on the primacy of what is seen over what is hidden),
then any disruption to the image, its power of illusion or address, simultaneously disrupts sexual difference, revealing the fact that it is incomplete and imperfect.[16] Psychoanalysis, then, shows the points at which
sexual categories are contested as well as produced, exposing the fact that
the relation between viewer and viewed is one of partial identification
and fracture, in which the fullness of vision and gender are both fantasies.

The image-reading that theories like psychoanalysis undertake cannot
simply be seen as a metalanguage, a way of describing or explaining the
visual from the outside, but as a mechanism that actually determines its
processes. Theory interacts with the significations of the specular: it is one
of the means by which vision and visuality acquire their meanings and
value in society, a way of learning to see, and not from one stable or

monolithic perspective but from different and conflicting vantages and viewpoints. And just as visuality is a theoretical construct and category, so theory itself is always invaded and informed by the visual, a dialectic that becomes apparent in many of the extracts reprinted in this anthology: in *Camera Lucida*, Barthes' last and most poignant text, which is itself a static and immovable photograph, the capture of a fleeting moment that anticipates and points back to the writer's own imminent death; in bell hooks's 'oppositional gaze' at white middle-class feminism; or in Foucault's panoptical theories of power and knowledge, which sweep, in the blink of an all-seeing eye, from one historical epoch to the next. All the essays reproduced here are self-reflexive, both in the sense that they are about 'reflection', modes of seeing, and in the fact that they view and refer to themselves, exploring the approaches available to a reader of visuality, and what it means to write about it. They stand as examples of theory's engagement with visuality, and as reminders that, while theory changes ways of seeing, it is itself something eminently seen. This, in fact, might be the only model of analysis available in a Reader that is also a 'viewer', a book that, in its very nature, occupies the visual and physical space of something to be looked at as well as read.

There is a way, therefore, in which the practice of 'reading images' always already deconstructs the apparent opposition between its two separate terms. For Derrida, the model for this is to be found in Eisenman's architecture, which challenges the binarism between textuality and visuality and anticipates the deconstruction of other prevalent systems of thought, embodying 'an economy in which we no longer have to exclude the invisible from the visible, to oppose the temporal and the spatial, discourse and architecture'.[17] Derrida's reference to the opposition between visible and the invisible, the spatial and temporal, is an allusion to Gotthold Lessing's influential book *Laocoön*, which in the eighteenth century emphasised the incommensurable differences between poetry and painting and marked one of the first attempts to divide the arts. But another method of ordering is allowed for in the different theoretical approaches that are on offer here, or at least a method which, while it might not resolve the tension between language and image, theory and vision, the social and the subjective, does expose the fact that such distinctions are never ideologically and politically neutral. Perhaps, indeed, this conflict is foregrounded in very different visual and architectural projects from those developed by Peter Eisenman: in the Wonderbra advertisement with its own play between picture and caption and negotiation of spectatorial relations; or even in those golden arches, at once letter and image, that both incite and return the viewer's gaze.

2

Perspective

Richard L. Gregory

In the Western world rooms are nearly always rectangular; and many objects, such as boxes, have right-angled corners. Again, many things, such as roads and railways, present long parallel lines converging by perspective. People living in the Western world have a visual environment rich in perspective cues to distance. We may ask whether people living in other environments, where there are few right angles and few long parallel lines, are subject to the illusions which we believe to be associated with perspective. Fortunately, several studies have been made on the perception of people living in such environments, and measurements have been made of their susceptibility to some of the illusion figures.

The people who stand out as living in a non-perspective world are the Zulus. Their world has been described as a 'circular culture' – their huts are round, and have round doors; they do not plough their land in straight furrows but in curves; and few of their possessions have corners or straight lines. They are thus ideal subjects for our purpose. It is found that they do experience the arrow illusion to a small extent, but they are hardly affected at all by the other illusion figures.

Studies of people living in dense forest have been made. Such people are interesting, in that they do not experience distant objects, because there are only small clearances in the forest. When they are taken out of their forest, and shown distant objects, they see these not as distant, but as small. People living in Western cultures experience a similar distortion when looking down from a height. From a high window objects look too small, though steeplejacks and men who work on the scaffolding and girder structure of skyscrapers are reported to see objects below them without distortion. It seems that actual touch is important in setting the visual scale of objects.

This point comes out in the study of a man who was blind as a baby but recovered sight by operation in middle life. Shortly after the operation he thought he could lower himself safely to the ground from his hospital window, some thirty or forty feet above the ground. Although he saw the ground as just below him, his appreciation of familiar horizontal distances was quite accurate. Like the Zulus, he did not suffer from any of the normal illusions except, to a small degree, the arrow illusion.

11

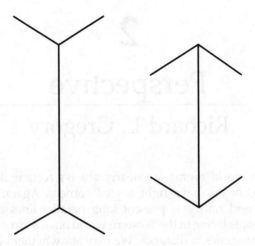

The Muller–Lyer, or *arrow illusion*. The figure with the outgoing fins looks longer than the figure with the ingoing fins. Why?

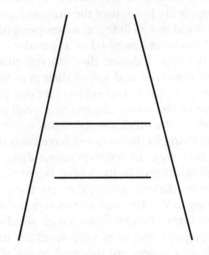

The Ponzo, or *railway lines illusion*. The upper horizontal line looks the longer. This same line continues to look longer in whichever orientation the figure is viewed. (Try rotating the book.)

The arrow illusion has been measured in some animals, notably the pigeon, and in fish. The technique is to train the experimental animals to select the longer of two lines, and when this is established, to present them with arrow figures in which the shafts are objectively equal. Do they then select the arrow which appears the longer to us? Positive results have been reported, both for pigeons and for the fish. It thus seems that animals are subject to the illusions.

(In fact this experiment is not as easy as it sounds, for it is important to establish that the animal is responding to the length of the shaft of the arrow and not to the length of the entire figure. This is done by training the animals with lines having various shapes added to their ends, to ensure that it is the length of the lines themselves and not the total length of the figures, which are being selected by the animals. In the training period, care is taken to use no additions to the lines which would produce an illusion. This is no doubt a hazardous experiment.)

The evidence from non-Western cultures in which there is little perspective (though there will always be some, if only perspective through motion parallax giving 'dynamic perspective') shows that the illusions are reduced, and largely absent, where perspective cues are meagre. The evidence from the man blind since infancy also suggests that illusions depend in part on previous visual experience. The evidence from animals suggests that illusions are not limited to the human perceptual system, but occur also in less developed eyes and brains. It would be interesting to bring animals up in a perspective-free environment and then measure their illusions. We might expect illusions to be absent. In fact, this experiment was tried in the author's laboratory, on fish. But unfortunately they died, though presumably not for perceptual reasons.

In connection with the non-Western people, it is perhaps worth adding that they make little or nothing of drawings or photographs of familiar objects, and this was also true of the blind man made to see. It is likely that perspective cues are made use of only after considerable experience, when they are related to touch, and that it is only then that appropriate perspective cues give rise to distortions of size in flat figures. There is some evidence that the illusion figures give rise to distortions of size as judged by touch. This is apparently true also of blind people touching these figures. The evidence for this is primarily on the arrow illusion, but this is perhaps not the best one to consider, for error of judged length in this figure could be due to the limited spatial acuity of the sense of touch tending to place the end of the line beyond the corner in the outgoing fins figure, and before the corner in the ingoing fins figure – so lengthening the first and shortening the second. As we have seen (in discussing the limited acuity theory) this is a most implausible explanation for illusions as *seen*, because of the high acuity of the eye; but it might be the explanation for touch where acuity is so low that the corners of the arrow figures may be displaced for this reason. This would be entirely trivial, and so we should not take touch illusions too seriously until we know more about them. But if indeed it is found that distortions do occur for touch apart from its limited acuity, then illusory distortions will appear even more general and basic than they do at present.

Perspective as we know it in Western art is extraordinarily recent. In all known primitive art, and in the art of all previous civilisations, there is no perspective until the Italian Renaissance. In the highly developed formalised painting of the ancient Egyptians, heads and feet are shown in profile, never foreshortened by perspective; which gives the figures a certain resemblance to child art. Chinese drawing and painting is most curious in this respect, for distance is represented by formal rules which contravene geometry, and which often give what we would regard as reversed perspective – lines diverging rather than converging with increasing distance. It is an extraordinary fact that simple geometrical perspective took so long to develop – far longer than fire or the wheel – and yet in a sense it has always been present for the seeing. But is perspective present in nature? Is perspective a discovery, or an invention of the Renaissance artists?

The laws and principles of perspective were first clearly described by Leonardo da Vinci (1452–1519) in his *Notebooks*, where he outlines a suitable course of study for the artist including, as well as perspective, the arrangement of surface muscles, the structure of the eyes of man and animals, and botany. He called perspective 'the bridle and rudder of painting,' describing it in the following way:

> Perspective is nothing else than the seeing of a plane behind a sheet of glass, smooth and quite transparent, on the surface of which all the things approach the point of the eye in pyramids, and these pyramids are intersected on the glass plane.

Leonardo treated the perspective of drawings as a branch of geometry. He described how perspective could actually be drawn directly on a sheet of glass; a technique used by the Dutch masters and, in a later form, with the *camera obscura* which employs a lens to form an image of the scene which may be traced directly. The projection is determined purely by the geometry of the situation and this constitutes so-called *geometrical perspective*; but as Leonardo realised more clearly than many later writers, there is more to the matter than the pure geometry of the situation. Leonardo included in his account of perspective such effects as increasing haze and blueness with increasing distance; the importance of shadows and shading in drawings to represent the orientation of objects. These considerations go beyond pure geometry. But, as we shall see, they are highly relevant to the use of perspective, being essential to prevent its being ambiguous.

Any perspective projection is ambiguous – correct perspective may be a necessary but is never a sufficient condition for indicating depth. Consider a simple ellipse. This might represent an elliptical object seen normally or a circular object seen obliquely. This figure does not uniquely indicate any one kind of object: it could be a projection of any of an infinite variety of objects, each seen from a certain angle of view. The art of the draughtsman and painter is, in large part, to make us accept just one out of the infinite set of possible interpretations of a figure, to make us see a certain shape from a certain point of view. This is where geometry goes out and perception comes in. To limit the ambiguity of perspective, the artist must make use of perceptual distance cues available to a single eye. He is forbidden the binocular cues of convergence and disparity, and also motion parallax. Indeed these cues will work against him. Paintings are generally more compelling in depth when viewed with a single eye, and the head held still.

We have to consider a double reality. The painting is itself a physical object, and our eyes will see it as such, flat on the wall, but it can also evoke quite other objects – people, ships, buildings – lying in space. It is the artist's task to make us reject the first reality, while conveying the second, so that we see his world and not mere patches of colour on a flat surface.

As we have seen from the example of the ellipse, a figure can represent a given object from one viewing position, or any of an infinite set of somewhat different objects seen in some other orientations. This means that for the figure to represent something unambiguously, we must know what the object really is – what its shape is – or how it lies in space. It is very much easier to represent familiar than unfamiliar objects. When we know what the object is, then we know how it must be lying to give the projection given by the artist. For example, if we know that the ellipse is representing a circular object, then we know that this must be lying at a certain oblique angle – the angle giving the eccentricity drawn on the flat plane by the artist. We all know that wheels, dinner plates, the pupil of the human eye, etc., are circular objects, and for such familiar objects the artist's task is easy. We may see how easy it is from the power that very simple line drawings have in indicating form, orientation and distance – when we know what the object is. [...]

When an artist employs geometrical perspective he does not draw what he sees – he represents his retinal image. As we know, these are very different, for what is seen is affected by constancy. A photograph represents the retinal image, not how the scene appears. By comparing a drawing with a photograph taken from exactly the same position, we could determine just how far the artist adopts perspective and how far he draws the world as he sees it after his retinal images are scaled by his constancy. In general, distant objects look too small in a photograph – it is a common and sad experience that a grand mountain range comes out looking like a pitiful row of mole hills.

The situation here is curious. The camera gives true geometrical perspective, but because we do not see the world as it is projected on the retina, or a camera, the photograph looks wrong. It should not surprise us that primitive people make little or nothing of photographs. Indeed it is fortunate that perspective was invented before the camera, or we might have had great difficulty in accepting photographs as other than weird distortions. As it is, photographs can look quite wrong, particularly when the camera is not held horizontally. Aiming a camera upwards, to take in a tall building, gives the impression of the building falling backwards. And yet this is the true perspective. The towers do look slightly converging though not so much as in a photograph taken from the same position and with the camera tilted at the same angle as the eyes. Some architects have recognised that the visual compensation for distance is less efficient when looking upwards, and have built their towers to diverge slightly from the bottom to the top. The most notable example is the magnificent Campanile at Florence, designed by Giotto. Here the artist as architect has applied reversed perspective to reality, to compensate for the eye's inadequacy in correcting for perspective. There are examples of this on the horizontal plane also, notably the Piazza San Marco in Venice which is not a true rectangle but diverges towards the cathedral, so that it appears to be a true rectangle when the cathedral is viewed from across the Piazza. We find similar 'distortions' of reality to suit the eye and brain in some of the temples of ancient Greece. This is true of the Parthenon.

We begin to see why it took so long for perspective to be adopted by painters. In an important sense perspective representations of three dimensions are wrong, for they do not depict the world as it is seen but rather the (idealised) images on the retina. But we do not see our retinal images; and we do not see the world according to the size or shapes of the retinal images, for these are effectively modified by constancy.

3

Monster Metaphors: Notes on Michael Jackson's *Thriller*

Kobena Mercer

Michael Jackson, megastar. His LP, *Thriller*, made in 1982, has sold over thirty-five million copies worldwide and is said to be the biggest selling album in the history of pop. At the age of twenty-six Jackson is reputed to have amassed a personal fortune of some seventy-five million dollars. Even more remarkably, he has been a star since he was eleven and sang lead with his brothers in The Jackson Five, the biggest selling group on the Tamla Motown label in the 1970s. The Jacksons practically invented the genre of 'teenybopper' pop, cashed in upon by white idols like Donny Osmond. While such figures have faded from popular memory, classic Jackson Five tunes like 'I Want You Back' and 'ABC' can still evoke the enthusiasm which marked the assertive mood of the Black Pride era.

After he and his brothers left Motown in the mid-seventies, and took more artistic control over their own productions, Jackson developed as a singer, writer and stage performer in his own right. His 1979 *Off the Wall* LP, which established him as a solo star, demonstrates the lithe, sensual texture of his voice and its mastery over a diverse range of musical styles and idioms, from romantic ballad to rock. Just what is it that makes this young, gifted and black man so different, so appealing?

Undoubtedly it is the voice which lies at the heart of his appeal. Rooted in the Afro-American soul tradition, Jackson's vocal performance is characterised by breathy gasps, squeaks, sensual sighs and other wordless sounds which have become his stylistic signature. The way in which this style punctuates the emotional resonance and bodily sensuality of the music corresponds to what Roland Barthes called the 'grain' of the voice – 'the grain is the body in the voice as it sings'.[1] The emotional and erotic expressiveness of the voice is complemented by the sensual grace and sheer dynamism of Jackson's dancing style: even as a child his stage performance provoked comparisons with Jackie Wilson and James Brown.

But there is another element to Jackson's popularity – his image. Jackson's individual style fascinates and attracts attention. The ankle-cut jeans, the single-gloved hand and, above all, the curly-perm hairstyle which have become his visual trademarks have influenced the sartorial

repertoires of black and white youth cultures and have been incorporated
into mainstream fashion. Most striking is the change in Jackson's physical
appearance as he has grown. The cute child dressed in gaudy flower-
power gear and sporting a huge Afro hairstyle has become, as a young
adult, a paragon of racial and sexual ambiguity. Michael reclines across
the gatefold sleeve of the *Thriller* LP dressed in crisp black and white on a
glossy metallic surface against a demure pink background. Look closer –
the glossy sheen of his complexion appears lighter in colour than
before; the nose seems sharper, more aquiline, less rounded and 'African', and the lips seem tighter, less pronounced. Above all, the large
Afro has dissolved into a shock of wet-look curls and a new stylistic
trademark, a single lock over the forehead, appears.

What makes this reconstruction of Jackson's star image more intriguing
is the mythology built up around it, in which it is impossible or simply
beside the point to distinguish truth from falsehood. It is said that he has
undergone cosmetic surgery in order to adopt a more white, European
look, although Jackson himself denies it.[2] But the definite sense of racial
ambiguity writ large in his new image is at the same time, and by the
same token, the site of a sexual ambiguity bordering on androgyny. He
may sing as sweet as Al Green, dance as hard as James Brown, but he
looks more like Diana Ross than any black male soul artist. The media
have seized upon these ambiguities and have fabricated a persona, a
private self behind the public image, which has become the subject of
mass speculation and rumour. Such mythologisation has culminated in
the construction of a Peter Pan figure. We are told that behind the star's
image is a lonely 'lost boy', whose life is shadowed by morbid obsessions
and anxieties. He lives like a recluse and is said to 'come alive' only when
he is on stage in front of his fans. The media's exploitation of public
fascination with Jackson the celebrity has even reached the point of
'pathologising' his personal eccentricities:

> Even Michael Jackson's millions of fans find his lifestyle strange. It's
> just like one of his hit songs, Off The Wall. People in the know say – His
> biggest thrill is taking trips to Disneyland. His closest friends are zoo
> animals. He talks to tailor's dummies in his lounge. He fasts every
> Sunday and then dances in his bedroom until he drops of exhaustion.
> So showbusiness folk keep asking the question: Is Jacko Wacko? Two
> top American psychiatrists have spent hours examining a detailed
> dossier on Jackson. Here is their on-the-couch report. (*The Sun*, 9
> April 1984, p. 5)

In particular, Jackson's sexuality and sexual preference have been the
focus of intense public scrutiny, as a business associate of his, Shirley
Brooks, complains:

He doesn't and won't make public statements about his sex life, because he believes – and he is right – that is none of anyone else's business. Michael and I had a long conversation about it, and he felt that anytime you're in the public eye and don't talk to the press, they tend to make up these rumours to fill their pages.[3]

Neither child nor adult, not clearly either black or white, and with an androgynous image that is neither masculine nor feminine, Jackson's star image is a 'social hieroglyph', as Marx said of the commodity form, which demands, yet defies, decoding. This article offers a reading of the music video *Thriller* from the point of view of the questions raised by the phenomenal popularity of this star, whose image is a spectacle of racial and sexual indeterminacy.

REMAKE, REMODEL: VIDEO IN THE MARKETING OF *THRILLER*

In recent years the new, hybrid medium of music video has come to occupy a central importance in the sale and significance of pop music. As ads to promote records, videos are now prerequisites to break singles into the charts. As industrial product, the medium – now institutionalised in America's cable network MTV, owned by Warner Communications and American Express – has revitalised the declining profitability of the singles market by capitalising on new patterns of consumption created by the use, on a mass scale, of video technologies.[4] From its inception in 1981, however, MTV maintained an unspoken policy of excluding black artists. Jackson's videos for singles from the *Thriller* LP were among the first to penetrate this invisible racial boundary.

Videos for 'Billy Jean' and 'Beat It' stand out in the way they foreground Jackson's new star image. 'Billy Jean', directed by Steve Barron, visualises the cinematic feel of the music track and its narrative of a false paternity claim by creating, through a studio-set scenario, sharp editing and various effects, an ambience that complements rather than illustrates the song. Taking its cue from the LP cover, it stresses Jackson's style in his dress and in his dance. Paving stones light up as Jackson twists, kicks and turns through the performance, invoking the 'magic' of his stardom. 'Beat It', directed by Bob Giraldi (who made TV commercials for McDonald's hamburgers and Dr Pepper soft drinks), visualises the antimacho lyric of the song. Shots alternate between 'juvenile delinquent' gangs about to start a fight, and Michael, fragile and alone in his bedroom. The singer then disarms the street gangs with his superior charm as he leads the all-male cast through a choreographic sequence that synthesises the cinematic imagery of *The Warriors* and *West Side Story*.

These videos – executed from storyboards by Jackson himself – and others in which he appears, such as 'Say, Say, Say' by Paul McCartney and 'Can You Feel it' by The Jacksons, are important aspects of the commercial success of *Thriller*, because they breach the boundaries of race on which the music industry is based. Unlike stars such as Lionel Richie, Jackson has not 'crossed over' from black to white markets to end up in the middle of the road: his success has popularised black music among white audiences by explicitly *playing* with visual imagery and style which has always been central to the mass marketing of pop. In so doing, Jackson's experimentation in music video has reopened a space in which new stars like Prince are operating, at the interface of cultural boundaries defined by 'race'.

'Thriller', the title track, was released as the third single from the album. The accompanying video went beyond the then-established conventions and limitations of the medium. According to Dave Laing, these conventions have been tied to the economic imperative of the pop sales process:

> first, the visuals were subordinated to the soundtrack, which they were there to sell; second, music video as a medium for marketing immediately inherited an aesthetic and a set of techniques from the pre-existing and highly developed form of television commercials.[5]

Thus one key convention, that of rapid editing derived from the montage codes of television advertising, has been overlaid with another: that of an alternation between naturalistic or 'realist' modes of representation (in which the song is performed 'live' or in a studio and mimed to by the singer or group), and 'constructed' or fantastic modes of representation (in which the singer/group acts out imaginary roles implied by the lyrics or by the atmosphere of the music). 'Thriller' incorporates such montage and alternation conventions, but organises the image flow by framing it with a powerful *storytelling* or *narrational* direction which provides continuity and closure. Since 'Thriller', this storytelling code has itself become a music video convention: Julian Temple's 'Undercover of the Night' (Rolling Stones, 1983) and 'Jazzin' for Blue Jean' (David Bowie, 1984) represent two of the more imaginative examples of this narrativisation of music by the direction of the flow of images. 'Thriller', moreover, is distinguished not only by its internal and formal structure at the level of *mise-en-scène*, but also by the fact that it is 'detached' from a primary economic imperative or rationale. The LP was already a 'monster' of a success before its title track became a single: there was no obvious need for a 'hard sell'. Thus the 'Thriller' video does not so much seek to promote the record as a primary product, but rather *celebrates the stardom* which the LP has brought to Michael Jackson. In the absence of a direct economic imperative, the video can indulge Jackson's own interest in acting: its use of cinematic codes thus provides a narrative framework in which Jackson may perform as a 'movie star'. Jackson himself had acted before, in *The Wiz* (1977), Motown's all-black remake of *The Wizard of Oz* in which he played the Scarecrow. He professes a deep fascination with acting *per se*:

> I love it so much. It's escape. It's fun. It's just neat to become another thing, another person. Especially when you really believe it and it's not like you're acting. I always hated the word 'acting' – to say, 'I am an actor'. It should be more than that. It should be more like a believer.[6]

In 'Thriller', Jackson enacts a variety of roles as the video engages in a playful parody of the stereotypes, codes and conventions of the horror genre. The intertextual dialogues between film, dance and music which the video articulates also draw us, the spectators, into the *play* of signs and meanings at work in the 'constructedness' of the star's image. The following reading considers the specificity of the music track, asks how video 'visualises' the music and then goes on to examine the internal structure of the video as an intertext of sound, image and style.

'THRILLER': A READING

Consider first the specificity of the music track. The title, which gives the LP its title as well, is the name for a particular genre of film – the 'murder-mystery-suspense' film, the detective story, the thriller. But the lyrics of the song are not 'about' film or cinema. The track is a mid-tempo funk number, written by Rod Temperton, and recalls similar numbers by that songwriter, such as 'Off the Wall'. The lyrics evoke allusions and references to the cinematic genre of horror films, but only to play on the meaning of the word 'thriller'. The lyrics weave a little story, which could be summarised as 'a night of viewing some ... gruesome horror movies with a lady friend'[7] and narrate such a fictional scene by speaking in the first person:

> It's close to midnight and somethin' evil's lurkin' in the dark
> ... You try to scream, but terror takes the sound before you make it
> You start to freeze, as horror looks you right between the eyes
> You're paralyzed.

Who is this 'you' being addressed? The answer comes in the semantic turnaround of the third verse and chorus, in which the pun on the title is made evident:

Now is the time for you and I to cuddle close together
All thru' the night, I'll save you from the terror on the screen
I'll make you see, that [Chorus]
This is thriller, thriller-night, 'cause I could thrill you more than any
ghost would dare to try
Girl, this is thriller, thriller-night . . . So let me hold you close and share
a killer, thriller, tonight.[8]

Thus the lyrics play on a *double entendre* of the meaning of 'thrill'.

As Iain Chambers has observed: 'Distilled into the metalanguage
of soul and into the clandestine cultural liberation of soul music is the
regular employment of a sexual discourse.'[9] Along with the emotional
complexity of intimate relationships, sexuality is perhaps *the* central
preoccupation of the soul tradition. But, as Chambers suggests, the
power of soul as a cultural form to express sexuality does not so much
lie in the literal meanings of the words but in the passion of the
singer's voice and vocal performance. The explicit meanings of the lyrics
are in this sense secondary to the sensual resonance of the individual character of the voice, its 'grain'. While the 'grain' of the voice
encodes the contradictions of sexual relationships, their pleasures and
pain, the insistence of the rhythm is an open invitation to the body to
dance. Dance, as cultural form and erotic ritual, is a mode of decoding
the sound and meaning generated in the music. In its incitement of the
listener to dance, to become an active participant in the texture of voice,
words and rhythm, soul music is not merely 'about' sexuality, but
is itself a musical means for the eroticisation of the body.[10] In 'Thriller'
it is the 'grain' of Jackson's voice that expresses and plays with this
sexual subtext and it is this dimension that transgresses the denotation
of the lyrics and escapes analytic reduction. Jackson's interpretation
of Temperton's lyric inflects the allusions to cinema in order to
thematise a discourse on sexuality, rather than film, and the 'story'
evoked by the lyrics sets up a reverberation between two semantic
poles: the invocation of macabre movies is offset by the call to 'cuddle
close together'.

The element of irony set in motion by this semantic polarity is the
'literary' aspect of the sense of parody that pervades the song.
Sound effects – creaking doors and howling dogs – contribute to the
pun on the title. Above all, the play of parody spreads out in Vincent
Price's rap, which closes the tune. The idea of a well-established, white,
movie actor like Price delivering a rap, a distinctly black, urban, music
form, is funny enough. But the fruity, gurgling tones of the actor's voice,
which immediately evoke the semi-comic self-parody of 'horror' he
has become, express the playful sense of humour that underpins the
song:

Darkness falls across the land. The midnight hour is close at hand.
Creatures crawl in search of blood, to terrorize y'all's neighborhood.
And whosoever shall be found, without a soul for getting down,
must stand and face the hounds of hell, and rot inside a corpse's shell.

The parody at play here lies in the quotation of soul argot – 'get down',
'midnight hour', 'funk of forty thousand years' – in the completely
different context of the horror genre. The almost camp quality of refined
exaggeration in Price's voice and his 'British' accent is at striking odds
with the discourse of black American soul music.

As we 'listen' to the production of meanings in the music track, the
various 'voices' involved in the process (Jackson, Temperton, Price,
Quincy Jones) are audibly combined into parodic play. One way of
approaching the transition from music to video, then, would be to suggest that John Landis, its director, brings aspects of his own 'voice' as a
Hollywood auteur into this dialogue. It seems to me that Landis's voice
contributes to the puns and play on the meaning of 'thriller' by drawing
on the filmic conventions of the horror genre.

STORY, PLOT AND PARODY

Landis introduces two important elements from film into the medium of
music video: a narrative direction to the image flow, and special-effects
techniques associated with the pleasures of the horror film. These effects
are used in the two scenes that show the metamorphosis of Michael into,
first, a werewolf, and then, a zombie. Such cinematic technologies, which
introduce the dimension of the fantasmatic, clearly distinguish 'Thriller'
from other music videos. Moreover, it is in this way that 'Thriller' gives
the video audiences *real thrills* – the 'thrill' of tension, anxiety and fear
whose release underlines the distinct pleasures offered by the horror
genre. The spectacle of the visceral transformation of cute, lovable
Michael Jackson into a howlin' wolf of a monster is disturbing precisely
because it seems so convincing and 'real' as a result of these techniques.
As Philip Brophy remarks: 'The pleasure of the (horror) text is, in fact,
getting the shit scared out of you – and loving it: an exchange mediated
by adrenaline.'[11]

Both special effects and narrative return us to the authorial voice of
John Landis, who directed *An American Werewolf in London* (1979). *American Werewolf* is actually a horror-comedy; it recalls the folkloric werewolf
myth, setting its protagonists as tourists in England attacked by a strange
animal, into which one of them turns during the full moon. The film
employs pop tunes to exacerbate its underlying parody of this mythology
– 'Moondance' (Van Morrison), 'Bad Moon Rising' (Creedence

Clearwater Revival) and 'Blue Moon' (Frankie Lymon and the Teen-agers). And this humour is combined with the verisimilitude of special effects and makeup techniques which show the bodily metamorphosis of man to wolf in 'real time', as opposed to less credible time-lapse techniques. 'Thriller' not only alludes to this film, but to other generic prede-cessors, including *Night of the Living Dead* (1969) by George Romero and *Halloween* (1978) by John Carpenter. Indeed, in keeping with the genre, the video is strewn with allusions to horror films. As Brophy observes:

> It is a genre which mimics itself mercilessly – because its statement is coded in its very mimicry. . . . It is not so much that the modern horror film refutes or ignores the conventions of genre, but it is involved in a violent awareness of itself as a saturated genre.[12]

Thus cinematic horror seems impelled towards parody of its own codes and conventions as a constitutive aspect of its own generic identity.[13] With hindsight it is tempting to suggest that 'Thriller''s music track was almost made to be filmed, as it seems to cue these cinematic references. Certain moments within the video appear to be straightforward transpo-sitions from the song: 'They're out to get you, there's demons closin' in on ev'ry side...Night creatures call and the dead start to walk in their masquerade', and so on. But it is at the level of its *narrative structure* that the video engages in an intertextual dialogue with the music track.[14]

Unlike most pop videos, 'Thriller' does not begin with the first notes of the song, but with a long panning shot of a car driving through woods at night and the 'cinematic' sound of recorded silence. This master-shot, establishing the all-seeing but invisible eye of the camera, is comparable to the discursive function of third-person narration. The shot/reverse-shot series which frames the opening dialogue between the two protagonists (about the car running out of gas) establishes 'point-of-view' camera angles, analogous to subjective, first-person modes of enunciation. These specific cinematic codes of narration structure the entire flow of images, and thus give the video a beginning, a middle and an end. 'Thriller' incorporates the pop video convention of switching from 'realist' to 'fantastic' modes of representation, but binds this into continuity and closure through its narrative. The two metamorphosis sequences are of crucial importance to this narrative structure; the first disrupts the equilibrium of the opening sequence, and the second repeats but differs from the first in order to bring the flow of images to an end and thus re-establish equilibrium. Within the storytelling conventions of generic horror the very appearance of the monster/werewolf/vampire/alien signals the violation of equilibrium: the very presence of the mon-ster activates the narrative dynamic whose goal or ending is achieved by an act of counterviolence that eliminates it.[15]

In the opening sequence equilibrium is established and then disrupted. The dialogue and exchange of glances between Michael and 'the girl' (as the male and female protagonists of the story) establish 'romance' as the narrative pretext. The girl's look at Michael as the car stops hints at a question, answered by the expression of bemused incredulity on his face. Did he stop the car on purpose? Was it a romantic ruse, to lure her into a trap? The girl's coquettish response to Michael's defence ('Honestly, we're out of gas') lingers sensually on the syllables, 'So . . . what are we going to do now?' Her question, and his smile in return, hint at and exacerbate the underlying erotic tension of romantic intrigue between the two characters. Michael's dialogue gives a minimal 'character' to his role as the boyfriend: he appears a somewhat shy, very proper and polite 'boy next door'. The girl, on the other hand, is not so much a character as the 'girlfriend' type. At another level, their clothes – a pastiche fifties retro style – connote youthful innocence, the couple as archetypical teen lovers. But this innocent representation is unsettled by Michael's statement: 'I'm not like other guys.' The statement implies a question posed on the terrain of gender, and masculinity in particular: why is he different from 'other guys'?

The sequence provides an answer in the boyfriend's transformation into a monster. But, although the metamorphosis resolves the question, it is at the cost of disrupting the equilibrium of 'romance' between the two protagonists, which is now converted into a relation of terror between monster and victim. The ensuing chase through the woods is the final sequence of this 'beginning' of the narrative. The subsequent scene, returning to Michael and the girl as a couple in the cinema, re-establishes the equation of romance and repositions the protagonists as girlfriend and boyfriend, but at another level of representation.

In structural terms this shift in modes of representation, from a fantastic level (in which the metamorphosis and chase take place) to a realist level (in which the song is performed), is important because it retrospectively implies that the entire opening sequence was a film within a film, or rather, a film within the video. More to the point, the narrative 'beginning' is thus revealed to be a *parody of 1950s B-movie horror*. This had been signalled by the self-conscious 'acting' mannerisms that Jackson employs and by the pastiche of fifties teenager styles. The shift from a parody of a fifties horror movie to the cinema audience watching the film and the long shot of the cinema showing the 'film', visually acknowledge this 'violent awareness of itself as saturated genre'. The cultural history it taps into has been described as follows:

While Hammer were reviving the Universal monsters . . . American International Pictures began a cycle whose appreciation was almost entirely tongue-in-cheek – a perfect example of 'camp' manufacture and reception of the iconography of terror.

The first film in this series bore the (now notorious) title *I Was a Teenage Werewolf* (1957). ... The absurdity of the plot and acting, and the relentless pop music that filled the soundtrack, gave various kinds of pleasure to young audiences and encouraged the film-makers to follow this pilot movie with *I Was A Teenage Frankenstein* and with *Teenage Monster* and *Teenage Zombie*, creations that were as awful to listen to as they were to see.[16]

Parody depends on an explicit self-consciousness: in 'Thriller' this informs the dialogue, dress style and acting in the opening sequence. In its parody of a parody it also acknowledges that there is no 'plot' as such: the narrative code that structures the video has no story to tell. Rather it creates a simulacrum of a story in its stylistic send-up of genre conventions. But it is precisely at the level of its self-consciousness that 'Thriller''s mimicry of the *gender roles* of the horror genre provides an anchor for the way it visualises the sexual discourse, the play on the meaning of the word 'thriller' on the music track.

GENRE AND GENDER: 'THRILLER''S SEXUAL SUBTEXT

As the video switches from fantastic to realist modes of representation, the roles played by the two protagonists shift accordingly. The fictional film within the video, with its narrative pretext of 'romance', positions Michael and the girl as boyfriend and girlfriend, and within this the horrifying metamorphosis transforms the relation into one of terror between monster and victim. If we go back to Michael's statement made in this scene, 'I'm not like other guys', we can detect a confusion about the role he is playing.

The girl's initial reply, 'Of course not. That's why I love you', implies that it is obvious that he is 'different' because *he* is the real Michael Jackson. When, in her pleasure at his proposal, she calls him by his proper name she interpellates him in two roles at once – as fictional boyfriend and real superstar. This ambiguity of reference acknowledges Jackson's self-conscious acting style: we, the video audience, get the impression he is playing at playing a role, and we 'know' that Jackson the singer, the star, is playing at the role of a 'movie star'. Michael's outfit and its stylistic features – the wet-look hairstyle, the ankle-cut jeans and the letter 'M' emblazoned on his jacket – reinforce this metatextual superimposition of roles. If Michael, as the male protagonist, is both boyfriend and star, his female counterpart is both the girlfriend and, at this metatextual level, the fan. The girl is in two places at once: on screen and in the audience. As spectator to the film within the video she is horrified by the image on the screen and gets up to leave. 'Fooled' by the violent spectacle of the metamorphosis, she mistakes the fantastic for the real, she forgets that 'it's only a movie'. The girl's positions in the fictional and realist scenes mirror those of the video spectator – the effects which generate thrills for the audience are the events, in the story world, that generate terror for the girl.

The girl occupies a mediated position between the audience and the star image which offers a clue to the way the video visualises the music track. In the middle section, as the couple walk away from the cinema and Michael begins the song, the narrative roles of boyfriend and girl-friend are re-established, but now subordinated to the song's perfor-mance. This continuity of narrative function is underlined by the differentiation of costume style: Michael now wears a flashy red and black leather jacket cut in a futuristic style and her ensemble is also contemporary – T-shirt, flight jacket and a head of curls like Michael's own. This imagery echoes publicity images of Jackson the stage per-former. As the song gets under way Jackson becomes 'himself', the star. The girl becomes the 'you' in the refrain, 'Girl, I could thrill you more than any ghost would dare to try'.

On the music track, the 'you' could be the listener, since the personal and direct mode of enunciation creates a space for the listener to enter and take part in the production of meanings. In the video, it is the girl who takes this place and, as the addressee of the sexual subtext encoded in the song, her positions in the video-text create possibilities for spectat-orial identification. These lines of identification are hinted at in the open-ing scene, in which the girl's response to Michael's seduction enacts the 'fantasy of being a pop star's girlfriend', a fantasy which is realised in this section of the video.[17]

BEAUTY AND THE BEAST: MASKS, MONSTERS AND MASCULINITY

The conventions of horror inscribe a fascination with sexuality, with gender identity codified in terms that revolve around the symbolic pre-sence of the monster. Women are invariably the victims of the acts of terror unleashed by the werewolf/vampire/alien/'thing': the monster as non-human Other. The destruction of the monster establishes male pro-tagonists as heroes, whose object and prize is of course the woman. But as the predatory force against which the hero has to compete, the monster itself occupies a 'masculine' position in relation to the female victim.

'Thriller''s rhetoric of parody presupposes a degree of self-conscious-ness on the part of the spectator, giving rise to a supplementary com-mentary on the sexuality and sexual identity of its star. Thus, the warning, 'I'm not like other guys,' can be read by the audience as a reference to Jackson's sexuality. Inasmuch as the video audience is conscious of the gossip which circulates around his star image, the statement of difference provokes other meanings: is he homosexual, transsexual or somehow asexual?

In the first metamorphosis Michael becomes a werewolf. As the film *Company of Wolves* (director Neil Jordan, 1984) demonstrates, werewolf mythology – lycanthropy – concerns the representation of male sexuality as 'naturally' predatory, bestial, aggressive, violent – in a word, 'monstrous'. Like 'Thriller', *Company of Wolves* employs similar special effects to show the metamorphosis of man to wolf in real time. And like the Angela Carter story on which it is based, the film can be read as a rewriting of the European folktale of Little Red Riding Hood to reveal its concerns with subjects of menstruation, the moon and the nature of male sexuality. In the fictional opening scene of 'Thriller' the connotation of innocence around the girl likens her to Red Riding Hood. But is Michael a big, bad wolf?

In the culmination of the chase sequence through the woods the girl takes the role of victim. Here, the disposition of point-of-view angles between the monster's dominant position and the supine position of the victim suggests rape, fusing the underlying sexual relation of romance with terror and violence. As the monster, Michael's transformation might suggest that beneath the boy-next-door image there is a 'real' man waiting to break out, a man whose masculinity is measured by a rapacious sexual appetite, 'hungry like the wolf'. But such an interpretation is undermined and subverted by the final shot of the metamorphosis. Michael-as-werewolf lets out a bloodcurdling howl, but this is in hilarious counterpoint to the collegiate 'M' on his jacket. What does it stand for? Michael? Monster? Macho Man? More like Mickey Mouse! The incongruity between the manifest signifier and the symbolic meaning of the monster opens up a gap in the text, to be filled with laughter.

Animals are regularly used to signify human attributes, with the wolf, lion, snake and eagle all understood as symbols of male sexuality. Jackson's subversion of this symbolism is writ large on the *Thriller* LP cover. Across the star's knee lies a young tiger cub, a brilliant little metaphor for the ambiguity of Jackson's image as a black male pop star. This plays on the star's 'man-child' image, and suggests a domesticated animality, hinting at menace beneath the cute and cuddly surface. Jackson's sexual ambiguity makes a mockery out of the menagerie of received images of masculinity.[18]

In the second metamorphosis Michael becomes a zombie. Less dramatic and horrifying than the first, this transformation cues the spectacular dance sequence that frames the chorus of the song. While the dance, choreographed by Michael Peters, makes visual one of the lines from the lyric, 'Night creatures crawl and the dead start to walk in their masquerade', it foregrounds Jackson-the-dancer, and his performance breaks loose from the narrative. As the ghouls begin to dance, the sequence elicits the same kind of parodic humour provoked by Vincent Price's rap. A visual equivalent of the incongruity between Price's voice and the argot of black soul culture is here created by the spectacle of the living dead performing with Jackson a funky dance routine. The sense of parody is intensified by the macabre makeup of the ghouls, bile dripping from their mouths. Jackson's makeup, casting a ghostly pallor over his skin and emphasising the contour of the skull, alludes to one of the paradigmatic masks of the horror genre, that of Lon Chaney in *The Phantom of the Opera* (1925).

Unlike the werewolf, the figure of the zombie, the undead corpse, does not represent sexuality so much as asexuality or antisexuality, suggesting the sense of *neutral eroticism* in Jackson's style as dancer. As has been observed:

> The movie star Michael most resembles is Fred Astaire – that *paragon of sexual vagueness*. Astaire never fit a type, hardly ever played a traditional romantic lead. He created his own niche by the sheer force of his tremendous talent.[19]

The dance sequence can be read as cryptic writing on this 'sexual vagueness' of Jackson's body in movement, in counterpoint to the androgyny of his image. The dance breaks out of the narrative structure, and Michael's body comes alive in movement, a rave from the grave: the scene can thus be seen as a commentary on the notion that as a star Jackson only 'comes alive' when he is on stage performing. The living dead evoke an existential liminality which corresponds to both the sexual indeterminacy of Jackson's dance and the somewhat morbid life-style that reportedly governs his off-stage existence. Both meanings are buried in the video 'cryptogram'.[20]

METAPHOR-MORPHOSIS

Finally, I feel compelled to return to the scene of the first metamorphosis. It enthralls and captivates, luring the spectator's gaze and petrifying it in wonder. This sense of both fear and fascination is engineered by the video's special effects. By showing the metamorphosis in 'real time' the spectacle violently distorts the features of Jackson's face. The horror effect of his monstrous appearance depends on the 'suspension of disbelief': we know that the monster is a fiction, literally a mask created by mechanical techniques, but repress or disavow this knowledge in order to participate in the 'thrills', the pleasures expected from the horror text. Yet in this splitting of levels of belief which the horror film presupposes, it is the credibility of the techniques themselves that is at stake in making the 'otherness' of the monster believable.[21]

The Making of Michael Jackson's Thriller (1984) demonstrates the special effects used in the video. We see makeup artists in the process of applying the 'mask' that will give Jackson the appearance of the monster. Of particular interest is the makeup artists' explanation of how the werewolf mask was designed and constructed: a series of transparent cells, each with details of the animal features of the mask, are gradually superimposed on a publicity image of Jackson from the cover of *Rolling Stone* magazine. It is this superimposition of fantastic and real upon Jackson's face that offers clues as to why the metamorphosis is so effective. Like the opening parody of the 1950s horror movie and its layering of roles that Jackson is playing (boyfriend/star), there is a slippage between different levels of belief on the part of the spectator.

The metamorphosis achieves a horrifying effect because the monster does not just mutilate the appearance of the boyfriend, but plays on the audience's awareness of Jackson's double role; thus, the credibility of the special effects violates the image of the star himself. At this metatextual level, the drama of the transformation is heightened by other performance signs that foreground Jackson as star. The squeaks, cries and other wordless sounds which emanate from his throat as he grips his stomach grotesquely mimic the sounds which are the stylistic trademark of Jackson's voice, and thus reinforce the impression that it is the 'real' Michael Jackson undergoing this mutation. Above all, the very first shots of the video highlight the makeup on his face – the lighting emphasises the pallor of his complexion and reveals the eerie sight of his skull beneath the curly-perm hairstyle. The very appearance of Jackson draws attention to the artificiality of his own image. As the monstrous mask is, literally, a construction made out of makeup and cosmetic 'work', the fictional world of the horror film merely appropriates what is already an artifice. In this sense, I suggest that the metamorphosis be seen as *a metaphor for the aesthetic reconstruction of Michael Jackson's face*.

The literal construction of the fantastic monster mask refers to other images of the star: the referent of the mask, as a sign in its own right, is a commonplace publicity image taken from the cover of a magazine. In this sense the mask refers not to the real person or private self, but to Michael-Jackson-as-an-image. The metamorphosis could thus be seen as an accelerated allegory of the morphological transformation of Jackson's facial features: from child to adult, from boyfriend to monster, from star to megastar – the sense of wonder generated by the video's special effects forms an allegory for the fascination with which the world beholds his reconstructed star image.

In 1983 Jackson took part in a TV special celebrating Motown's twenty-fifth anniversary, in which vintage footage was intercut with each act's live performance; the film was then edited and used as a support act on Motown artists' tours in England. This is how the reception of the film was described:

> The audience almost visibly tensed as Michael's voice...took complete control, attacking the songs with that increased repertoire of whoops, hiccups and gasps, with which he punctuates the lyric to such stylish, relaxing effect. And then he danced. The cocky strut of a superconfident child had been replaced by a lithe, menacing grace, and his impossibly lean frame, still boyishly gangly, when galvanised by the music, assumed a hypnotic, androgynous sexuality. Certainly, it was the first time in a long, long time I'd heard girls scream at a film screen.[22]

Amid all the screaming elicited by 'Thriller' it is possible to hear an ambiguous echo of those fans' response. As a pop idol Michael Jackson has been the object of such screaming since he was eleven years old – and surely such fandom is, for the star himself, a source of both pleasure and terror.

In 'The Face of Garbo' Barthes[23] sought to explore the almost universal appeal of film stars like Chaplin, Hepburn and Garbo by describing their faces as *masks*: aesthetic surfaces on which a society writes large its own preoccupations. Jackson's face may also be seen as such a mask, for his image has garnered the kind of cultural fascination that makes him more like a movie star than a modern-day rhythm and blues artist. The racial and sexual ambiguity of his image can also be seen as pointing to a range of questions about images of race and gender in popular culture and pop music. If we regard his face not as the manifestation of personality traits, but as a surface of artistic and social inscription, the ambiguities of Jackson's star image call into question received ideas about what black male artists in popular music should look like. Seen from this angle his experimentation with imagery represents a creative incursion upon a terrain in pop culture more visibly mapped out by white male stars like Mick Jagger, David Bowie or Boy George. At best, these stars have used androgyny and sexual ambiguity as part of their style in ways which question prevailing definitions of male sexuality and sexual identity. Key songs on *Thriller* highlight a similar problematisation of masculinity: on 'Wanna Be Startin' Somethin'' the narrator replies to rumour and speculation about his sexual preference, on 'Billy Jean' – a story about a fan who claims he is the father of her son – he refuses the paternal model of masculinity, and on 'Beat It' – 'Don't wanna see no blood, Don't be a macho man' – he explicitly deflates a bellicose model of manliness.

What makes Jackson's use of androgyny more compelling is that his work is located entirely in the Afro-American tradition of popular music, and thus must be seen in the context of imagery of black men and black male sexuality. Jackson not only questions dominant stereotypes of black masculinity,[24] but also gracefully steps outside the existing range of 'types' of black men. In so doing his style reminds us how some black men in the rhythm and blues tradition, such as Little Richard, used 'camp', in the sense that Susan Sontag calls 'the love of the unnatural: of artifice and exaggeration'[25] long before white pop stars began to exploit its shock value or subversive potential. Indeed, 'Thriller' is reminiscent of the camp excess of the originator of the music and horror combination in pop culture, Screamin' Jay Hawkins.

Horror imagery has fascinated the distinctly white male musical genre of 'heavy metal', in which acts like Alice Cooper and Ozzy Osbourne (Black Sabbath) consume themselves in self-parody. But like Hawkins, whose 'I Put a Spell on You' (1956) borrowed imagery from horror mythologies to articulate a scream, 'that found its way out of my big mouth *directly* through my heart and guts',[26] Jackson expresses another sort of screaming, one that articulates the erotic materiality of the human voice, its 'grain'. Writing about a musical tradition radically different from soul, Barthes coined this term to give 'the impossible account of an individual thrill that I constantly experience in listening to singing'.[27] 'Thriller' celebrates the fact that this thrill is shared by millions.

4

The Look

Rosalind Coward

'I adore women and my eyes are in love with them'
J. H. Lartigue, photographer

Mirror image/photographic image – pivotal points in the organisation of female desire. Women's experience of sexuality rarely strays far from ideologies and feelings about self-image. There's a preoccupation with the visual image – of self and others – and a concomitant anxiety about how these images measure up to a socially prescribed ideal.

The preoccupation with visual images might appear to be the effect of a culture which generally gives priority to visual impact rather than other sensual impressions. The dominance of the visual regime has been augmented by the media surrounding us. Film, photography and television all offer forms of entertainment and communication based on the circulation of visual images, on the sale of the images and the meanings conveyed by them. With the development of techniques of mechanical reproduction and the technology of visual recording, Western culture has become obsessed with looking and recording images of what is seen.

This preoccupation with visual images strikes at women in a very particular way. For looking is not a neutral activity. Human beings don't all look at things in the same way, innocently as it were. In this culture, the look is largely controlled by men. Privileged in general in this society, men also control the visual media. The film and television industries are dominated by men, as is the advertising industry. The photographic profession is no less a bastion of the values of male professionalism. While I don't wish to suggest there's an intrinsically male way of making images, there can be little doubt that entertainment as we know it is crucially predicated on a masculine investigation of women, and a circulation of women's images for men.

The camera in contemporary media has been put to use as an extension of the male gaze at women on the streets. Here, men can and do stare at women; men assess, judge and make advances on the basis of these visual impressions. The ability to scrutinise is premised on power. Indeed the look confers power; women's inability to return such a critical and aggressive look is a sign of subordination, of being the recipients of

Reading Images

another's assessment. Women, in the flesh, often feel embarrassed, irritated or downright angered by men's persistent gaze. But not wanting to risk male attention turning to male aggression, women avert their eyes and hurry on their way. Those women on the billboards, though; they look back. Those fantasy women stare off the walls with a look of urgent availability.

Some people – those concerned with maintaining the status quo – say that men's scrutiny of women is just part of the natural order. Man the hunter, a sort of cross between a rutting stag and David Bailey, roams the street, pouncing on whatever appeals to his aesthetic sensibility. Women, meanwhile, cultivate their looks, make themselves all the more appealing and siren-like, and lure men to a terrible fate – monogamy and the marital home. Such a theory appears to be a distortion – in reality, men often seem far more dependent on monogamous romantic sexual commitment than do women. But the theory also wilfully obscures the way in which sexual behaviour is formed according to social conventions and structures.

In this society, looking has become a crucial aspect of sexual relations, not because of any natural impulse, but because it is one of the ways in which domination and subordination are expressed. The relations involved in looking enmesh with coercive beliefs about the appropriate sexual behaviour for men and women. The saturation of society with images of women has nothing to do with men's natural appreciation of objective beauty, their aesthetic appreciation, and everything to do with an obsessive recording and use of women's images in ways which make men comfortable. Clearly this comfort is connected with feeling secure or powerful. And women are bound to this power precisely because visual impressions have been elevated to the position of holding the key to our psychic well-being, our social success, and indeed to whether or not we will be loved.

Men defend their scrutiny of women in terms of the aesthetic appeal of women. But this so-called aesthetic appreciation of women is nothing less than a decided preference for a 'distanced' view of the female body. The aesthetic appeal of women disguises a preference for *looking* at women's bodies, for keeping women separate, at a distance, and the ability to do this. Perhaps this sex-at-a-distance is the only complete secure relation which men can have with women. Perhaps other forms of contact are too unsettling.

Thus the profusion of images of women which characterises contemporary society could be seen as an obsessive distancing of women, a form of voyeurism.[1] Voyeurism is a way of taking sexual pleasure by looking at rather than being close to a particular object of desire, like a Peeping Tom. And Peeping Toms can always stay in control. Whatever may be going on, the Peeping Tom can always determine his own meanings for what he sees. Distanced he may be, but secure he remains. Is this why one of the startling 'discoveries' made by twentieth-century sexology was the widespread use of sexual imagery, even during sexual intercourse itself? Turning back the sheets on the twentieth-century bed, sexology found a spectacle of incompetent fumbling and rampant discontent with 'doing it'. Heterosexuality it seemed was hovering on the edge of extinction, saved only by porn in the sock drawer, or by the widespread availability of images which could be substituted in fantasy for the real things. Perhaps in the images, the meanings are fixed and reassuring; perhaps only in the images could true controlling security be reached?

Attraction to images of women's bodies presented as ideal types is none other than an attraction to a sight which is in some way reassuringly pleasurable. And we've seen that the prevailing visual ideal is invariably an aesthetic ideal which conveys the prevailing values about sexual behaviour. Today's ideal is immaturity, a modern variant of feminine passivity. Because the female body is the main object of attention, it is on women's bodies, on women's looks, that prevailing sexual definitions are placed. The 'aesthetic sex' is the subordinate sex because beauty like truth is one of those empty terms, filled by the values of a particular society at a given historical moment. So when a woman is upheld by society as beautiful, we can be sure she expresses, with her body, the values currently surrounding women's sexual behaviour. The emphasis on women's looks becomes a crucial way in which society exercises control over women's sexuality.

Strict control over women's sexuality seems to be a characteristic of male-dominated societies. Marriage, for instance, often operates to secure women's labour and reproductive capacity to the advantage of men. In some societies the control of women is very direct – restrictions on movement, like foot-binding, rituals of exclusion, like purdah, the imposition of terrible punishments for adultery. In our society, the coercion is much more hidden and probably all the more insidious. The last hundred years have seen less and less direct control on women's morality and fertility. Indeed, Western society prides itself on its 'advanced' morality. Some of the West's boasts of 'freedom' are based precisely on a boast of sexual freedom, a freedom from archaic traditional morality. Sexual freedom is supposed to mean that individuals are free to follow their preference for sexual partners without reference to the wishes of the community, the family or the state. Individuals are supposed to be drawn to one another without having to take into account property considerations or political considerations.

Here in the West, then, we have a spontaneous and true sexual morality. Untrammelled by ancient conventions, Cupid's dart is free to enter where it will. But the coercion exercised on women by the cultural obsession with women's appearances is precisely what is disguised by such beliefs. When we hear talk of freedom to choose sexual partners, we can be sure we'll also hear talk of visual appeal, the mysterious alchemy which strikes from the blue at the most awkward moments. And here's the coercion. Because women are compelled to make themselves attractive in certain ways, and those ways involve submitting to the culture's beliefs about appropriate sexual behaviour, women's appearances are laden down with cultural values, and women have to form their identities within these values, or, with difficulty, against them.

There's no simple matter of men imposing these meanings on women who can then take them or leave them depending on what they had for breakfast. Women are, more often than not, preoccupied with images, their own and other people's. However unconsciously, most members of this society get the message that there's a lot at stake in visual impact. Most women know to their cost that appearance is perhaps the crucial way by which men form opinions of women. For that reason, feelings about self-image get mixed up with feelings about security and comfort. Self-image in this society is enmeshed with judgments about desirability. And because desirability has been elevated to being the crucial reason for sexual relations, it sometimes appears to women that the whole possibility of being loved and comforted hangs on how their appearance will be received.

Surely, it is this meshing with visual appearance of questions of desirability and promises about security and comfort that accounts for women's deep fascination with the visual images? This would surely account for what has previously been recorded as women's narcissism. Narcissism is certainly a useful notion, but it is crucially limited as an explanation of women's relation to images. Narcissus, it will be remembered, was a mythological character who was captivated by, indeed fell in love with, his own self-image, his reflection in a pool. It has been suggested that all children pass through a narcissistic phase where they become entranced by their own self-image.[2] The phase is supposedly characterised by the infant's fascination with its mirror image. This mirror phase in fact offers the child the first possibility of a unified sense of self, a unified identity, whereas prior to this stage the child had been dominated by motor unco-ordination and was awash with contradictory impulses over which it had little control. This glorious self-love provides the child with the first possibilities of an identity, with a self which could act on its surroundings and manipulate things to its advantage. In so-called normal development, another libido arises, existing beside this self-love. The other libido is that directed outwards towards another person or object.

Freud casually added to his account of the development of all humans that women were, however, 'more narcissistic'; 'nor does (their) need lie in the direction of loving, but of being loved; and the man who fulfils this condition is the one who finds favour with them'.[3] This assertion of women's greater narcissism has been left largely unchallenged, because at one level it appears so accurate. Indeed, the term has even been adopted to explain the process which is supposed to occur when women are bombarded with images of other women – in films, on TV, in the bulk of advertisements. As with the use of women's faces as icons on women's magazines, it is often assumed that women *identify* with these images rather than *desire* them, as men might confronted with similiar images. A narcissistic identification is supposed to take place; women like looking at glamorous and highly sexualised images of other women because these images are meant to function like a mirror. The image like a mirror reflects back to women their own fascination with their own image.

True though it is that women, especially young women, are deeply concerned with their own images, it is radically incorrect to liken women's relation with media images to the happy state of Narcissus. Women's relation to their own self-image is much more likely to be dominated by discontent. We have only to turn to the problem pages of *Jackie*, the magazine for teenage girls, to hear a howl of dissatisfaction – 'I'm not attractive enough.' And Jane Fonda (in her *Work Out Book*) summarises the disappointment, leading so quickly to obsession, which characterises adolescence:

> From as early as I can remember my mother, her friends, my grand-mother, my governess, my sister – all the women who surrounded me – talked anxiously of the pros and cons of their physiques. Hefty thighs, small breasts, a biggish bottom – there was always some per-ceived imperfection to focus on. None of them seemed happy the way they were which bewildered me because the way they were seemed fine to my young eyes.
>
> In pursuit of 'the feminine ideal' – exemplified by voluptuous film stars and skinny fashion models – women it seemed were even pre-pared to do violence to themselves. My mother, for example, who was a rather slender, beautiful woman, was terrified of getting fat. She once said if she ever gained weight she'd have the excess flesh cut off!

Fascination there may be, but there's certainly no straightforward identification which women experience with the multitude of images of glamour women. Instead, advertisements, health and beauty advice, fashion tips are effective precisely because somewhere, perhaps even subconsciously, an anxiety, rather than a pleasurable identification, is awakened. We take an interest, yes. But these images do not give back a glow of self-love as the image in the pool did for Narcissus. The faces that look back imply a criticism.

Women's relation to these cultural ideals, and therefore to their own images, is more accurately described as a relation of narcissistic damage. Even women's relation to their own mirror image is retrospectively damaged by that critical glance of the cultural ideal. Over the mirror always hangs the image of the socially approved, massively consumed, widely circulated image of the generic Woman. She alone it seems is guaranteed an easy ride through life, guaranteed the approval of all and safe in expecting uncritical love. Only she is guaranteed to recapture that happy childhood state, where child and adults alike gloried in the child's image.

Advertising in this society builds precisely on the creation of an anxiety to the effect that, unless we measure up, we will not be loved. We are set to work on an ever-increasing number of areas of the body, labouring to perfect and eroticise an ever-increasing number of erotogenic zones. Every minute region of the body is now exposed to this scrutiny by the ideal. Mouth, hair, eyes, eyelashes, nails, fingers, hands, skin, teeth, lips, cheeks, shoulders, arms, legs, feet – all these and many more have become areas requiring work. Each area requires potions, moisturisers, conditioners, night creams, creams to cover up blemishes. Moisturise, display, clean off, rejuvenate – we could well be at it all day, preparing the face to meet the faces that we meet.

This is not only the strict grip of the cultural ideal; it is also the multiplication of areas of the body accessible to marketing. Here, areas not previously seen as sexual have been sexualised. And being sexualised, they come under the scrutiny of the ideal. New areas constructed as sensitive and sexual, capable of stimulation and excitation, capable of attracting attention, are new areas requiring *work* and *products*. Advertisements set in motion work and the desire for products; narcissistic damage is required to hold us in this axis of work and consumption.

Any visit to a hairdresser's tends to deliver up a little drama, an exemplary spectacle about the relation between the cultural ideal and the work women do on themselves. The mini-drama is always conducted around the mirror. First the client is sat in front of the mirror – 'How would you like it?' Then the mirror disappears – 'Come this way and have your hair washed.' Bedraggled but hopeful, the client returns to the mirror – the work is about to begin. And the final product? Well, how many times have you seen, or been, the client who to the amazement of the assembled company berates the hairdresser for the disaster visited on her head? Is it that in disappearing from the mirror the client imagines the *ideal* transformation, the work that will bring her mirror image into line with what she imagines it could be? Is the anger and disappointment just rage at the distance between self-image and that critical ideal that hangs menacingly beside us?

There is then, for women, an ambivalence between fascination and damage in looking at themselves and images of other women. The adult woman near totally abandons the love which the little girl had for her own image, in the period of narcissistic glory. But this culture damages the glory, turns it into a guilty secret. The girl-child discovers herself to be scrutinised, discovers herself to be the defined sex, the sex on which society seeks to write its sexual and moral ideals. She learns that in this scrutiny might lie the answer to whether she will be loved.

Where women's behaviour was previously controlled directly by state, family or church, control of women is now also effected through the scrutiny of women by visual ideals. Photography, film and television offer themselves as transparent recordings of reality. But it is in these media where the definitions are tightest, where the female body is most carefully scripted with the prevailing ideals. Women internalise the damage created by these media; it is the damage of being the differentiated and therefore the defined sex. Women become *the sex*, the sex differentiated from the norm which is masculine. Women are the sex which is constantly questioned, explained, defined. And as the defined sex, women are put to work by the images. The command created by an image-obsessed culture is 'Do some work! Transform Yourself! Look Better! Be more erotic!' And through this command to meet the ideal, our society writes one message loud and clear across the female body. *Do not act. Do not desire. Wait for men's attention.*

5

In Plato's Cave

Susan Sontag

Humankind lingers unregenerately in Plato's cave, still revelling, its age-old habit, in mere images of the truth. But being educated by photographs is not like being educated by older, more artisanal images. For one thing, there are a great many more images around, claiming our attention. The inventory started in 1839 and since then just about everything has been photographed, or so it seems. This very insatiability of the photographing eye changes the terms of confinement in the cave, our world. In teaching us a new visual code, photographs alter and enlarge our notions of what is worth looking at and what we have a right to observe. They are a grammar and, even more importantly, an ethics of seeing. Finally, the most grandiose result of the photographic enterprise is to give us the sense that we can hold the whole world in our heads – as an anthology of images.

To collect photographs is to collect the world. Movies and television programmes light up walls, flicker, and go out; but with still photographs the image is also an object, lightweight, cheap to produce, easy to carry about, accumulate, store. In Godard's *Les Carabiniers* (1963), two sluggish lumpen-peasants are lured into joining the King's Army by the promise that they will be able to loot, rape, kill, or do whatever else they please to the enemy, and get rich. But the suitcase of booty that Michel-Ange and Ulysse triumphantly bring home, years later, to their wives turns out to contain only picture postcards, hundreds of them, of Monuments, Department Stores, Mammals, Wonders of Nature, Methods of Transport, Works of Art, and other classified treasures from around the globe. Godard's gag vividly parodies the equivocal magic of the photographic image. Photographs are perhaps the most mysterious of all the objects that make up, and thicken, the environment we recognise as modern. Photographs really are experience captured, and the camera is the ideal arm of consciousness in its acquisitive mood.

To photograph is to appropriate the thing photographed. It means putting oneself into a certain relation to the world that feels like knowledge – and, therefore, like power. A now notorious first fall into alienation, habituating people to abstract the world into printed words, is supposed to have engendered that surplus of Faustian energy and psychic damage needed to build modern, inorganic societies. But print seems a less treacherous form of leaching out the world, of turning it into a mental object, than photographic images, which now provide most of the knowledge people have about the look of the past and the reach of the present. What is written about a person or an event is frankly an interpretation, as are handmade visual statements, like paintings and drawings. Photographed images do not seem to be statements about the world so much as pieces of it, miniatures of reality that anyone can make or acquire.

Photographs, which fiddle with the scale of the world, themselves get reduced, blown up, cropped, retouched, doctored, tricked out. They age, plagued by the usual ills of paper objects; they disappear; they become valuable, and get bought and sold; they are reproduced. Photographs, which package the world, seem to invite packaging. They are stuck in albums, framed and set on tables, tacked on walls, projected as slides. Newspapers and magazines feature them; cops alphabetise them; museums exhibit them; publishers compile them.

For many decades the book has been the most influential way of arranging (and usually miniaturising) photographs, thereby guaranteeing them longevity, if not immortality – photographs are fragile objects, easily torn or mislaid – and a wider public. The photograph in a book is, obviously, the image of an image. But since it is, to begin with, a printed, smooth object, a photograph loses much less of its essential quality when reproduced in a book than a painting does. Still, the book is not a wholly satisfactory scheme for putting groups of photographs into general circulation. The sequence in which the photographs are to be looked at is proposed by the order of pages, but nothing holds readers to the recommended order or indicates the amount of time to be spent on each photograph. Chris Marker's film, *Si j'avais quatre dromadaires* (1966), a brilliantly orchestrated meditation on photographs of all sorts and themes, suggests a subtler and more rigorous way of packaging (and enlarging) still photographs. Both the order and the exact time for looking at each photograph are imposed; and there is a gain in visual legibility and emotional impact. But photographs transcribed in a film cease to be collectable objects, as they still are when served up in books.

Photographs furnish evidence. Something we hear about, but doubt, seems proven when we're shown a photograph of it. In one version of its utility, the camera record incriminates. Starting with their use by the Paris police in the murderous roundup of Communards in June 1871, photographs became a useful tool of modern states in the surveillance and control of their increasingly mobile populations. In another version of its utility, the camera record justifies. A photograph passes for incontrovertible proof that a given thing happened. The picture may distort;

but there is always a presumption that something exists, or did exist, which is like what's in the picture. Whatever the limitations (through amateurism) or pretensions (through artistry) of the individual photographer, a photograph – any photograph – seems to have a more innocent, and therefore more accurate, relation to visible reality than do other mimetic objects. Virtuosi of the noble image like Alfred Stieglitz and Paul Strand, composing mighty, unforgettable photographs decade after decade, still want, first of all, to show something 'out there', just like the Polaroid owner for whom photographs are a handy, fast form of note-taking, or the shutterbug with a Brownie who takes snapshots as souvenirs of daily life.

While a painting or a prose description can never be other than a narrowly selective interpretation, a photograph can be treated as a narrowly selective transparency. But despite the presumption of veracity that gives all photographs authority, interest, seductiveness, the work that photographers do is no generic exception to the usually shady commerce between art and truth. Even when photographers are most concerned with mirroring reality, they are still haunted by tacit imperatives of taste and conscience. The immensely gifted members of the Farm Security Administration photographic project of the late 1930s (among them Walker Evans, Dorothea Lange, Ben Shahn, Russell Lee) would take dozens of frontal pictures of one of their sharecropper subjects until satisfied that they had gotten just the right look on film – the precise expression on the subject's face that supported their own notions about poverty, light, dignity, texture, exploitation, and geometry. In deciding how a picture should look, in preferring one exposure to another, photographers are always imposing standards on their subjects. Although there is a sense in which the camera does indeed capture reality, not just interpret it, photographs are as much an interpretation of the world as paintings and drawings are. Those occasions when the taking of photographs is relatively undiscriminating, promiscuous, or self-effacing do not lessen the didacticism of the whole enterprise. This very passivity – and ubiquity – of the photographic record is photography's 'message', its aggression.

Images which idealise (like most fashion and animal photography) are no less aggressive than work which makes a virtue of plainness (like class pictures, still lifes of the bleaker sort, and mug shots). There is an aggression implicit in every use of the camera. This is as evident in the 1840s and 1850s, photography's glorious first two decades, as in all the succeeding decades, during which technology made possible an ever increasing spread of that mentality which looks at the world as a set of potential photographs. Even for such early masters as David Octavius Hill and Julia Margaret Cameron who used the camera as a means of getting painterly images, the point of taking photographs was a vast departure from the aims of painters. From its start, photography implied the capture of the largest possible number of subjects. Painting never had so imperial a scope. The subsequent industrialisation of camera technology only carried out a promise inherent in photography from its very beginning: to democratise all experiences by translating them into images.

That age when taking photographs required a cumbersome and expensive contraption – the toy of the clever, the wealthy, and the obsessed – seems remote indeed from the era of sleek pocket cameras that invite anyone to take pictures. The first cameras, made in France and England in the early 1840s, had only inventors and buffs to operate them. Since there were then no professional photographers, there could not be amateurs either, and taking photographs had no clear social use; it was a gratuitous, that is, an artistic activity, though with few pretensions to being an art. It was only with its industrialisation that photography came into its own as art. As industrialisation provided social uses for the operations of the photographer, so the reaction against these uses reinforced the self-consciousness of photography-as-art.

Recently, photography has become almost as widely practised an amusement as sex and dancing – which means that, like every mass art form, photography is not practised by most people as an art. It is mainly a social rite, a defence against anxiety, and a tool of power.

Memorialising the achievements of individuals considered as members of families (as well as of other groups) is the earliest popular use of photography. For at least a century, the wedding photograph has been as much a part of the ceremony as the prescribed verbal formulae. Cameras go with family life. According to a sociological study done in France, most households have a camera, but a household with children is twice as likely to have at least one camera as a household in which there are no children. Not to take pictures of one's children, particularly when they are small, is a sign of parental indifference, just as not turning up for one's graduation picture is a gesture of adolescent rebellion.

Through photographs, each family constructs a portrait-chronicle of itself – a portable kit of images that bears witness to its connectedness. It hardly matters what activities are photographed so long as photographs get taken and are cherished. Photography becomes a rite of family life just when, in the industrialising countries of Europe and America, the very institution of the family starts undergoing radical surgery. As that claustrophobic unit, the nuclear family, was being carved out of a much larger family aggregate, photography came along to memorialise, to restate symbolically, the imperilled continuity and vanishing extendedness of family life. Those ghostly traces, photographs, supply the token presence of the dispersed relatives. A family's photograph album is generally about the extended family – and, often, is all that remains of it.

As photographs give people an imaginary possession of a past that is unreal, they also help people to take possession of space in which they are insecure. Thus, photography develops in tandem with one of the most characteristic of modern activities: tourism. For the first time in history, large numbers of people regularly travel out of their habitual environments for short periods of time. It seems positively unnatural to travel for pleasure without taking a camera along. Photographs will offer indisputable evidence that the trip was made, that the programme was carried out, that fun was had. Photographs document sequences of consumption carried on outside the view of family, friends, neighbours. But dependence on the camera, as the device that makes real what one is experiencing, doesn't fade when people travel more. Taking photographs fills the same need for the cosmopolitans accumulating photograph-trophies of their boat trip up the Albert Nile or their fourteen days in China as it does for lower-middle-class vacationers taking snapshots of the Eiffel Tower or Niagara Falls.

A way of certifying experience, taking photographs is also a way of refusing it – by limiting experience to a search for the photogenic, by converting experience into an image, a souvenir. Travel becomes a strategy for accumulating photographs. The very activity of taking pictures is soothing, and assuages general feelings of disorientation that are likely to be exacerbated by travel. Most tourists feel compelled to put the camera between themselves and whatever is remarkable that they encounter. Unsure of other responses, they take a picture. This gives shape to experience: stop, take a photograph, and move on. The method especially appeals to people handicapped by a ruthless work ethic – Germans, Japanese, and Americans. Using a camera appeases the anxiety which the work-driven feel about not working when they are on vacation and supposed to be having fun. They have something to do that is like a friendly imitation of work: they can take pictures.

People robbed of their past seem to make the most fervent picture takers, at home and abroad. Everyone who lives in an industrialised society is obliged gradually to give up the past, but in certain countries, such as the United States and Japan, the break with the past has been particularly traumatic. In the early 1970s, the fable of the brash American tourist of the 1950s and 1960s, rich with dollars and Babbittry, was replaced by the mystery of the group-minded Japanese tourist, newly released from his island prison by the miracle of overvalued yen, who is generally armed with two cameras, one on each hip.

Photography has become one of the principal devices for experiencing something, for giving an appearance of participation. One full-page ad shows a small group of people standing pressed together, peering out of the photograph, all but one looking stunned, excited, upset. The one who wears a different expression holds a camera to his eye; he seems self-possessed, is almost smiling. While the others are passive, clearly alarmed spectators, having a camera has transformed one person into something active, a voyeur: only he has mastered the situation. What do these people see? We don't know. And it doesn't matter. It is an Event: something worth seeing – and therefore worth photographing. The adcopy, white letters across the dark lower third of the photograph like news coming over a teletype machine, consists of just six words: '...Prague...Woodstock...Vietnam...Sapporo...Londonderry ...LEICA'. Crushed hopes, youth antics, colonial wars, and winter sports are alike – are equalised by the camera. Taking photographs has set up a chronic voyeuristic relation to the world which levels the meaning of all events.

A photograph is not just the result of an encounter between an event and a photographer; picture-taking is an event in itself, and one with ever more peremptory rights – to interfere with, to invade, or to ignore whatever is going on. Our very sense of situation is now articulated by the camera's interventions. The omnipresence of cameras persuasively suggests that time consists of interesting events, events worth photographing. This, in turn, makes it easy to feel that any event, once underway, and whatever its moral character, should be allowed to complete itself – so that something else can be brought into the world, the photograph. After the event has ended, the picture will still exist, conferring on the event a kind of immortality (and importance) it would never otherwise have enjoyed. While real people are out there killing themselves or other real people, the photographer stays behind his or her camera, creating a tiny element of another world: the imagine-world that bids to outlast us all.

Photographing is essentially an act of non-intervention. Part of the horror of such memorable coups of contemporary photojournalism as the pictures of a Vietnamese bonze reaching for the gasoline can, of a Bengali guerrilla in the act of bayoneting a trussed-up collaborator, comes from the awareness of how plausible it has become, in situations where the photographer has the choice between a photograph and a life, to choose the photograph. The person who intervenes cannot record; the person who is recording cannot intervene. Dziga Vertov's great film, *Man with a Movie Camera* (1929), gives the ideal image of the photographer as someone in perpetual movement, someone moving through a panorama of disparate events with such agility and speed that any intervention is out of the question. Hitchcock's *Rear Window* (1954) gives the complementary image: the photographer played by James Stewart has an intensified relation to one event, through his camera, precisely because he has a broken leg and is confined to a wheelchair; being temporarily immobilised prevents him from acting on what he sees, and makes it even more important to take pictures. Even if incompatible with intervention in a physical sense, using a camera is still a form of participation. Although the camera is an observation station, the act of photographing is more than passive observing. Like sexual voyeurism, it is a way of at least tacitly, often explicitly, encouraging whatever is going on to keep on happening. To take a picture is to have an interest in things as they are, in the status quo remaining unchanged (at least for as long as it takes to get a 'good' picture), to be in complicity with whatever makes a subject interesting, worth photographing – including, when that is the interest, another person's pain or misfortune.

'I always thought of photography as a naughty thing to do – that was one of my favourite things about it', Diane Arbus wrote, 'and when I first did it I felt very perverse.' Being a professional photographer can be thought of as naughty, to use Arbus's pop word, if the photographer seeks out subjects considered to be disreputable, taboo, marginal. But naughty subjects are harder to find these days. And what exactly is the perverse aspect of picture-taking? If professional photographers often have sexual fantasies when they are behind the camera, perhaps the perversion lies in the fact that these fantasies are both plausible and so inappropriate. In *Blowup* (1966), Antonioni has the fashion photographer hovering convulsively over Verushka's body with his camera clicking. Naughtiness, indeed! In fact, using a camera is not a very good way of getting at someone sexually. Between photographer and subject, there has to be distance. The camera doesn't rape, or even possess, though it may presume, intrude, trespass, distort, exploit, and, at the farthest reach of metaphor, assassinate – all activities that, unlike the sexual push and shove, can be conducted from a distance, and with some detachment.

There is a much stronger sexual fantasy in Michael Powell's extraordinary movie *Peeping Tom* (1960), which is not about a Peeping Tom but about a psychopath who kills women with a weapon concealed in his camera, while photographing them. Not once does he touch his subjects. He doesn't desire their bodies; he wants their presence in the form of filmed images – those showing them experiencing their own death – which he screens at home for his solitary pleasure. The movie assumes connections between impotence and aggression, professionalised looking and cruelty, which point to the central fantasy connected with the camera. The camera as phallus is, at most, a flimsy variant of the inescapable metaphor that everyone unselfconsciously employs. However hazy our awareness of this fantasy, it is named without subtlety whenever we talk about 'loading' and 'aiming' a camera, about 'shooting' a film.

The old-fashioned camera was clumsier and harder to reload than a brown Bess musket. The modern camera is trying to be a ray gun. One ad reads:

The Yashica Electro-35 GT is the spaceage camera your family will love. Take beautiful pictures day or night. Automatically. Without any nonsense. Just aim, focus and shoot. The GT's computer brain and electronic shutter will do the rest.

Like a car, a camera is sold as a predatory weapon – one that's as automated as possible, ready to spring. Popular taste expects an easy, an invisible technology. Manufacturers reassure their customers that taking pictures demands no skill or expert knowledge, that the machine is all-knowing, and responds to the slightest pressure of the will. It's as simple as turning the ignition key or pulling the trigger.

Like guns and cars, cameras are fantasy-machines whose use is addictive. However, despite the extravagances of ordinary language and advertising, they are not lethal. In the hyperbole that markets cars like guns, there is at least this much truth: except in wartime, cars kill more people than guns do. The camera/gun does not kill, so the ominous metaphor seems to be all bluff – like a man's fantasy of having a gun, knife, or tool between his legs. Still, there is something predatory in the act of taking a picture. To photograph people is to violate them, by seeing them as they never see themselves, by having knowledge of them they can never have; it turns people into objects that can be symbolically possessed. Just as the camera is a sublimation of the gun, to photograph someone is a sublimated murder – a soft murder, appropriate to a sad, frightened time.

Eventually, people might learn to act out more of their aggressions with cameras and fewer with guns, with the price being an even more image-choked world. One situation where people are switching from bullets to film is the photographic safari that is replacing the gun safari in East Africa. The hunters have Hasselblads instead of Winchesters; instead of looking through a telescopic sight to aim a rifle, they look through a viewfinder to frame a picture. In end-of-the-century London, Samuel Butler complained that 'there is a photographer in every bush, going about like a roaring lion seeking whom he may devour'. The photographer is now charging real beasts, beleaguered and too rare to kill. Guns have metamorphosed into cameras in this earnest comedy, the ecology safari, because nature has ceased to be what it always had been – what people needed protection from. Now nature – tamed, endangered, mortal – needs to be protected from people. When we are afraid, we shoot. But when we are nostalgic, we take pictures.

It is a nostalgic time right now, and photographs actively promote nostalgia. Photography is an elegiac art, a twilight art. Most subjects photographed are, just by virtue of being photographed, touched with pathos. An ugly or grotesque subject may be moving because it has been dignified by the attention of the photographer. A beautiful subject can be the object of rueful feelings, because it has aged or decayed or no longer exists. All photographs are *memento mori*. To take a photograph is to participate in another person's (or thing's) mortality, vulnerability, mutability. Precisely by slicing out this moment and freezing it, all photographs testify to time's relentless melt.

Cameras began duplicating the world at that moment when the human landscape started to undergo a vertiginous rate of change: while an untold number of forms of biological and social life are being destroyed in a brief span of time, a device is available to record what is disappearing. The moody, intricately textured Paris of Atget and Brassaï is mostly gone. Like the dead relatives and friends preserved in the family album, whose presence in photographs exorcises some of the anxiety and remorse prompted by their disappearance, so the photographs of neighbourhoods now torn down, rural places disfigured and made barren, supply our pocket relation to the past.

A photograph is both a pseudo-presence and a token of absence. Like a wood fire in a room, photographs – especially those of people, of distant landscapes and faraway cities, of the vanished past – are incitements to reverie. The sense of the unattainable that can be evoked by photographs feeds directly into the erotic feelings of those for whom desirability is enhanced by distance. The lover's photograph hidden in a married woman's wallet, the poster photograph of a rock star tacked up over an adolescent's bed, the campaign-button image of a politician's face pinned on a voter's coat, the snapshots of a cabdriver's children clipped to the visor – all such talismanic uses of photographs express a feeling both sentimental and implicitly magical: they are attempts to contact or lay claim to another reality.

Photographs can abet desire in the most direct, utilitarian way – as when someone collects photographs of anonymous examples of the desirable as an aid to masturbation. The matter is more complex when photographs are used to stimulate the moral impulse. Desire has no history – at least, it is experienced in each instance as all foreground, immediacy. It is aroused by archetypes and is, in that sense, abstract. But moral feelings are embedded in history, whose personae are concrete, whose situations are always specific. Thus, almost opposite rules hold true for the use of the photograph to awaken desire and to awaken conscience. The images that mobilise conscience are always linked to a given historical situation. The more general they are, the less likely they are to be effective.

A photograph that brings news of some unsuspected zone of misery cannot make a dent in public opinion unless there is an appropriate context of feeling and attitude. The photographs Mathew Brady and his colleagues took of the horrors of the battlefields did not make people any less keen to go on with the Civil War. The photographs of ill-clad, skeletal prisoners held at Andersonville inflamed Northern public opinion – against the South. (The effect of the Andersonville photographs must have been partly due to the very novelty, at that time, of seeing photographs.) The political understanding that many Americans came to in the 1960s would allow them, looking at the photographs Dorothea Lange took of Nisei on the West Coast being transported to internment camps in 1942, to recognise their subject for what it was – a crime committed by the government against a large group of American citizens. Few people who saw those photographs in the 1940s could have had so unequivocal a reaction; the grounds for such a judgment were covered over by the pro-war consensus. Photographs cannot create a moral position, but they can reinforce one – and can help build a nascent one.

Photographs may be more memorable than moving images, because they are a neat slice of time, not a flow. Television is a stream of under-selected images, each of which cancels its predecessor. Each still photograph is a privileged moment, turned into a slim object that one can keep and look at again. Photographs like the one that made the front page of most newspapers in the world in 1972 – a naked South Vietnamese child just sprayed by American napalm, running down a highway toward the camera, her arms open, screaming with pain – probably did more to increase the public revulsion against the war than a hundred hours of televised barbarities.

One would like to imagine that the American public would not have been so unanimous in its acquiescence to the Korean War if it had been confronted with photographic evidence of the devastation of Korea, an ecocide and genocide in some respects even more thorough than those inflicted on Vietnam a decade later. But the supposition is trivial. The public did not see such photographs because there was, ideologically, no space for them. No one brought back photographs of daily life in Pyongyang, to show that the enemy had a human face, as Felix Greene and Marc Riboud brought back photographs of Hanoi. Americans did have access to photographs of the suffering of the Vietnamese (many of which came from military sources and were taken with quite a different use in mind) because journalists felt backed in their efforts to obtain those photographs, the event having been defined by a significant number of people as a savage colonialist war. The Korean War was understood differently – as part of the just struggle of the Free World against the Soviet Union and China – and, given that characterisation, photographs of the cruelty of unlimited American firepower would have been irrelevant.

Though an event has come to mean, precisely, something worth photographing, it is still ideology (in the broadest sense) that determines what constitutes an event. There can be no evidence, photographic or otherwise, of an event until the event itself has been named and characterised.

And it is never photographic evidence which can construct – more properly, identify – events; the contribution of photography always follows the naming of the event. What determines the possibility of being affected morally by photographs is the existence of a relevant political consciousness. Without a politics, photographs of the slaughter-bench of history will most likely be experienced as, simply, unreal or as a demoralising emotional blow.

The quality of feeling, including moral outrage, that people can muster in response to photographs of the oppressed, the exploited, the starving, and the massacred also depends on the degree of their familiarity with these images. Don McCullin's photographs of emaciated Biafrans in the early 1970s had less impact for some people than Werner Bischof's photographs of Indian famine victims in the early 1950s because those images had become banal, and the photographs of Tuareg families dying of starvation in the sub-Sahara that appeared in magazines everywhere in 1973 must have seemed to many like an unbearable replay of a now familiar atrocity exhibition.

Photographs shock insofar as they show something novel. Unfortunately, the ante keeps getting raised – partly through the very proliferation of such images of horror. One's first encounter with the photographic inventory of ultimate horror is a kind of revelation, the prototypically modern revelation, a negative epiphany. For me, it was photographs of Bergen-Belsen and Dachau which I came across by chance in a bookstore in Santa Monica in July 1945. Nothing I have seen – in photographs or in real life – ever cut me as sharply, deeply, instantaneously. Indeed, it seems plausible to me to divide my life into two parts, before I saw those photographs (I was twelve) and after, though it was several years before I understood fully what they were about. What good was served by seeing them? They were only photographs – of an event I had scarcely heard of and could do nothing to affect, of suffering I could hardly imagine and could do nothing to relieve. When I looked at those photographs, something broke. Some limit had been reached, and not only that of horror; I felt irrevocably grieved, wounded, but a part of my feelings started to tighten; something went dead; something is still crying.

To suffer is one thing; another thing is living with the photographed images of suffering, which does not necessarily strengthen conscience and the ability to be compassionate. It can also corrupt them. Once one has seen such images, one has started down the road of seeing more – and more. Images transfix. Images anaesthetise. An event known through photographs certainly becomes more real than it would have been if one had never seen the photographs – think of the Vietnam War. (For a counter-example, think of the Gulag Archipelago, of which we have no photographs.) But after repeated exposure to images it also becomes less real.

The same law holds for evil as for pornography. The shock of photographed atrocities wears off with repeated viewings, just as the surprise and bemusement felt the first time one sees a pornographic movie wear off after one sees a few more. The sense of taboo which makes us indignant and sorrowful is not much sturdier than the sense of taboo that regulates the definition of what is obscene. And both have been sorely tried in recent years. The vast photographic catalogue of misery and injustice throughout the world has given everyone a certain familiarity with atrocity, making the horrible seem more ordinary – making it appear familiar, remote ('it's only a photograph'), inevitable. At the time of the first photographs of the Nazi camps, there was nothing banal about these images. After thirty years, a saturation point may have been reached. In these last decades, 'concerned' photography has done at least as much to deaden conscience as to arouse it.

The ethical content of photographs is fragile. With the possible exception of photographs of those horrors, like the Nazi camps, that have gained the status of ethical reference points, most photographs do not keep their emotional charge. A photograph of 1900 that was affecting then because of its subject would, today, be more likely to move us because it is a photograph taken in 1900. The particular qualities and intentions of photographs tend to be swallowed up in the generalised pathos of time past. Aesthetic distance seems built into the very experience of looking at photographs, if not right away, then certainly with the passage of time. Time eventually positions most photographs, even the most amateurish, at the level of art.

The industrialisation of photography permitted its rapid absorption into rational – that is, bureaucratic – ways of running society. No longer toy images, photographs became part of the general furniture of the environment – touchstones and confirmations of that reductive approach to reality which is considered realistic. Photographs were enrolled in the service of important institutions of control, notably the family and the police, as symbolic objects and as pieces of information. Thus, in the bureaucratic cataloguing of the world, many important documents are not valid unless they have, affixed to them, a photograph-token of the citizen's face.

The 'realistic' view of the world compatible with bureaucracy redefines knowledge – as techniques and information. Photographs are valued because they give information. They tell one what there is; they make an inventory. To spies, meteorologists, coroners, archaeologists, and other information professionals, their value is inestimable. But in the situations in which most people use photographs, their value as information is of the same order as fiction. The information that photographs can give starts to seem very important at that moment in cultural history when everyone is thought to have a right to something called news. Photographs were seen as a way of giving information to people who do not take easily to reading. The *Daily News* still calls itself 'New York's Picture Newspaper', its bid for populist identity. At the opposite end of the scale, *Le Monde*, a newspaper designed for skilled, well-informed readers, runs no photographs at all. The presumption is that, for such readers, a photograph could only illustrate the analysis contained in an article.

A new sense of the notion of information has been constructed around the photographic image. The photograph is a thin slice of space as well as time. In a world ruled by photographic images, all borders ('framing') seem arbitrary. Anything can be separated, can be made discontinuous, from anything else. All that is necessary is to frame the subject differently. (Conversely, anything can be made adjacent to anything else.) Photography reinforces a nominalist view of social reality as consisting of small units of an apparently infinite number – as the number of photographs that could be taken of anything is unlimited. Through photographs, the world becomes a series of unrelated, freestanding particles; and history, past and present, a set of anecdotes and *faits divers*. The camera makes reality atomic, manageable, and opaque. It is a view of the world which denies interconnectedness, continuity, but which confers on each moment the character of a mystery. Any photograph has multiple meanings; indeed, to see something in the form of a photograph is to encounter a potential object of fascination. The ultimate wisdom of the photographic image is to say: 'There is the surface. Now think – or rather feel, intuit – what is beyond it, what the reality must be like if it looks this way.' Photographs, which cannot themselves explain anything, are inexhaustible invitations to deduction, speculation, and fantasy.

Photography implies that we know about the world if we accept it as the camera records it. But this is the opposite of understanding, which starts from *not* accepting the world as it looks. All possibility of understanding is rooted in the ability to say no. Strictly speaking, one never understands anything from a photograph. Of course, photographs fill in blanks in our mental pictures of the present and the past: for example, Jacob Riis's images of New York squalor in the 1880s are sharply instructive to those unaware that urban poverty in late-nineteenth-century America was really that Dickensian. Nevertheless, the camera's rendering of reality must always hide more than it discloses. As Brecht points out, a photograph of the Krupp works reveals virtually nothing about that organisation. In contrast to the amorous relation, which is based on how something looks, understanding is based on how it functions. And functioning takes place in time, and must be explained in time. Only that which narrates can make us understand.

The limit of photographic knowledge of the world is that, while it can goad conscience, it can, finally, never be ethical or political knowledge.

The knowledge gained through still photographs will always be some kind of sentimentalism, whether cynical or humanist. It will be a knowledge at bargain prices – a semblance of knowledge, a semblance of wisdom; as the act of taking pictures is a semblance of appropriation, a semblance of rape. The very muteness of what is, hypothetically, comprehensible in photographs is what constitutes their attraction and provocativeness. The omnipresence of photographs has an incalculable effect on our ethical sensibility. By furnishing this already crowded world with a duplicate one of images, photography makes us feel that the world is more available than it really is.

Needing to have reality confirmed and experience enhanced by photographs is an aesthetic consumerism to which everyone is now addicted. Industrial societies turn their citizens into image-junkies; it is the most irresistible form of mental pollution. Poignant longings for beauty, for an end to probing below the surface, for a redemption and celebration of the body of the world – all these elements of erotic feeling are affirmed in the pleasure we take in photographs. But other, less liberating feelings are expressed as well. It would not be wrong to speak of people having a *compulsion* to photograph: to turn experience itself into a way of seeing. Ultimately, having an experience becomes identical with taking a photograph of it, and participating in a public event comes more and more to be equivalent to looking at it in photographed form. That most logical of nineteenth-century aesthetes, Mallarmé, said that everything in the world exists in order to end in a book. Today everything exists to end in a photograph.

6

Camera Lucida: Reflections on Photography

Roland Barthes

There I was, alone in the apartment where she had died, looking at these pictures of my mother, one by one, under the lamp, gradually moving back in time with her, looking for the truth of the face I had loved. And I found it.

The photograph was very old. The corners were blunted from having been pasted into an album, the sepia print had faded, and the picture just managed to show two children standing together at the end of a little wooden bridge in a glassed-in conservatory, what was called a Winter Garden in those days. My mother was five at the time (1898), her brother seven. He was leaning against the bridge railing, along which he had extended one arm; she, shorter than he, was standing a little back, facing the camera; you could tell that the photographer had said, 'Step forward a little so we can see you'; she was holding one finger in the other hand, as children often do, in an awkward gesture. The brother and sister, united, as I knew, by the discord of their parents, who were soon to divorce, had posed side by side, alone, under the palms of the Winter Garden (it was the house where my mother was born, in Chennevières-sur-Marne).

I studied the little girl and at last rediscovered my mother. The distinctness of her face, the naïve attitude of her hands, the place she had docilely taken without either showing or hiding herself, and finally her expression, which distinguished her, like Good from Evil, from the hysterical little girl, from the simpering doll who plays at being a grown-up – all this constituted the figure of a sovereign *innocence* (if you will take this word according to its etymology, which is: 'I do no harm'), all this had transformed the photographic pose into that untenable paradox which she had nonetheless maintained all her life: the assertion of a gentleness. In this little girl's image I saw the kindness which had formed her being immediately and forever, without her having inherited it from anyone; how could this kindness have proceeded from the imperfect parents who had loved her so badly – in short: from a family? Her kindness was specifically *out-of-play*, it belonged to no system, or at least it was located at the limits of a morality (evangelical, for instance); I could not define it better than by this feature (among others): that during the whole of our life together, she never made a single 'observation'. This extreme and particular circumstance, so abstract in relation to an image, was nonetheless present in the face revealed in the photograph I had just discovered. 'Not a just image, just an image', Godard says. But my grief wanted a just image, an image which would be both justice and accuracy – *justesse*: just an image, but a just image. Such, for me, was the Winter Garden Photograph.

For once, photography gave me a sentiment as certain as remembrance, just as Proust experienced it one day when, leaning over to take off his boots, there suddenly came to him his grandmother's true face, 'whose living reality I was experiencing for the first time, in an involuntary and complete memory'. The unknown photographer of Chennevières-sur-Marne had been the mediator of a truth, as much as Nadar making of his mother (or of his wife – no one knows for certain) one of the loveliest photographs in the world; he had produced a supererogatory photograph which contained more than what the technical being of photography can reasonably offer. Or again (for I am trying to express this truth) this Winter Garden Photograph was for me like the last music Schumann wrote before collapsing, that first *Gesang der Frühe* which accords with both my mother's being and my grief at her death; I could not express this accord except by an infinite series of adjectives, which I omit, convinced however that this photograph collected all the possible predicates from which my mother's being was constituted and whose suppression or partial alteration, conversely, had sent me back to these photographs of her which had left me so unsatisfied. These same photographs, which phenomenology would call 'ordinary' objects, were merely analogical, provoking only her identity, not her truth; but the Winter Garden Photograph was indeed essential, it achieved for me, utopically, *the impossible science of the unique being*.

Nor could I omit this from my reflection: that I had discovered this photograph by moving back through Time. The Greeks entered into Death backward: what they had before them was their past. In the same way I worked back through a life, not my own, but the life of someone I love. Starting from her latest image, taken the summer before her death (so tired, so noble, sitting in front of the door of our house, surrounded by my friends), I arrived, traversing threequarters of a century, at the image of a child: I stare intensely at the Sovereign Good of childhood, of the mother, of the mother-as-child. Of course I was then losing her twice over, in her final fatigue and in her first photograph, for me the last; but it was also at this moment that everything turned around and I discovered her *as into herself* ... (... *eternity changes her*, to complete Mallarmé's verse).

This movement of the Photograph (of the order of photographs) I have experienced in reality. At the end of her life, shortly before the moment when I looked through her pictures and discovered the Winter Garden Photograph, my mother was weak, very weak. I lived in her weakness (it was impossible for me to participate in a world of strength, to go out in the evenings; all social life appalled me). During her illness, I nursed her, held the bowl of tea she liked because it was easier to drink from than from a cup; she had become my little girl, uniting for me with that essential child she was in her first photograph. In Brecht, by a reversal I used to admire a good deal, it is the son who (politically) educates the mother; yet I never educated my mother, never converted her to anything at all; in a sense I never 'spoke' to her, never 'discoursed' in her presence, for her; we supposed, without saying anything of the kind to each other, that the frivolous insignificance of language, the suspension of images must be the very space of love, its music. Ultimately I experienced her, strong as she had been, my inner law, as my feminine child. Which was my way of resolving Death. If, as so many philosophers have said, Death is the harsh victory of the race, if the particular dies for the satisfaction of the universal, if after having been reproduced as other than himself, the individual dies, having thereby denied and transcended himself, I who had not procreated, I had, in her very illness, engendered my mother. Once she was dead I no longer had any reason to attune myself to the progress of the superior Life Force (the race, the species). My particularity could never again universalise itself (unless, utopically, by writing, whose project henceforth would become the unique goal of my life). From now on I could do no more than await my total, undialectical death.

That is what I read in the Winter Garden Photograph.

Something like an essence of the Photograph floated in this particular picture. I therefore decided to 'derive' all Photography (its 'nature') from the only photograph which assuredly existed for me, and to take it somehow as a guide for my last investigation. All the world's photographs formed a Labyrinth. I knew that at the centre of this Labyrinth I would find nothing but this sole picture, fulfilling Nietzsche's prophecy: 'A labyrinthine man never seeks the truth, but only his Ariadne.' The Winter Garden Photograph was my Ariadne, not because it would help me discover a secret thing (monster or treasure), but because it would tell me what constituted that thread which drew me toward Photography. I had understood that henceforth I must interrogate the evidence of Photography, not from the viewpoint of pleasure, but in relation to what we romantically call love and death.

(I cannot reproduce the Winter Garden Photograph. It exists only for me. For you, it would be nothing but an indifferent picture, one of the thousand manifestations of the 'ordinary'; it cannot in any way constitute the visible object of a science; it cannot establish an objectivity, in the positive sense of the term; at most it would interest your *studium*: period, clothes, photogeny; but in it, for you, no wound.)

From the beginning, I had determined on a principle for myself: never to reduce myself-as-subject, confronting certain photographs, to the disincarnated, disaffected *socius* which science is concerned with. This principle obliged me to 'forget' two institutions: the Family, the Mother.

An unknown person has written me: 'I hear you are preparing an album of family photographs' (rumour's extravagant progress). No: neither album nor family. For a long time, the family, for me, was my mother and, at my side, my brother; beyond that, nothing (except the memory of grandparents); no 'cousin', that unit so necessary to the constitution of the family group. Besides, how opposed I am to that scientific way of treating the family as if it were uniquely a fabric of constraints and rites: either we code it as a group of immediate allegiances or else we make it into a knot of conflicts and repressions. As if our experts cannot conceive that there are families 'whose members love one another'.

And no more than I would reduce my family to the Family, would I reduce my mother to the Mother. Reading certain general studies, I saw that they might apply quite convincingly to my situation: commenting on Freud (*Moses and Monotheism*), J. J. Goux explains that Judaism rejected the image in order to protect itself from the risk of worshipping the Mother; and that Christianity, by making possible the representation of the maternal feminine, transcended the rigour of the Law for the sake of the Image-Repertoire. Although growing up in a religion-without-images where the Mother is not worshipped (Protestantism) but doubtless formed culturally by Catholic art, when I confronted the Winter Garden Photograph I gave myself up to the Image, to the Image-Repertoire. Thus I could understand my generality; but having understood it, invincibly I escaped from it. In the Mother, there was a radiant, irreducible core: my mother. It is always maintained that I should suffer more because I have spent my whole life with her; but my suffering proceeds from *who she was*; and it is because she was who she was that I lived with her. To the Mother-as-Good, she had added that grace of being an individual soul. I might say, like the Proustian Narrator at his grandmother's death: 'I did not insist only upon suffering, but upon respecting the originality of my suffering'; for this originality was the reflection of what was absolutely irreducible in her, and thereby lost forever. It is said that mourning, by its gradual labour, slowly erases pain; I could not, I cannot believe this; because for me, Time eliminates the emotion of loss (I do not weep), that is all. For the rest, everything has remained motionless. For what I have lost is not a Figure (the Mother), but a being; and not a being, but a *quality* (a soul): not the indispensable, but the irreplaceable. I could live without the Mother (as we all do, sooner or later); but what life remained would be absolutely and entirely *unqualifiable* (without quality).

What I had noted at the beginning, in a free and easy manner, under cover of method, i.e., that every photograph is somehow co-natural with its referent, I was rediscovering, overwhelmed by the truth of the image. Henceforth I would have to consent to combine two voices: the voice of banality (to say what everyone sees and knows) and the voice of singularity (to replenish such banality with all the élan of an emotion which belonged only to myself). It was as if I were seeking the nature of a verb which had no infinitive, only tense and mode.

First of all I had to conceive, and therefore if possible express properly (even if it is a simple thing) how Photography's Referent is not the same as the referent of other systems of representation. I call 'photographic referent' not the *optionally* real thing to which an image or a sign refers but the *necessarily* real thing which has been placed before the lens, without which there would be no photograph. Painting can feign reality without having seen it. Discourse combines signs which have referents, of course, but these referents can be and are most often 'chimeras'. Contrary to these imitations, in Photography I can never deny that *the thing has been there*. There is a superimposition here: of reality and of the past. And since this constraint exists only for Photography, we must consider it, by reduction, as the very essence, the *noeme* of Photography. What I intentionalise in a photograph (we are not yet speaking of film) is neither Art nor Communication, it is Reference, which is the founding order of Photography.

The name of Photography's *noeme* will therefore be: 'That-has-been', or again: the Intractable. In Latin (a pedantry necessary because it illuminates certain nuances), this would doubtless be said: *interfuit*: what I see has been here, in this place which extends between infinity and the subject (*operator* or *spectator*); it has been here, and yet immediately separated; it has been absolutely, irrefutably present, and yet already deferred. It is all this which the verb *intersum* means.

In the daily flood of photographs, in the thousand forms of interest they seem to provoke, it may be that the *noeme* 'That-has-been' is not repressed (a *noeme* cannot be repressed) but experienced with indifference, as a feature which goes without saying. It is this indifference which the Winter Garden Photograph had just roused me from. According to a paradoxical order – since usually we verify things before declaring them 'true' – under the effect of a new experience, that of intensity, I had induced the truth of the image, the reality of its origin; I had identified truth and reality in a unique emotion, in which I henceforth placed the nature – the genius – of Photography, since no painted portrait, supposing that it seemed 'true' to me, could compel me to believe its referent had really existed.

I might put this differently: what founds the nature of Photography is the pose. The physical duration of this pose is of little consequence; even in the interval of a millionth of a second (Edgerton's drop of milk) there has still been a pose, for the pose is not, here, the attitude of the target or even a technique of the *Operator*, but the term of an 'intention' of reading: looking at a photograph, I inevitably include in my scrutiny the thought of that instant, however brief, in which a real thing happened to be motionless in front of the eye. I project the present photograph's immobility upon the past shot, and it is this arrest which constitutes the pose. This explains why the Photograph's *noeme* deteriorates when this Photograph is animated and becomes cinema: in the Photograph, something *has posed* in front of the tiny hole and has remained there forever (that is my feeling); but in cinema, something *has passed* in front of this same tiny hole: the pose is swept away and denied by the continuous series of images: it is a different phenomenology, and therefore a different art which begins here, though derived from the first one.

In Photography, the presence of the thing (at a certain past moment) is never metaphoric; and in the case of animated beings, their life as well, except in the case of photographing corpses; and even so: if the photograph then becomes horrible, it is because it certifies, so to speak, that the corpse is alive, as *corpse*: it is the living image of a dead thing. For the photograph's immobility is somehow the result of a perverse confusion between two concepts: the Real and the Live: by attesting that the object has been real, the photograph surreptitiously induces belief that it is alive, because of that delusion which makes us attribute to Reality an absolutely superior, somehow eternal value; but by shifting this reality to the past ('this-has-been'), the photograph suggests that it is already dead. Hence it would be better to say that Photography's inimitable feature (its *noeme*) is that someone has seen the referent (even if it is a matter of objects) *in flesh and blood*, or again *in person*. Photography, moreover, began, historically, as an art of the Person: of identity, of civil status, of what we might call, in all senses of the term, the body's *formality*. Here again, from a phenomenological viewpoint, the cinema begins to differ from the Photograph; for the (fictional) cinema combines two poses: the actor's 'this-has-been' and the role's, so that (something I would not experience before a painting) I can never see or see again in a film certain actors whom I know to be dead without a kind of melancholy: the melancholy of Photography itself (I experience this same emotion listening to the recorded voices of dead singers).

I think again of the portrait of William Casby, 'born a slave', photographed by Avedon. The *noeme* here is intense; for the man I see here *has been* a slave: he certifies that slavery has existed, not so far from us; and he certifies this not by historical testimony but by a new, somehow experiential order of proof, although it is the past which is in question – a proof no longer merely induced: the proof-according-to-St-Thomas-seeking-to-touch-the-resurrected-Christ. I remember keeping for a long time a photograph I had cut out of a magazine – lost subsequently, like everything too carefully put away – which showed a slave market: the slave-master, in a hat, standing; the slaves, in loincloths, sitting. I repeat: a photograph, not a drawing or engraving; for my horror and my fascination as a child came from this: that there was a *certainty* that such a thing had existed: not a question of exactitude, but of reality: the historian was no longer the mediator, slavery was given without mediation, the fact was established *without method*.

It is often said that it was the painters who invented Photography (by bequeathing it their framing, the Albertian perspective, and the optic of the *camera obscura*). I say: no, it was the chemists. For the *noeme* 'That-has-been' was possible only on the day when a scientific circumstance (the discovery that silver halogens were sensitive to light) made it possible to recover and print directly the luminous rays emitted by a variously lighted object. The photograph is literally an emanation of the referent. From a real body, which was there, proceed radiations which ultimately touch me, who am here; the duration of the transmission is insignificant; the photograph of the missing being, as Sontag says, will touch me like the delayed rays of a star. A sort of umbilical cord links the body of the photographed thing to my gaze: light, though impalpable, is here a carnal medium, a skin I share with anyone who has been photographed.

It seems that in Latin 'photograph' would be said 'imago lucis opera expressa'; which is to say: image revealed, 'extracted', 'mounted', 'expressed' (like the juice of a lemon) by the action of light. And if Photography belonged to a world with some residual sensitivity to myth, we should exult over the richness of the symbol: the loved body is immortalised by the mediation of a precious metal, silver (monument and luxury); to which we might add the notion that this metal, like all the metals of Alchemy, is alive.

Perhaps it is because I am delighted (or depressed) to know that the thing of the past, by its immediate radiations (its luminances), has really touched the surface which in its turn my gaze will touch, that I am not very fond of Colour. An anonymous daguerreotype of 1843 shows a man and a woman in a medallion subsequently tinted by the miniaturists on the staff of the photographic studio: I always feel (unimportant what actually occurs) that in the same way, colour is a coating applied *later on* to the original truth of the black-and-white photograph. For me, colour is an artifice, a cosmetic (like the kind used to paint corpses). What matters to me is not the photograph's 'life' (a purely ideological notion) but the certainty that the photographed body touches me with its own rays and not with a superadded light.

(Hence the Winter Garden Photograph, however pale, is for me the treasury of rays which emanated from my mother as a child, from her hair, her skin, her dress, her gaze, *on that day*.)

7

The Work of Art in the Age of Mechanical Reproduction

Walter Benjamin

Our fine arts were developed, their types and uses were established, in times very different from the present, by men whose power of action upon things was insignificant in comparison with ours. But the amazing growth of our techniques, the adaptability and precision they have attained, the ideas and habits they are creating, make it a certainty that profound changes are impending in the ancient craft of the Beautiful. In all the arts there is a physical component which can no longer be considered or treated as it used to be, which cannot remain unaffected by our modern knowledge and power. For the last twenty years neither matter nor space nor time has been what it was from time immemorial. We must expect great innovations to transform the entire technique of the arts, thereby affecting artistic invention itself and perhaps even bring about an amazing change in our very notion of art.

Paul Valéry, PIÈCES SUR L'ART.
'La Conquète de l'ubiquité', Paris[1]

PREFACE

When Marx undertook his critique of the capitalistic mode of production, this mode was in its infancy. Marx directed his efforts in such a way as to give them prognostic value. He went back to the basic conditions underlying capitalistic production and through his presentation showed what could be expected of capitalism in the future. The result was that one could expect it not only to exploit the proletariat with increasing intensity, but ultimately to create conditions which would make it possible to abolish capitalism itself.

The transformation of the superstructure, which takes place far more slowly than that of the substructure, has taken more than half a century to manifest in all areas of culture the change in the conditions of production. Only today can it be indicated what form this has taken. Certain prognostic requirements should be met by these statements. However, theses about the art of the proletariat after its assumption of power or about the art of a classless society would have less bearing on these demands than theses about the developmental tendencies of art under present conditions of production. Their dialectic is no less noticeable in the superstructure than in the economy. It would therefore be wrong to underestimate the value of such theses as a weapon. They brush aside a number of outmoded concepts, such as creativity and genius, eternal value and mystery – concepts whose uncontrolled (and at present almost uncontrollable) application would lead to a processing of data in the Fascist sense. The concepts which are introduced into the theory of art in what follows differ from the more familiar terms in that they are completely useless for the purposes of Fascism. They are, on the other hand, useful for the formulation of revolutionary demands in the politics of art.

I

In principle a work of art has always been reproducible. Manmade artifacts could always be imitated by men. Replicas were made by pupils in practice of their craft, by masters for diffusing their works, and, finally, by third parties in the pursuit of gain. Mechanical reproduction of a work of art, however, represents something new. Historically, it advanced intermittently and in leaps at long intervals, but with accelerated intensity. The Greeks knew only two procedures of technically reproducing works of art: founding and stamping. Bronzes, terra cottas, and coins were the only art works which they could produce in quantity. All others were unique and could not be mechanically reproduced. With the woodcut graphic art became mechanically reproducible for the first time, long before script became reproducible by print. The enormous changes which printing, the mechanical reproduction of writing, has brought about in literature are a familiar story. However, within the phenomenon which we are here examining from the perspective of world history, print is merely a special, though particularly important, case. During the Middle Ages engraving and etching were added to the woodcut; at the beginning of the nineteenth century lithography made its appearance.

With lithography the technique of reproduction reached an essentially new stage. This much more direct process was distinguished by the tracing of the design on a stone rather than its incision on a block of wood or its etching on a copperplate and permitted graphic art for the first time to put its products on the market, not only in large numbers as hitherto, but also in daily changing forms. Lithography enabled graphic art to illustrate everyday life, and it began to keep pace with printing. But only a few decades after its invention, lithography was surpassed by photography. For the first time in the process of pictorial reproduction, photography freed the hand of the most important artistic functions which henceforth devolved only upon the eye looking into a lens. Since the eye perceives more swiftly than the hand can draw, the process of pictorial reproduction was accelerated so enormously that it could keep pace with speech. A film operator shooting a scene in the studio captures the images at the speed of an actor's speech. Just as lithography virtually implied the illustrated newspaper, so did photography foreshadow the sound film. The technical reproduction of sound was tackled at the end of the last century. These convergent endeavours made predictable a situation which Paul Valéry pointed up in this sentence: 'Just as water, gas, and electricity are brought into our houses from far off to satisfy our needs in response to a minimal effort, so we shall be supplied with visual or auditory images, which will appear and disappear at a simple movement of the hand, hardly more than a sign' (*Aesthetics*, p. 226). Around 1900 technical reproduction had reached a standard that not only permitted it to reproduce all transmitted works of art and thus to cause the most profound change in their impact upon the public; it also had captured a place of its own among the artistic processes. For the study of this standard nothing is more revealing than the nature of the repercussions that these two different manifestations – the reproduction of works of art and the art of the film – have had on art in its traditional form.

II

Even the most perfect reproduction of a work of art is lacking in one element: its presence in time and space, its unique existence at the place where it happens to be. This unique existence of the work of art determined the history to which it was subject throughout the time of its existence. This includes the changes which it may have suffered in physical condition over the years as well as the various changes in its ownership.[2] The traces of the first can be revealed only by chemical or physical analyses which it is impossible to perform on a reproduction; changes of ownership are subject to a tradition which must be traced from the situation of the original.

The presence of the original is the prerequisite to the concept of authenticity. Chemical analyses of the patina of a bronze can help to establish this, as does the proof that a given manuscript of the Middle Ages stems from an archive of the fifteenth century. The whole sphere of authenticity is outside technical – and, of course, not only technical – reproducibility.[3] Confronted with its manual reproduction, which was usually branded as a forgery, the original preserved all its authority; not so *vis-à-vis* technical reproduction. The reason is twofold. First, process reproduction is more independent of the original than manual reproduction. For example, in photography, process reproduction can bring out those aspects of the original that are unattainable to the naked eye yet accessible to the lens, which is adjustable and chooses its angle at will. And photographic reproduction, with the aid of certain processes, such as enlargement or slow motion, can capture images which escape natural vision. Secondly, technical reproduction can put the copy of the original into situations which would be out of reach for the original itself. Above all, it enables the original to meet the beholder halfway, be it in the form of a photograph or a phonograph record. The cathedral leaves its locale to be received in the studio of a lover of art; the choral production, performed in an auditorium or in the open air, resounds in the drawing room.

The situations into which the product of mechanical reproduction can be brought may not touch the actual work of art, yet the quality of its presence is always depreciated. This holds not only for the art work but also, for instance, for a landscape which passes in review before the spectator in a movie. In the case of the art object, a most sensitive nucleus – namely, its authenticity – is interfered with whereas no natural object is vulnerable on that score. The authenticity of a thing is the essence of all that is transmissible from its beginning, ranging from its substantive duration to its testimony to the history which it has experienced. Since the historical testimony rests on the authenticity, the former, too, is jeopardised by reproduction when substantive duration ceases to matter. And what is really jeopardised when the historical testimony is affected is the authority of the object.[4]

One might subsume the eliminated element in the term 'aura' and go on to say: that which withers in the age of mechanical reproduction is the aura of the work of art. This is a symptomatic process whose significance points beyond the realm of art. One might generalise by saying: the technique of reproduction detaches the reproduced object from the domain of tradition. By making many reproductions it substitutes a plurality of copies for a unique existence. And in permitting the reproduction to meet the beholder or listener in his own particular situation, it reactivates the object reproduced. These two processes lead to a tremendous shattering of tradition which is the obverse of the contemporary crisis and renewal of mankind. Both processes are intimately connected with the contemporary mass movements. Their most powerful agent is the film. Its social significance, particularly in its most positive form, is inconceivable without its destructive, cathartic aspect, that is, the liquidation of the traditional value of the cultural heritage. This phenomenon is most palpable in the great historical films. It extends to ever new positions. In 1927 Abel Gance exclaimed enthusiastically: 'Shakespeare,

Rembrandt, Beethoven will make films...all legends, all mythologies
and all myths, all founders of religion, and the very religions...await
their exposed resurrection, and the heroes crowd each other at the gate.'[5]
Presumably without intending it, he issued an invitation to a far-reaching
liquidation.

III

During long periods of history, the mode of human sense perception
changes with humanity's entire mode of existence. The manner in
which human sense perception is organised, the medium in which it is
accomplished, is determined not only by nature but by historical circumstances as well. The fifth century, with its great shifts of population, saw
the birth of the late Roman art industry and the Vienna Genesis, and there
developed not only an art different from that of antiquity but also a new
kind of perception. The scholars of the Viennese school, Riegl and Wickh-
off, who resisted the weight of classical tradition under which these later
art forms had been buried, were the first to draw conclusions from them
concerning the organisation of perception at the time. However far-reaching their insight, these scholars limited themselves to showing the significant, formal hallmark which characterised perception in late Roman
times. They did not attempt – and, perhaps, saw no way – to show the
social transformations expressed by these changes of perception. The
conditions for an analogous insight are more favourable in the present.
And if changes in the medium of contemporary perception can be com-
prehended as decay of the aura, it is possible to show its social causes.

The concept of aura which was proposed above with reference to
historical objects may usefully be illustrated with reference to the aura
of natural ones. We define the aura of the latter as the unique phenomenon of a distance, however close it may be. If, while resting on a summer
afternoon, you follow with your eyes a mountain range on the horizon or
a branch which casts its shadow over you, you experience the aura of
those mountains, of that branch. This image makes it easy to comprehend
the social bases of the contemporary decay of the aura. It rests on two
circumstances, both of which are related to the increasing significance of
the masses in contemporary life. Namely, the desire of contemporary
masses to bring things 'closer' spatially and humanly, which is just as
ardent as their bent toward overcoming the uniqueness of every reality
by accepting its reproduction.[6] Every day the urge grows stronger to get
hold of an object at very close range by way of its likeness, its reproduction. Unmistakably, reproduction as offered by picture magazines and
newsreels differs from the image seen by the unarmed eye. Uniqueness
and permanence are as closely linked in the latter as are transitoriness

and reproducibility in the former. To pry an object from its shell, to destroy its aura, is the mark of a perception whose 'sense of the universal equality of things' has increased to such a degree that it extracts it even from a unique object by means of reproduction. Thus is manifested in the field of perception what in the theoretical sphere is noticeable in the increasing importance of statistics. The adjustment of reality to the masses and of the masses to reality is a process of unlimited scope, as much for thinking as for perception.

IV

The uniqueness of a work of art is inseparable from its being imbedded in the fabric of tradition. This tradition itself is thoroughly alive and extremely changeable. An ancient statue of Venus, for example, stood in a different traditional context with the Greeks, who made it an object of veneration, than with the clerics of the Middle Ages, who viewed it as an ominous idol. Both of them, however, were equally confronted with its uniqueness, that is, its aura. Originally the contextual integration of art in tradition found its expression in the cult. We know that the earliest art works originated in the service of a ritual – first the magical, then the religious kind. It is significant that the existence of the work of art with reference to its aura is never entirely separated from its ritual function.[7] In other words, the unique value of the 'authentic' work of art has its basis in ritual, the location of its original use value. This ritualistic basis, however remote, is still recognisable as secularised ritual even in the most profane forms of the cult of beauty.[8] The secular cult of beauty, developed during the Renaissance and prevailing for three centuries, clearly showed that ritualistic basis in its decline and the first deep crisis which befell it. With the advent of the first truly revolutionary means of reproduction, photography, simultaneously with the rise of socialism, art sensed the approaching crisis which has become evident a century later. At the time, art reacted with the doctrine of *l'art pour l'art*, that is, with a theology of art. This gave rise to what might be called a negative theology in the form of the idea of 'pure' art, which not only denied any social function of art but also any categorising by subject matter. (In poetry, Mallarmé was the first to take this position.)

An analysis of art in the age of mechanical reproduction must do justice to these relationships, for they lead us to an all-important insight: for the first time in world history, mechanical reproduction emancipates the work of art from its parasitical dependence on ritual. To an ever greater degree the work of art reproduced becomes the work of art designed for reproducibility.[9] From a photographic negative, for example, one can make any number of prints; to ask for the 'authentic' print makes no sense. But the instant the criterion of authenticity ceases to be applicable to artistic production, the total function of art is reversed. Instead of being based on ritual, it begins to be based on another practice – politics.

V

Works of art are received and valued on different planes. Two polar types stand out: with one, the accent is on the cult value; with the other, on the exhibition value of the work.[10] Artistic production begins with ceremonial objects destined to serve in a cult. One may assume that what mattered was their existence, not their being on view. The elk portrayed by the man of the Stone Age on the walls of his cave was an instrument of magic. He did expose it to his fellow men, but in the main it was meant for the spirits. Today the cult value would seem to demand that the work of art remain hidden. Certain statues of gods are accessible only to the priest in the cella; certain Madonnas remain covered nearly all year round; certain sculptures on medieval cathedrals are invisible to the spectator on ground level. With the emancipation of the various art practices from ritual go increasing opportunities for the exhibition of their products. It is easier to exhibit a portrait bust that can be sent here and there than to exhibit the statue of a divinity that has its fixed place in the interior of a temple. The same holds for the painting as against the mosaic or fresco that preceded it. And even though the public presentability of a mass originally may have been just as great as that of a symphony, the latter originated at the moment when its public presentability promised to surpass that of the mass.

With the different methods of technical reproduction of a work of art, its fitness for exhibition increased to such an extent that the quantitative shift between its two poles turned into a qualitative transformation of its nature. This is comparable to the situation of the work of art in prehistoric times when, by the absolute emphasis on its cult value, it was, first and foremost, an instrument of magic. Only later did it come to be recognised as a work of art. In the same way today, by the absolute emphasis on its exhibition value the work of art becomes a creation with entirely new functions, among which the one we are conscious of, the artistic function, later may be recognised as incidental.[11] This much is certain: today photography and the film are the most serviceable exemplifications of this new function.

VI

In photography, exhibition value begins to displace cult value all along the line. But cult value does not give way without resistance. It retires into an ultimate retrenchment: the human countenance. It is no accident that the portrait was the focal point of early photography. The cult of remembrance of loved ones, absent or dead, offers a last refuge for the cult value of the picture. For the last time the aura emanates from the early photographs in the fleeting expression of a human face. This is what constitutes their melancholy, incomparable beauty. But as man withdraws from the photographic image, the exhibition value for the first time shows its superiority to the ritual value. To have pinpointed this new stage constitutes the incomparable significance of Atget, who, around 1900, took photographs of deserted Paris streets. It has quite justly been said of him that he photographed them like scenes of crime. The scene of a crime, too, is deserted; it is photographed for the purpose of establishing evidence. With Atget, photographs become standard evidence for historical occurrences, and acquire a hidden political significance. They demand a specific kind of approach; free-floating contemplation is not appropriate to them. They stir the viewer; he feels challenged by them in a new way. At the same time picture magazines begin to put up signposts for him, right ones or wrong ones, no matter. For the first time, captions have become obligatory. And it is clear that they have an altogether different character than the title of a painting. The directives which the captions give to those looking at pictures in illustrated magazines soon become even more explicit and more imperative in the film where the meaning of each single picture appears to be prescribed by the sequence of all preceding ones.

VII

The nineteenth-century dispute as to the artistic value of painting versus photography today seems devious and confused. This does not diminish its importance, however; if anything, it underlines it. The dispute was in fact the symptom of a historical transformation the universal impact of which was not realised by either of the rivals. When the age of mechanical reproduction separated art from its basis in cult, the semblance of its autonomy disappeared forever. The resulting change in the function of art transcended the perspective of the century; for a long time it even escaped that of the twentieth century, which experienced the development of the film.

Earlier much futile thought had been devoted to the question of whether photography is an art. The primary question – whether the very invention of photography had not transformed the entire nature of art – was not raised. Soon the film theoreticians asked the same ill-considered question with regard to the film. But the difficulties which photography caused traditional aesthetics were mere child's play as compared to those raised by the film. Whence the insensitive and forced character of early theories of the film. Abel Gance, for instance, compares the film with hieroglyphs: 'Here, by a remarkable regression, we have come back to the level of expression of the Egyptians...Pictorial language has not yet matured because our eyes have not yet adjusted to it. There is as yet insufficient respect for, insufficient cult of, what it expresses.'[12] Or, in the words of Séverin-Mars: 'What art has been granted a dream more poetical and more real at the same time! Approached in this fashion the film might represent an incomparable means of expression. Only the most high-minded persons, in the most perfect and mysterious moments of their lives, should be allowed to enter its ambience.'[13] Alexandre Arnoux concludes his fantasy about the silent film with the question: 'Do not all the bold descriptions we have given amount to the definition of prayer?'[14] It is instructive to note how their desire to class the film among the 'arts' forces these theoreticians to read ritual elements into it – with a striking lack of discretion. Yet when these speculations were published, films like *L'Opinion publique* and *The Gold Rush* had already appeared. This, however, did not keep Abel Gance from adducing hieroglyphs for purposes of comparison, nor Séverin-Mars from speaking of the film as one might speak of paintings by Fra Angelico. Characteristically, even today ultrareactionary authors give the film a similar contextual significance – if not an outright sacred one, then at least a supernatural one. Commenting on Max Reinhardt's film version of *A Midsummer Night's Dream*, Werfel states that undoubtedly it was the sterile copying of the exterior world with its streets, interiors, railroad stations, restaurants, motorcars, and beaches which until now had obstructed the elevation of the film to the realm of art. 'The film has not yet realised its true meaning, its real possibilities...these consist in its unique faculty to express by natural means and with incomparable persuasiveness all that is fairylike, marvellous, supernatural.'[15]

VIII

The artistic performance of a stage actor is definitely presented to the public by the actor in person; that of the screen actor, however, is presented by a camera, with a twofold consequence. The camera that presents the performance of the film actor to the public need not respect the performance as an integral whole. Guided by the cameraman, the camera continually changes its position with respect to the performance. The sequence of positional views which the editor composes from the material supplied him constitutes the completed film. It comprises certain factors of movement which are in reality those of the camera, not to mention special camera angles, close-ups, etc. Hence, the performance of the actor is subjected to a series of optical tests. This is the first consequence of the fact that the actor's performance is presented by means of a camera. Also, the film actor lacks the opportunity of the stage actor to adjust to the audience during his performance, since he does not present his performance to the audience in person. This permits the audience to take the position of a critic, without experiencing any personal contact with the actor. The audience's identification with the actor is really an identification with the camera. Consequently the audience takes the position of the camera; its approach is that of testing.[16] This is not the approach to which cult values may be exposed.

IX

For the film, what matters primarily is that the actor represents himself to the public before the camera, rather than representing someone else. One of the first to sense the actor's metamorphosis by this form of testing was Pirandello. Though his remarks on the subject in his novel *Si Gira* were limited to the negative aspects of the question and to the silent film only, this hardly impairs their validity. For in this respect, the sound film did not change anything essential. What matters is that the part is acted not for an audience but for a mechanical contrivance – in the case of the sound film, for two of them. 'The film actor,' wrote Pirandello, 'feels as if in exile – exiled not only from the stage but also from himself. With a vague sense of discomfort he feels inexplicable emptiness: his body loses its corporeality, it evaporates, it is deprived of reality, life, voice, and the noises caused by his moving about, in order to be changed into a mute image, flickering an instant on the screen, then vanishing into silence ... The projector will play with his shadow before the public, and he himself must be content to play before the camera.'[17] This situation might also be characterised as follows: for the first time – and this is the effect of the film – man has to operate with his whole living person, yet forgoing its aura. For aura is tied to his presence; there can be no replica of it. The aura which, on the stage, emanates from Macbeth, cannot be separated for the spectators from that of the actor. However, the singularity of the shot in the studio is that the camera is substituted for the public. Consequently, the aura that envelops the actor vanishes, and with it the aura of the figure he portrays.

It is not surprising that it should be a dramatist such as Pirandello who, in characterising the film, inadvertently touches on the very crisis in which we see the theatre. Any thorough study proves that there is indeed no greater contrast than that of the stage play to a work of art that is completely subject to or, like the film, founded in mechanical reproduction. Experts have long recognised that in the film 'the greatest effects are almost always obtained by "acting" as little as possible...' In 1932 Rudolf Arnheim saw 'the latest trend...in treating the actor as a stage prop chosen for its characteristics and...inserted at the proper place.'[18] With this idea something else is closely connected. The stage actor identifies himself with the character of his role. The film actor very often is denied this opportunity. His creation is by no means all of a piece; it is composed of many separate performances. Besides certain fortuitous considerations, such as cost of studio, availability of fellow players, décor, etc., there are elementary necessities of equipment that split the actor's work into a series of mountable episodes. In particular, lighting and its installation require the presentation of an event that, on the screen, unfolds as a rapid and unified scene, in a sequence of separate shootings which may take hours at the studio; not to mention more obvious montage. Thus a jump from the window can be shot in the studio as a jump from a scaffold, and the ensuing flight, if need be, can be shot weeks later when outdoor scenes are taken. Far more paradoxical cases can easily be construed. Let us assume that an actor is supposed to be startled by a knock at the door. If his reaction is not satisfactory, the director can resort to an expedient: when the actor happens to be at the studio again he has a shot fired behind him without his being forewarned of it. The frightened reaction can be shot now and be cut into the screen version. Nothing more strikingly shows that art has left the realm of the 'beautiful semblance' which, so far, had been taken to be the only sphere where art could thrive.

X

The feeling of strangeness that overcomes the actor before the camera, as Pirandello describes it, is basically of the same kind as the estrangement felt before one's own image in the mirror. But now the reflected image has become separable, transportable. And where is it transported? Before the public.[19] Never for a moment does the screen actor cease to be conscious of this fact. While facing the camera he knows that ultimately he will face the public, the consumers who constitute the market. This market, where he offers not only his labour but also his whole self, his heart and soul, is beyond his reach. During the shooting he has as little contact with it as any article made in a factory. This may contribute to that oppression, that new anxiety which, according to Pirandello, grips the actor before the camera. The film responds to the shrivelling of the aura with an artificial build-up of the 'personality' outside the studio. The cult of the movie star, fostered by the money of the film industry, preserves not the unique aura of the person but the 'spell of the personality', the phony spell of a commodity. So long as the movie-makers' capital sets the fashion, as a rule no other revolutionary merit can be accredited to today's film than the promotion of a revolutionary criticism of traditional concepts of art. We do not deny that in some cases today's films can also promote revolutionary criticism of social conditions, even of the distribution of property. However, our present study is no more specifically concerned with this than is the film production of Western Europe.

It is inherent in the technique of the film as well as that of sports that everybody who witnesses its accomplishments is somewhat of an expert. This is obvious to anyone listening to a group of newspaper boys leaning on their bicycles and discussing the outcome of a bicycle race. It is not for nothing that newspaper publishers arrange races for their delivery boys. These arouse great interest among the participants, for the victor has an opportunity to rise from delivery boy to professional racer. Similarly, the newsreel offers everyone the opportunity to rise from passer-by to movie extra. In this way any man might even find himself part of a work of art, as witness Vertoff's *Three Songs About Lenin* or Ivens' *Borinage*. Any man today can lay claim to being filmed. This claim can best be elucidated by a comparative look at the historical situation of contemporary literature.

For centuries a small number of writers were confronted by many thousands of readers. This changed toward the end of the last century. With the increasing extension of the press, which kept placing new political, religious, scientific, professional, and local organs before the readers, an increasing number of readers became writers – at first, occasional ones. It began with the daily press opening to its readers space for 'letters to the editor'. And today there is hardly a gainfully employed European who could not, in principle, find an opportunity to publish somewhere or other comments on his work, grievances, documentary reports, or that sort of thing. Thus, the distinction between author and public is about to lose its basic character. The difference becomes merely functional; it may vary from case to case. At any moment the reader is ready to turn into a writer. As expert, which he had to become willy-nilly in an extremely specialised work process, even if only in some minor respect, the reader gains access to authorship. In the Soviet Union work itself is given a voice. To present it verbally is part of a man's ability to perform the work. Literary licence is now founded on polytechnic rather than specialised training and thus becomes common property.[20]

All this can easily be applied to the film, where transitions that in literature took centuries have come about in a decade. In cinematic practice, particularly in Russia, this change-over has partially become established reality. Some of the players whom we meet in Russian films are not actors in our sense but people who portray *themselves* – and primarily in their own work process. In Western Europe the capitalistic exploitation of the film denies consideration to modern man's legitimate claim to being reproduced. Under these circumstances the film industry is trying hard to spur the interest of the masses through illusion-promoting spectacles and dubious speculations.

XI

The shooting of a film, especially of a sound film, affords a spectacle unimaginable anywhere at any time before this. It presents a process in which it is impossible to assign to a spectator a viewpoint which would exclude from the actual scene such extraneous accessories as camera equipment, lighting machinery, staff assistants, etc. – unless his eye were on a line parallel with the lens. This circumstance, more than any other, renders superficial and insignificant any possible similarity between a scene in the studio and one on the stage. In the theatre one is well aware of the place from which the play cannot immediately be detected as illusionary. There is no such place for the movie scene that is being shot. Its illusionary nature is that of the second degree, the result of cutting. That is to say, in the studio the mechanical equipment has penetrated so deeply into reality that its pure aspect freed from the foreign substance of equipment is the result of a special procedure, namely, the shooting by the specially adjusted camera and the mounting of the shot together with other similar ones. The equipment-free aspect of reality here has become the height of artifice; the sight of immediate reality has become an orchid in the land of technology.

Even more revealing is the comparison of these circumstances, which differ so much from those of the theatre, with the situation in painting. Here the question is: How does the cameraman compare with the painter? To answer this we take recourse to an analogy with a surgical operation. The surgeon represents the polar opposite of the magician. The magician heals a sick person by the laying on of hands; the surgeon cuts into the patient's body. The magician maintains the natural distance between the patient and himself; though he reduces it very slightly by the laying on of hands, he greatly increases it by virtue of his authority. The surgeon does exactly the reverse; he greatly diminishes the distance between himself and the patient by penetrating into the patient's body, and increases it but little by the caution with which his hand moves among the organs. In short, in contrast to the magician – who is still hidden in the medical practitioner – the surgeon at the decisive moment abstains from facing the patient man to man; rather, it is through the operation that he penetrates into him.

Magician and surgeon compare to painter and cameraman. The painter maintains in his work a natural distance from reality, the cameraman penetrates deeply into its web.[21] There is a tremendous difference between the pictures they obtain. That of the painter is a total one, that of the cameraman consists of multiple fragments which are assembled under a new law. Thus, for contemporary man the representation of reality by the film is incomparably more significant than that of the painter, since it offers, precisely because of the thoroughgoing permeation of reality with mechanical equipment, an aspect of reality which is free of all equipment. And that is what one is entitled to ask from a work of art.

8

Panopticism

Michel Foucault

The following, according to an order published at the end of the seventeenth century, were the measures to be taken when the plague appeared in a town.[1]

First, a strict spatial partitioning: the closing of the town and its outlying districts, a prohibition to leave the town on pain of death, the killing of all stray animals; the division of the town into distinct quarters, each governed by an intendant. Each street is placed under the authority of a syndic, who keeps it under surveillance; if he leaves the street, he will be condemned to death. On the appointed day, everyone is ordered to stay indoors: it is forbidden to leave on pain of death. The syndic himself comes to lock the door of each house from the outside; he takes the key with him and hands it over to the intendant of the quarter; the intendant keeps it until the end of the quarantine. Each family will have made its own provisions; but, for bread and wine, small wooden canals are set up between the street and the interior of the houses, thus allowing each person to receive his ration without communicating with the suppliers and other residents; meat, fish and herbs will be hoisted up into the houses with pulleys and baskets. If it is absolutely necessary to leave the house, it will be done in turn, avoiding any meeting. Only the intendants, syndics and guards will move about the streets and also, between the infected houses, from one corpse to another, the 'crows', who can be left to die: these are 'people of little substance who carry the sick, bury the dead, clean and do many vile and abject offices'. It is a segmented, immobile, frozen space. Each individual is fixed in his place. And, if he moves, he does so at the risk of his life, contagion or punishment.

Inspection functions ceaselessly. The gaze is alert everywhere: 'A considerable body of militia, commanded by good officers and men of substance', guards at the gates, at the town hall and in every quarter to ensure the prompt obedience of the people and the most absolute authority of the magistrates, 'as also to observe all disorder, theft and extortion'. At each of the town gates there will be an observation post; at the end of each street sentinels. Every day, the intendant visits the quarter in his charge, inquires whether the syndics have carried out their tasks, whether the inhabitants have anything to complain of; they 'observe their actions'. Every day, too, the syndic goes into the street for which he is responsible; stops before each house: gets all the inhabitants to appear at the windows (those who live overlooking the courtyard will be allocated a window looking onto the street at which no one but they may show themselves); he calls each of them by name; informs himself as to the state of each and every one of them – 'in which respect the inhabitants will be compelled to speak the truth under pain of death'; if someone does not appear at the window, the syndic must ask why: 'In this way he will find out easily enough whether dead or sick are being concealed.' Everyone locked up in his cage, everyone at his window, answering to his name and showing himself when asked – it is the great review of the living and the dead.

This surveillance is based on a system of permanent registration: reports from the syndics to the intendants, from the intendants to the magistrates or mayor. At the beginning of the 'lock up', the role of each of the inhabitants present in the town is laid down, one by one; this document bears 'the name, age, sex of everyone, notwithstanding his condition': a copy is sent to the intendant of the quarter, another to the office of the town hall, another to enable the syndic to make his daily roll call. Everything that may be observed during the course of the visits – deaths, illnesses, complaints, irregularities – is noted down and transmitted to the intendants and magistrates. The magistrates have complete control over medical treatment; they have appointed a physician in charge; no other practitioner may treat, no apothecary prepare medicine, no confessor visit a sick person without having received from him a written note 'to prevent anyone from concealing and dealing with those sick of the contagion, unknown to the magistrates'. The registration of the pathological must be constantly centralised. The relation of each individual to his disease and to his death passes through the representatives of power, the registration they make of it, the decisions they take on it.

Five or six days after the beginning of the quarantine, the process of purifying the houses one by one is begun. All the inhabitants are made to leave; in each room 'the furniture and goods' are raised from the ground or suspended from the air; perfume is poured around the room; after carefully sealing the windows, doors and even the keyholes with wax, the perfume is set alight. Finally, the entire house is closed while the perfume is consumed; those who have carried out the work are searched, as they were on entry, 'in the presence of the residents of the house, to see that they did not have something on their persons as they left that they did not have on entering'. Four hours later, the residents are allowed to re-enter their homes.

This enclosed, segmented space, observed at every point, in which the individuals are inserted in a fixed place, in which the slightest movements are supervised, in which all events are recorded, in which an uninterrupted work of writing links the centre and periphery, in which power is exercised without division, according to a continuous hierarch-ical figure, in which each individual is constantly located, examined and distributed among the living beings, the sick and the dead – all this constitutes a compact model of the disciplinary mechanism. The plague is met by order; its function is to sort out every possible confusion: that of the disease, which is transmitted when bodies are mixed together; that of the evil, which is increased when fear and death overcome prohibi-tions. It lays down for each individual his place, his body, his disease and his death, his well-being, by means of an omnipresent and omniscient power that subdivides itself in a regular, uninterrupted way even to the ultimate determination of the individual, of what characterises him, of what belongs to him, of what happens to him. Against the plague, which is a mixture, discipline brings into play its power, which is one of analysis. A whole literary fiction of the festival grew up around the plague: suspended laws, lifted prohibitions, the frenzy of passing time, bodies mingling together without respect, individuals unmasked, aban-doning their statutory identity and the figure under which they had been recognised, allowing a quite different truth to appear. But there was also a political dream of the plague, which was exactly its reverse: not the collective festival, but strict divisions; not laws transgressed, but the penetration of regulation into even the smallest details of everyday life through the mediation of the complete hierarchy that assured the capil-lary functioning of power; not masks that were put on and taken off, but the assignment to each individual of his 'true' name, his 'true' place, his 'true' body, his 'true' disease. The plague as a form, at once real and imaginary, of disorder had as its medical and political correlative disci-pline. Behind the disciplinary mechanisms can be read the haunting memory of 'contagions', of the plague, of rebellions, crimes, vagabon-dage, desertions, people who appear and disappear, live and die in disorder.

If it is true that the leper gave rise to rituals of exclusion, which to a certain extent provided the model for and general form of the great Confinement, then the plague gave rise to disciplinary projects. Rather than the massive, binary division between one set of people and another, it called for multiple separations, individualising distributions, an organ-isation in depth of surveillance and control, an intensification and a ramification of power. The leper was caught up in a practice of rejection, of exile-enclosure; he was left to his doom in a mass among which it was useless to differentiate; those sick of the plague were caught up in a meticulous tactical partitioning in which individual differentiations were the constricting effects of a power that multiplied, articulated and subdivided itself; the great confinement on the one hand; the correct training on the other. The leper and his separation; the plague and its segmentations. The first is marked; the second analysed and distributed. The exile of the leper and the arrest of the plague do not bring with them the same political dream. The first is that of a pure community, the second that of a disciplined society. Two ways of exercising power over men, of controlling their relations, of separating out their dangerous mixtures. The plague-stricken town, traversed throughout with hierarchy, surveillance, observation, writing; the town immobilised by the functioning of an extensive power that bears in a distinct way over all individual bodies – this is the utopia of the perfectly governed city. The plague (envisaged as a possibility at least) is the trial in the course of which one may define ideally the exercise of disciplinary power. In order to make rights and laws function according to pure theory, the jurists place themselves in imagination in the state of nature; in order to see perfect disciplines functioning, rulers dreamt of the state of plague. Underlying disciplinary projects the image of the plague stands for all forms of confusion and disorder; just as the image of the leper, cut off from all human contact, underlies projects of exclusion.

They are different projects, then, but not incompatible ones. We see them coming slowly together, and it is the peculiarity of the nineteenth century that it applied to the space of exclusion of which the leper was the symbolic inhabitant (beggars, vagabonds, madmen and the disorderly formed the real population) the technique of power proper to disciplinary partitioning. Treat 'lepers' as 'plague victims', project the subtle segmentations of discipline onto the confused space of internment, combine it with the methods of analytical distribution proper to power, individualise the excluded, but use procedures of individualisation to mark exclusion – this is what was operated regularly by disciplinary power from the beginning of the nineteenth century in the psychiatric asylum, the penitentiary, the reformatory, the approved school and, to some extent, the hospital. Generally speaking, all the authorities exercising individual control function according to a double mode; that of binary division and branding (mad/sane; dangerous/harmless; normal/abnormal); and that of coercive assignment, of differential distribution (who he is; where he must be; how he is to be characterised; how he is to be recognised; how a constant surveillance is to be exercised over him in an individual way, etc.). On the one hand, the lepers are treated as plague victims; the tactics of individualising disciplines are imposed on the excluded; and, on the other hand, the universality of disciplinary controls makes it possible to brand the 'leper' and to bring into play against him the dualistic mechanisms of exclusion. The constant division between the normal and the abnormal, to which every individual is subjected, brings us back to our own time, by applying the binary branding and exile of the leper to quite different objects; the existence of a whole set of techniques and institutions for measuring, supervising and correcting the abnormal brings into play the disciplinary mechanisms to which the fear of the plague gave rise. All the mechanisms of power which, even today, are disposed around the abnormal individual, to brand him and to alter him, are composed of those two forms from which they distantly derive.

Bentham's *Panopticon* is the architectural figure of this composition (Plate 1). We know the principle on which it was based: at the periphery, an annular building; at the centre, a tower; this tower is pierced with wide windows that open onto the inner side of the ring; the peripheric building is divided into cells, each of which extends the whole width of the building; they have two windows, one on the inside, corresponding to the windows of the tower; the other, on the outside, allows the light to cross the cell from one end to the other. All that is needed, then, is to place a supervisor in a central tower and to shut up in each cell a madman, a patient, a condemned man, a worker or a schoolboy. By the effect of backlighting, one can observe from the tower, standing out precisely against the light, the small captive shadows in the cells of the periphery. They are like so many cages, so many small theatres, in which each actor is alone, perfectly individualised and constantly visible. The panoptic mechanism arranges spatial unities that make it possible to see constantly and to recognise immediately. In short, it reverses the principle of the dungeon; or rather of its three functions – to enclose, to deprive of light and to hide – it preserves only the first and eliminates the other two. Full lighting and the eye of a supervisor capture better than darkness, which ultimately protected. Visibility is a trap.

To begin with, this made it possible – as a negative effect – to avoid those compact, swarming, howling masses that were to be found in places of confinement, those painted by Goya or described by Howard. Each individual, in his place, is securely confined to a cell from which he is seen from the front by the supervisor; but the side walls prevent him from coming into contact with his companions. He is seen, but he does not see; he is the object of information, never a subject in communication. The arrangement of his room, opposite the central tower, imposes on him an axial visibility; but the divisions of the ring, those separated cells, imply a lateral invisibility. And this invisibility is a guarantee of order. If the inmates are convicts, there is no danger of a plot, an attempt at collective escape, the planning of new crimes for the future, bad reciprocal influences; if they are patients, there is no danger of contagion; if they are madmen there is no risk of their committing violence upon one another; if they are schoolchildren, there is no copying, no noise, no chatter, no waste of time; if they are workers, there are no disorders, no theft, no coalitions, none of those distractions that slow down the rate of

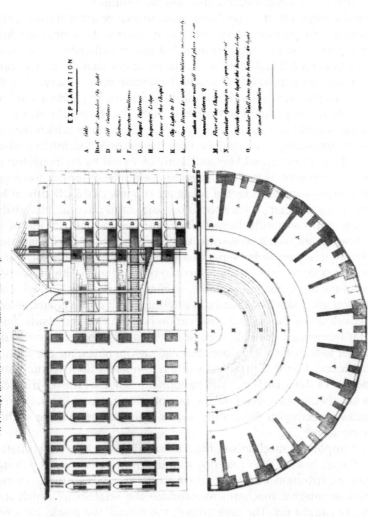

A General Idea of a *PENITENTIARY PANOPTICON* in an Improved, but as yet (Jan.y 23.d 1791) Unfinished State
See Postscript References to Plan Elevation & Section, being Plate referred to in N.º 2

EXPLANATION

A ...... Cells
B to C ...... Cell Annular Sky Light
D ...... Cell Gallaries
E ...... Entrance
F ...... Inspectors Gallaries
G ...... Chapel Gallaries
H ...... Inspectors Lodge
I ...... Dome or the Chapel
K ...... Sky Light to D.º
L ...... Store Rooms &c: with their entrance on
&c ...... doors: within the outer wall all round plate &c: an
&c ...... annular Cistern &c.
M ...... Floor of the Chapel.
N ...... Circular Openings in d.º upon except of
&c ...... Church tower to light the Inspector Lodge
O ...... Annular Well down top to bottom, to light
&c ...... air and operation

Plate 1 Plan of a Penitentiary Panopticon from John Bowring (ed.), *The Works of Jeremy Bentham*, vol. 4 (1843).
Reproduced courtesy of British Library Reproductions

work, make it less perfect or cause accidents. The crowd, a compact mass, a locus of multiple exchanges, individualities merging together, a collective effect, is abolished and replaced by a collection of separated individualities. From the point of view of the guardian, it is replaced by a multiplicity that can be numbered and supervised; from the point of view of the inmates, by a sequestered and observed solitude.[2]

Hence the major effect of the Panopticon: to induce in the inmate a state of conscious and permanent visibility that assures the automatic functioning of power. So to arrange things that the surveillance is permanent in its effects, even if it is discontinuous in its action; that the perfection of power should tend to render its actual exercise unnecessary; that this architectural apparatus should be a machine for creating and sustaining a power relation independent of the person who exercises it; in short, that the inmates should be caught up in a power situation of which they are themselves the bearers. To achieve this, it is at once too much and too little that the prisoner should be constantly observed by an inspector: too little, for what matters is that he knows himself to be observed; too much, because he has no need in fact of being so. In view of this, Bentham laid down the principle that power should be visible and unverifiable. Visible: the inmate will constantly have before his eyes the tall outline of the central tower from which he is spied upon. Unverifiable: the inmate must never know whether he is being looked at at any one moment; but he must be sure that he may always be so. In order to make the presence or absence of the inspector unverifiable, so that the prisoners, in their cells, cannot even see a shadow, Bentham envisaged not only venetian blinds on the windows of the central observation hall, but, on the inside, partitions that intersected the hall at right angles and, in order to pass from one quarter to the other, not doors but zig-zag openings; for the slightest noise, a gleam of light, a brightness in a half-opened door would betray the presence of the guardian.[3] The Panopticon is a machine for dissociating the see/being seen dyad: in the peripheric ring, one is totally seen, without ever seeing; in the central tower, one sees everything without ever being seen.[4]

It is an important mechanism, for it automatises and disindividualises power. Power has its principle not so much in a person as in a certain concerted distribution of bodies, surfaces, lights, gazes; in an arrangement whose internal mechanisms produce the relation in which individuals are caught up. The ceremonies, the rituals, the marks by which the sovereign's surplus power was manifested are useless. There is a machinery that assures dissymmetry, disequilibrium, difference. Consequently, it does not matter who exercises power. Any individual, taken almost at random, can operate the machine: in the absence of the director, his family, his friends, his visitors, even his servants (*P*, p. 45). Similarly, it does not matter what motive animates him: the curiosity of the indiscreet, the malice of a child, the thirst for knowledge of a philosopher who wishes to visit this museum of human nature, or the perversity of those who take pleasure in spying and punishing. The more numerous those anonymous and temporary observers are, the greater the risk for the inmate of being surprised and the greater his anxious awareness of being observed. The Panopticon is a marvellous machine which, whatever use one may wish to put it to, produces homogeneous effects of power.

A real subjection is born mechanically from a fictitious relation. So it is not necessary to use force to constrain the convict to good behaviour, the madman to calm, the worker to work, the schoolboy to application, the patient to the observation of the regulations. Bentham was surprised that panoptic institutions could be so light: there were no more bars, no more chains, no more heavy locks; all that was needed was that the separations should be clear and the openings well arranged. The heaviness of the old 'houses of security', with their fortress-like architecture, could be replaced by the simple, economic geometry of a 'house of certainty'. The efficiency of power, its constraining force have, in a sense, passed over to the other side – to the side of its surface of application. He who is subjected to a field of visibility, and who knows it, assumes responsibility for the constraints of power; he makes them play spontaneously upon himself; he inscribes in himself the power relation in which he simultaneously plays both roles; he becomes the principle of his own subjection. By this very fact, the external power may throw off its physical weight; it tends to the non-corporal; and, the more it approaches this limit, the more constant, profound and permanent are its effects: it is a perpetual victory that avoids any physical confrontation and which is always decided in advance.

Bentham does not say whether he was inspired, in his project, by Le Vaux's menagerie at Versailles: the first menagerie in which the different elements are not, as they traditionally were, distributed in a park.[5] At the centre was an octagonal pavilion which, on the first floor, consisted of only a single room, the king's *salon*; on every side large windows looked out onto seven cages (the eighth side was reserved for the entrance), containing different species of animals. By Bentham's time, this menagerie had disappeared. But one finds in the programme of the Panopticon a similar concern with individualising observation, with characterisation and classification, with the analytical arrangement of space. The Panopticon is a royal menagerie; the animal is replaced by man, individual distribution by specific grouping and the king by the machinery of a furtive power. With this exception, the Panopticon also does the work of a naturalist. It makes it possible to draw up differences: among patients, to observe the symptoms of each individual, without the proximity of beds, the circulation of miasmas, the effects of contagion confusing the clinical tables; among schoolchildren, it makes it possible to observe performances (without there being any imitation or copying), to map aptitudes, to assess characters, to draw up rigorous classifications and, in relation to normal development, to distinguish 'laziness and stubbornness' from 'incurable imbecility'; among workers, it makes it possible to note the aptitudes of each worker, compare the time he takes to perform a task, and if they are paid by the day, to calculate their wages (*P*, pp. 60–4).

So much for the question of observation. But the Panopticon was also a laboratory; it could be used as a machine to carry out experiments, to alter behaviour, to train or correct individuals. To experiment with medicines and monitor their effects. To try out different punishments on prisoners, according to their crimes and character, and to seek the most effective ones. To teach different techniques simultaneously to the workers, to decide which is the best. To try out pedagogical experiments – and in particular to take up once again the well-debated problem of secluded education, by using orphans. One would see what would happen when, in their sixteenth or eighteenth year, they were presented with other boys or girls; one could verify whether, as Helvetius thought, anyone could learn anything; one would follow 'the genealogy of every observable idea'; one could bring up different children according to different systems of thought, making certain children believe that two and two do not make four or that the moon is a cheese, then put them together when they are twenty or twenty-five years old; one would then have discussions that would be worth a great deal more than the sermons or lectures on which so much money is spent; one would have at least an opportunity of making discoveries in the domain of metaphysics. The Panopticon is a privileged place for experiments on men, and for analysing with complete certainty the transformations that may be obtained from them. The Panopticon may even provide an apparatus for supervising its own mechanisms. In this central tower, the director may spy on all the employees that he has under his orders: nurses, doctors, foremen, teachers, warders; he will be able to judge them continuously, alter their behaviour, impose upon them the methods he thinks best; and it will even be possible to observe the director himself. An inspector arriving unexpectedly at the centre of the Panopticon will be able to judge at a glance, without anything being concealed from him, how the entire establishment is functioning. And, in any case, enclosed as he is in the middle of this architectural mechanism, is not the director's own fate entirely bound up with it? The incompetent physician who has allowed contagion to spread, the incompetent prison governor or workshop manager will be the first victims of an epidemic or a revolt. ' "By every tie I could devise", said the master of the Panopticon, "my own fate had been bound up by me with theirs" ' (*P*, p. 177). The Panopticon functions as a kind of laboratory of power. Thanks to its mechanisms of observation, it gains in efficiency and in the ability to penetrate into men's behaviour;

knowledge follows the advances of power, discovering new objects of knowledge over all the surfaces on which power is exercised.

The plague-stricken town, the panoptic establishment – the differences are important. They mark, at a distance of a century and a half, the transformations of the disciplinary programme. In the first case, there is an exceptional situation: against an extraordinary evil, power is mobilised; it makes itself everywhere present and visible; it invents new mechanisms; it separates, it immobilises, it partitions; it constructs for a time what is both a counter-city and the perfect society; it imposes an ideal functioning, but one that is reduced, in the final analysis, like the evil that it combats, to a simple dualism of life and death: that which moves brings death, and one kills that which moves. The Panopticon, on the other hand, must be understood as a generalisable model of functioning; a way of defining power relations in terms of the everyday life of men. No doubt Bentham presents it as a particular institution, closed in upon itself. Utopias, perfectly closed in upon themselves, are common enough. As opposed to the ruined prisons, littered with mechanisms of torture, to be seen in Piranese's engravings, the Panopticon presents a cruel, ingenious cage. The fact that it should have given rise, even in our own time, to so many variations, projected or realised, is evidence of the imaginary intensity that it has possessed for almost two hundred years. But the Panopticon must not be understood as a dream building: it is the diagram of a mechanism of power reduced to its ideal form; its functioning, abstracted from any obstacle, resistance or friction, must be represented as a pure architectural and optical system: it is in fact a figure of political technology that may and must be detached from any specific use.

It is polyvalent in its applications; it serves to reform prisoners, but also to treat patients, to instruct schoolchildren, to confine the insane, to supervise workers, to put beggars and idlers to work. It is a type of location of bodies in space, of distribution of individuals in relation to one another, of hierarchical organisation, of disposition of centres and channels of power, of definition of the instruments and modes of intervention of power, which can be implemented in hospitals, workshops, schools, prisons. Whenever one is dealing with a multiplicity of individuals on whom a task or a particular form of behaviour must be imposed, the panoptic schema may be used. It is – necessary modifications apart – applicable 'to all establishments whatsoever, in which, within a space not too large to be covered or commanded by buildings, a number of persons are meant to be kept under inspection' (*P*, p. 40; although Bentham takes the penitentiary house as his prime example, it is because it has many different functions to fulfil – safe custody, confinement, solitude, forced labour and instruction).

In each of its applications, it makes it possible to perfect the exercise of power. It does this in several ways: because it can reduce the number of those who exercise it, while increasing the number of those on whom it is exercised. Because it is possible to intervene at any moment and because the constant pressure acts even before the offences, mistakes or crimes have been committed. Because, in these conditions, its strength is that it never intervenes, it is exercised spontaneously and without noise, it constitutes a mechanism whose effects follow from one another. Because, without any physical instrument other than architecture and geometry, it acts directly on individuals; it gives 'power of mind over mind'. The panoptic schema makes any apparatus of power more intense: it assures its economy (in material, in personnel, in time); it assures its efficacity by its preventative character, its continuous functioning and its automatic mechanisms. It is a way of obtaining from power 'in hitherto unexampled quantity', 'a great and new instrument of government...; its great excellence consists in the great strength it is capable of giving to *any* institution it may be thought proper to apply it to' (*P*, p. 66).

It's a case of 'it's easy once you've thought of it' in the political sphere. It can in fact be integrated into any function (education, medical treatment, production, punishment); it can increase the effect of this function, by being linked closely with it; it can constitute a mixed mechanism in which relations of power (and of knowledge) may be precisely adjusted, in the smallest detail, to the processes that are to be supervised; it can establish a direct proportion between 'surplus power' and 'surplus production'. In short, it arranges things in such a way that the exercise of power is not added on from the outside, like a rigid, heavy constraint, to the functions it invests, but is so subtly present in them as to increase their efficiency by itself increasing its own points of contact. The panoptic mechanism is not simply a hinge, a point of exchange between a mechanism of power and a function; it is a way of making power relations function in a function, and of making a function function through these power relations. Bentham's Preface to *Panopticon* opens with a list of the benefits to be obtained from his 'inspection-house': '*Morals reformed – health preserved – industry invigorated – instruction diffused – public burthens lightened* – Economy seated, as it were, upon a rock – the gordian knot of the Poor-Laws not cut, but untied – all by a simple idea in architecture!' (*P*, p. 39).

Furthermore, the arrangement of this machine is such that its enclosed nature does not preclude a permanent presence from the outside: we have seen that anyone may come and exercise in the central tower the functions of surveillance, and that, this being the case, he can gain a clear idea of the way in which the surveillance is practised. In fact, any panoptic institution, even if it is as rigorously closed as a penitentiary, may without difficulty be subjected to such irregular and constant inspections: and not only by the appointed inspectors, but also by the public; any member of society will have the right to come and see with his own eyes how the schools, hospitals, factories, prisons function. There is no risk, therefore, that the increase of power created by the panoptic machine may degenerate into tyranny; the disciplinary mechanism will be democratically controlled, since it will be constantly accessible 'to the great tribunal committee of the world'.[6] This Panopticon, subtly arranged so that an observer may observe, at a glance, so many different individuals, also enables everyone to come and observe any of the observers. The seeing machine was once a sort of dark room into which individuals spied; it has become a transparent building in which the exercise of power may be supervised by society as a whole.

The panoptic schema, without disappearing as such or losing any of its properties, was destined to spread throughout the social body; its vocation was to become a generalised function. The plague-stricken town provided an exceptional disciplinary model: perfect, but absolutely violent; to the disease that brought death, power opposed its perpetual threat of death; life inside it was reduced to its simplest expression; it was, against the power of death, the meticulous exercise of the right of the sword. The Panopticon, on the other hand, has a role of amplification; although it arranges power, although it is intended to make it more economic and more effective, it does so not for power itself, nor for the immediate salvation of a threatened society: its aim is to strengthen the social forces – to increase production, to develop the economy, spread education, raise the level of public morality; to increase and multiply.

How is power to be strengthened in such a way that, far from impeding progress, far from weighing upon it with its rules and regulations, it actually facilitates such progress? What intensificator of power will be able at the same time to be a multiplicator of production? How will power, by increasing its forces, be able to increase those of society instead of confiscating them or impeding them? The Panopticon's solution to this problem is that the productive increase of power can be assured only if, on the one hand, it can be exercised continuously in the very foundations of society, in the subtlest possible way, and if, on the other hand, it functions outside these sudden, violent, discontinuous forms that are bound up with the exercise of sovereignty. The body of the king, with its strange material and physical presence, with the force that he himself deploys or transmits to some few others, is at the opposite extreme of this new physics of power represented by panopticism; the domain of panopticism is, on the contrary, that whole lower region, that region of irregular bodies, with their details, their multiple movements, their heterogeneous forces, their spatial relations; what are required are mechanisms that analyse distributions, gaps, series, combinations, and which use instruments that render visible, record, differentiate and compare: a physics of a relational and multiple power, which has its maximum intensity not in the person of the king, but in the bodies that can be individualised by these relations. At the theoretical level, Bentham defines another way of analysing the social body and the power relations that traverse it; in terms of practice, he defines a procedure of subordination of bodies and forces that must increase the utility of power while dispensing with the need for the prince. Panopticism is the general principle of a new 'political anatomy' whose object and end are not the relations of sovereignty but the relations of discipline.

The celebrated, transparent, circular cage, with its high tower, powerful and knowing, may have been for Bentham a project of a perfect disciplinary institution; but he also set out to show how one may 'unlock' the disciplines and get them to function in a diffused, multiple, polyvalent way throughout the whole social body. These disciplines, which the classical age had elaborated in specific, relatively enclosed places – barracks, schools, workshops – and whose total implementation had been imagined only at the limited and temporary scale of a plague-stricken town, Bentham dreamt of transforming into a network of mechanisms that would be everywhere and always alert, running through society without interruption in space or in time. The panoptic arrangement provides the formula for this generalisation. It programmes, at the level of an elementary and easily transferable mechanism, the basic functioning of a society penetrated through and through with disciplinary mechanisms.

9

Semiology and Visual Interpretation

Norman Bryson

In this essay I want to sketch the outlines of a semiological approach to painting. Semiology approaches painting as a system of signs. The emphasis on *sign* may seem odd, but what this term in the first instance displaces is the term *perception*. The idea of painting as the record of a perception may be historically recent. Reynolds in the *Discourses*, for example, urges painters to rise *above* mere perception, and by abstraction to derive from perception its central forms, and to paint those. The hierarchy of genres gives pride of place to painting that sheds the particularity of perception in favour of the ideality of averaged or abstracted forms (in 'the grand manner'): the discarding or 'scraping away' of perception is regarded as the precondition of high art. But in Ruskin's *Modern Painters* painting is consistently approached *from* perception. Turner's paintings are said by Ruskin to record how Turner perceives what is there: some paintings by Turner may look 'visionary' – deviating from what is there – but, Ruskin argues, they are actually grounded in a perceiving consciousness 'on the heights' (yet perceiving clearly from those heights). Ruskin's commitment to this principle gets him into some famous knots. He notices, for example, that Turner often uses the same device for depicting a particular motif, say, a bridge. Ruskin argues that each new bridge Turner sees and paints reminds Turner of previous bridges he has seen, and that Turner's new perception of a bridge brings with it the train of all the bridges Turner has previously perceived: what is painted, Ruskin alleges, is the entire chain of associated perceptual memories in articulation with the new perception.[1] *That* is why Turner's bridges tend to look alike: because of their concatenation of perceptions; not because – as one might far more economically say – this is just Turner's way of painting bridges. Old concepts such as 'invention', 'manner' or 'central form' are transposed and re-expressed as the consequences of perception. This seems to be the dominant strategy of *Modern Painters*, a work which indicates how fully fledged a 'Perceptualist' account of art could be, in 1843.

To place the forms of painting in relation to a psychology of perception is a familiar move among 'the Critical Historians of Art'. Michael Podro has described for us the way that Hildebrand's *Das Problem der Form in der bildenen Kunst* (1893) accounts for artistic form as the structuring of (formless?) *experience*, analysed in terms of sensorium (optical and tactile registers in interplay). 'Optical' and 'tactile' have important work to do in Wölfflin's *Grundbegriffe* (1915), and Riegl's *Spätromische Kunstindustrie* (1901). Panofsky's third, iconological level of meaning – though for us it may throw the gates open to 'context' when we consider works of art – seems in the argument to reduce whatever may lie beyond the second, iconographic level to the psychology of an epoch.[2]

This tradition is still vigorous, notably at the point where German and English aesthetics meet, namely in Gombrich. *Art and Illusion* (1960) has had, in its own time, a centrality and inevitability comparable to Reynolds' *Discourses* in the late eighteenth century.[3] Gombrich's approach to art by way of a psychology of perception is fortified by twentieth-century cognitive psychology, as well as the 'making and matching' model taken from Popper. In a sense this work is the climax of the 'Perceptualist' tradition. Painting is viewed *principally* as the mimesis of perception, modified by a schema. The semiological perceptive questions this mimetic model by giving emphasis to the term *sign* rather than to *perception*; from this move follow a number of consequences.

It is still almost natural for us to think of painting as in some sense, if not completely, the record of perception, perception which – if we follow Gombrich on this point – is variously conditioned by the previous representations of perceptions that come to the artist from his or her tradition. Our ordinary assumptions here owe much to Gombrich, and it is not out of place to clarify some of the thinking we almost take for granted when we picture to ourselves what is involved when the representational painter sets out to create a painting. The thinking, as Gombrich is the first to point out, models itself on a certain understanding of observation in science. First there is an initial problem, which science intends to explore. A trial solution is proposed, in the form of the hypothesis most appropriate to the problem and the one likeliest to lead to the problem's solution. An experimental situation is devised in which the strengths and weaknesses of the hypothesis can be submitted to falsification. The resulting situation reveals new problems the existence or importance of which were not apparent at the commencement of the process. And so scientific observation continues, constantly testing its hypotheses against the observed world, and re-testing its scheme of things against perceptual disclosure.

In *Art and Illusion* Gombrich characterises the work of art along just these lines: as a continuous development consisting in what he calls the 'gradual modification of the traditional schematic conventions of image-making under the pressure of novel demands'. The pattern for art is the same as that for science. First there is the initial problem: Giotto, for example, sets out to record the appearance of the human face. Tradition suggests a particular formula or schema for its transcription onto canvas; let us imagine that it is an early Giotto where the influence of Cimabue is strongly felt. Giotto tests the schema against observation of the face. Observation reveals that here and there the Cimabue-schema is inadequate to the perceptual findings, and that the schema must be modified in accordance with the discrepant data. The modified schema in turn enters the repertoire of schemata and will in due course be subjected to similar tests and elaborations as its predecessor.

This conception of image-making, with its key terms of *schema, observation* and *testing*, can be called the Perceptualist account, because the essential transaction concerns the eye, and the accommodations the schema must make to new observations coming into the eye. The viewer, for his or her part, is defined by this Perceptualist account as performing an activity where those terms re-appear in more passive guise: the viewer confronting a new image mobilises the stock of perceptual memories, brings them to the new work for testing, and the visual schemata are in turn modified by the encounter between the new image and the viewer's gaze. And if we stand back a little and begin to ask questions of the Perceptualist account we will find that, crucially, it leaves no room for the question of the relationship between the image and power.

The account exhausts itself in a description of image-making that omits or brackets the social formation, for in the Perceptualist account the painter's task is to transcribe perceptions as accurately as he can, just as it is the viewer's task to receive those relayed perceptions as sensitively as possible, and with minimal interference or 'noise'. The painter perceives and the viewer re-perceives, and the form which unites them is a line of communication from one pole, replete with perception, the painter's vision, to the other pole, the viewer's gaze, eager for perception. The image is thought of as a channel, or stream of transmission, from a site dense in perception to another site, avid for perception. And if social power features anywhere, in this picture of things, it is as something which intervenes between the two sites or poles, which interposes itself and makes demands of another kind.

Power, social and political power, may utilise this channel and its object of perceptual transmission, the image, in various ways and according to its own ends. Its intervention may be construed as a positive and supportive nature, as when for example an individual or an institution – the patron, the Church – economically enables the painter to carry out his work. Or the intervention by social and political power may be of a negative and subtractive nature, appropriating the image to a particular ideology, of the Church, the State, the patron class. But either way the place of power is on the outside of this inward perceptual activity of painting and viewing. Power seizes, catches hold of, expropriates and deflects the channel of perception that runs from painter to viewer; perhaps it enables, supports, maintains, finances that channel; but however we view it, power is theorised by the Perceptualist account as always outside this relay of the visual image. Power is an external that moves in, and the forcefulness of power is measured by the degree to which it penetrates and overtakes the private transmission of percepts, where the essence of power manifests exactly in its exteriority.

Built into the Perceptualist account, whose fullest statement is Gombrich's *Art and Illusion*, is the idea of power as alien to the making of images, and accordingly a direction of enquiries into the relation of power to the image, *away* from the canvas and into institutions *outside* painting. Yet the connections between the image and power become instantly mysterious, for one is by definition outside the other: both are positioned in a mutual exteriority. A mystic simultaneity arises in which it can become acceptable practice to draw up two separate but nevertheless darkly inter-related columns, one of social events, and one of paintings painted. Clearly this 'two-column' approach is inadequate, so let us go back to the fundamentals of image-making and this time examine it from the other side – from the viewer's gaze.

It may indeed be the case when I look at a particularly life-like representation, I, the viewer, re-experience at one remove the original vision, retinal or imaginary, of its creator, the artist. There *might* be absolute congruence between the two mental fields of artist and spectator. Yet the recognition of a painting can hardly involve such congruence as a necessary criterion. While it might be possible for the painter to know that the image corresponds to his or her original vision or intention, no such knowledge is available to the viewer. Recognition, here, is not at all an act of cross-comparison between two mental fields, or cross-referral of perceptions from one end of the channel to another. It might well be true that when I look at a particular canvas I obtain a set of perceptions I can obtain from *this* canvas and no other, but the set of perceptions in the viewing gaze cannot of itself provide criteria of recognition. This is clear enough if we think of sign-systems other than painting. With mathematics, for example, I may have a vivid picture in my mind of a certain formula, but the criterion of my knowing that the picture was a *formula*, and not simply a tangle of numbers, would be my awareness of its mathematical application. The test of whether or not I had understood the formula would not consist in the examination of my private mental field, or even the comparison between my mental field and its counterpart in the mind of whoever produced the formula, but in seeing if I could place the formula in the general context of my knowledge of mathematical techniques, in my ability to carry out related calculations, and so forth: in short, in my executive *use* of the formula.

Again, in the case of a child learning to read, it is hard to determine the sense of the question, 'Which was the first word the child *read*?' The question seems to appeal to an inward accompaniment to the physical progress of the eye through the chain of characters, an accompaniment which at a particular point takes the form of a 'Now I can read!' sensation. Yet the criterion for right readings cannot be this. The child might indeed have such a sensation, yet be quite unable to read correctly; where reading, like the activity of mathematics, and like the recognition of an image, can be said to take place only when the individual is able to 'go on'; not to reveal to the world a secret event of the interior but to meet the executive demands placed upon the individual by his or her world.[4]

I hope the implications are becoming clear. Perceptualism, the doctrine whose most eloquent spokesman is undoubtedly Gombrich, describes image-making entirely in terms of these secret and private events, perceptions and sensations occurring in invisible recesses of the painter's and the viewer's mind. It is as though understanding in mathematics had been reduced to the occurrence of 'Now I see it!' experiences, or the test of whether or not someone read aright were whether he or she experienced a 'Now I can read!' sensation. The point is that mathematics and reading are activities of the sign, and that painting is, also. My ability to recognise an image neither involves, *nor makes necessary inference towards*, the isolated perceptual field of the image's creator. It is, rather, an ability which presupposes competence within social, that is, socially constructed, codes of recognition. And the crucial difference between the term 'perception' and the term 'recognition' is that the latter is *social*. It takes one person to experience a sensation, it takes (at least) two to recognise a sign. And when people look at representational painting and recognise what they see, their recognition does not unfold in the solitary recesses of the sensorium but through their activation of codes of recognition that are learnt by interaction with others, in the acquisition of human culture. One might put this another way and say that whereas in the Perceptualist account the image is said to span an arc that runs from the brush to the retina, an arc of inner vision or perception, the recognition of painting as sign spans an arc that extends from person to person and across *inter-individual space.*

A changeover from the account of painting in terms of perception to an account of painting as sign is nothing less than the relocation of painting within the field of power from which it had been excluded. In place of the transcendental comparison between the image and perceptual private worlds, stand the socially generated codes of recognition; and in place of the link, magical and illogical, that is alleged to extend from an outer world of things into recesses of inwardness and subjectivity, stands the link extending from individual to individual as consensual activity, in the *forum* of recognition. The social formation isn't, then, something which supervenes or appropriates or utilises the image so to speak *after* it has been made: rather painting, as an activity of the sign, unfolds within the social formation from the beginning. And from the inside – the social formation is inherently and immanently present in the image and not a fate or an external which clamps down on an image that might prefer to be left alone.

So far I have been addressing Perceptualism, the notion that artistic process can be described exclusively in terms of cognition, perception, and optical truth. What Perceptualism leads to is a picture of art in isolation from the rest of society's concerns, since essentially the artist is alone, watching the world as an ocular spectacle but never reacting to the world's meanings, basking in and recording his perceptions but apparently doing so in some extraterritorial zone, off the social map. Perceptualism always renders art banal, since its view never lifts above ocular accuracy, and always renders art trivial, since the making of images seems to go on, according to Perceptualism, out of society, at the margins of social concerns, in some eddy away from the flow of power. But one need not think this way: if we consider painting as an art of the sign, which is to say an art of discourse, then painting is coextensive with the flow of signs through both itself and the rest of the social formation. There is no marginalisation: painting is bathed in the same circulation of signs which permeates or ventilates the rest of the social structure.

This said, I think it equally important to address what might appear to be the opposite extreme, the position which says that art is to be approached in terms of social history, that art belongs to the superstructure and that the superstructure cannot be understood without analysis of the social, and in particular the economic, base. You might perhaps have supposed that in the claim for the immanently social character of the sign, a social history of art was necessarily being advocated, but that doesn't follow in any simple sense, and the reason it doesn't is once again that a strict economism is no better placed than Perceptualism to follow through the implications of what it means when we begin to think of paintings as signs.

The essential model here is inevitably that of *base* and *superstructure*. Taking the base-structure as consisting of the ultimately determinant economic apparatus of the society, and assuming the unified action of productive forces and relations of production, then 'art', alongside legal and political institutions and their ideological formations, is assigned firmly to the superstructure. If we want to understand painting, then first we must look to the base, to the questions of who owns the means of production and distribution of wealth, to what constitutes the dominant class, to the ideology this class uses to justify its power; and then to the arts, and to painting, as aspects of that legitimation and that monopoly.

The problem here is in interesting ways the same problem as that created by Perceptualism, because the question that needs most urgently to be addressed to the base–superstructure model is: In which tier of the model should we place the *sign*? Social history, in this view, is the expression in the superstructure of real, determinant events occurring in the economic base; legal institutions, political institutions, ideological formations, and among these the arts – and painting – are said to be secondary manifestations or epiphenomena of base action. Very well. But where shall one allocate the sign? Does the sign belong above, along with ideology, law, and other derivations? Or is it primary, down there next to the technology, the plant, the hard productive base?

It is indeed a crucial question. In the extreme statements of base–superstructure thinking, signs are no more than the *impress* of base on superstructure. The sign follows the base without deviation, which is also to say that the base *determines* discourse, that discourse takes its patterns from power and repeats them in another key, the key of ideologies. Signs, and discourse, are assumed to accept the impact of the material base as wax accepts the impress of a seal. The sign, and discourse, and painting as a discursive art, are the *expression* of the given reality, and, so to speak, its negative profile. First there is the original matrix of economic reality, then out of that matrix there appears the *inscription*, the writing into art of what is happening in the base. But as soon as this picture is fully drawn in we can see how difficult it is to understand how the model is to work in practice. The base–superstructure conception posits a material base that of *itself* engenders the sign, at its every point of change. The picture proposes a mystery of spontaneous generation of signs directly out of material substance. Yet it is clear that the economic or material base never *has* produced meanings in this uncanny sense; the world does not bear upon its surface signs which are then simply *read* there. And while the base–superstructure model may *seem* to lead to a social history of art, and to concede the social character of the sign on which I was earlier laying stress, in fact the iron-clad pronouncement that the sign belongs to the superstructure omits its social history. It is in matter – in the prior contour of material reality – that the sign is said to arise, as its negative relief, or stencilled echo. Yet the sign's *own* materiality, its status as material practice, is sublimed or vaporised just as drastically as in the Perceptualist account. The global body of signs – discourse – is said to be part of the cloud of ideas and ideologies hovering over and obscuring the real material base, as though discourse were the transcendental accompaniment, floating and hazy, to a real material world. What the economist position is forced to deny is that the sign, that discourse, is material *also*, and as much entails material work and elaboration as the activities of the alleged base.

In the case of painting, the material character of the sign is far more evident than it is in the case of language, and it is therefore perhaps easier to think of the image in non-idealist terms, than it is to think of the word in non-idealist terms. The problem here is that although the material character of painting cannot be ignored, that materiality tends to be equated with substance, pigment, with the brush and the canvas. And if one sets side by side the picture of a factory turning out machines, and a studio turning out paintings, then it will seem as though all the power is in the factory and none in the studio, and that the social history of art must first describe the hard reality of production, ownership, capital, and dominant and dominated classes, and then trace the repercussions of this hard reality in the *atelier*. Once again, painting is off the map, or at least relegated to the margin, just as it was in Gombrich. But figurative painting isn't just the material work of brush and pigment on canvas. Nonfigurative painting may tend in that direction, but for as long as the images one is dealing with involve recognition, for as long as they are *representations*, then they are material signs, and not simply material shapes. And as signs, as complex statements in signs and as material transformations of the sign, paintings are part of a flow of discourse traversing both the studio and the factory.

Discourse doesn't appear spontaneously out of matter: it is the product of human work and human labour. It is an institution that can't be simply derived from the alleged economic base. Like economic activity, discursive activity is nothing less than the transformation of matter through work, and though the economic sphere and the discursive sphere may interact, and in fact can hardly be conceived outside their interaction, to think of discourse as a floating, hazy, transcendental cloud hovering above the machinery amounts to a mystification of the material operation of ideology. To put this another way: to theorise the image as a nebulous superstructural accompaniment to a hard and necessary base is to deny the institution of discourse as a cultural form which interacts with the other, legal, political, economic forms in the social world.

The crucial reformulation here involves breaking the barrier between base and superstructure which in effect places the sign in exteriority to the social formation – an exteriority that merely repeats, in a different register, the Perceptualist separation of the image from social process. What is needed, then, is a form of analysis sufficiently global to include within the same framework *both* the economic practices which Historical Materialism assigns to the base, *and* the signifying practices which are marginalised as superstructural imprint. And the topology must be clear. The base – superstructure model can't easily cope with the question of the sign, and the problems that arise as soon as one tries to work out which tier of the model the sign is supposed to fit into are enormous. The difficulties make clear the need for a form of analysis in art history dialectical enough, and subtle enough, to comprehend as *interaction* the relationship between discursive, economic and political practices.

In discussing the visual arts at the moment the need is, I think, an urgent one. In one vigorous theorisation of painting – Perceptualism – the social formation has little part to play except as intervention or utilisation. The inherently social character of the painterly sign is eclipsed by the picture of the artist alone in the studio, immersed in the privacy of perceptions, the only link with the outer world consisting of optical contact with the surface of things, and the only major difficulty being the accommodation of the schema to the influx of new sensations. In Historical Materialism the same sequestration of art from the public domain is reinstated, for although the social history of art wants the *atelier* to come into contact with the rest of society, the contact can now be seen as *narrowly* economic. Out there, in the social base, an economic apparatus is generating dominant and dominated classes, is organising the means of production and distribution of wealth, and is forging the determinants over the superstructure. In here, in the hush of the studio, the painter passively transcribes on to canvas the visual echo of those far-off events. Or let us say that economic determination is less ambitious, and that it examines instead the more local relation that exists between the painter and his patron or patron-class. This is certainly an improve-ment on Perceptualism's relegation of the painter into social limbo, and hardly less of an improvement on the attempt by a dogmatic Historical Materialism to transform the painter into an echo of the distant rumble of history. The lines of capital that link the painter to his patron or patron-class are real and of enormous importance. But they are not the only lines that link the painter to the rest of the social world, for there is another flow that traverses the painter, and the patron class, and all those who participate in the codes of recognition: the flow of signs, of discourse, of discursive power.

It is a flow in two directions, for the painter can work on the discursive material, can elaborate it, transform it through labour, and return it to the social domain as an alteration or revision of the society's discursive field. I stress this because neither Perceptualism nor the economism underlying the 'two column' social history of art has much to say about creativity, or innovation, or more simply (and perhaps more accurately) the *work* of the sign. If the task of the artist is, in Gombrich's words, the 'modification of the schema under the pressure of novel [visual] demands', then the effort of image-making consists in making and matching against what is already and pre-existently there. The problem for the image becomes a matter of catching up with reality, of discarding those elements within the schema that occlude the limpid registration of the world. The image doesn't have the power to inaugurate, to commence, to molest the given structures. And again with a strict economism in its full, base–superstructure expression, the image can only at best repeat the larger and truer events of history. Capital flows into the *atelier*, power flows in, but the flow is in one direction, and it becomes difficult, if not impossible, to conceive of the reverse of this process, in which the image could be seen as self-empowered and out-flowing, or as an independent intervention within the social fabric.

A virtue of considering the visual image as sign is that having relocated painting within the social domain, inherently and not only as a result of its instrumental placing there by some other agency, it becomes possible to think of the image as discursive work which returns into the society. The painter assumes the society's codes of recognition, and performs his or her activity within their constraints, but the codes permit the elaboration of new combinations of the sign, further evolution in the discursive formation. The result of painting's signifying *work*, these are then recirculated into society as fresh and renewing currents of discourse. The configuration of signs which constitutes a particular image may or may not correspond to configurations in the economic and political spheres, but it need not have first been read there, or match events which only by an act of arbitrary election are privileged as the truth of social history.

It is usually at this point that one encounters the objection that the power of the image to intervene in the social fabric is severely limited, that the image possesses in-built strategic inadequacies, and that unless images articulate their local acts of innovation with the stronger, the major movements and activities within the social formation, they are insignificant (where that word operates as a term of quantity, a measure of instrumental efficacy). No one is so misguided or so out of touch as to claim otherwise. If we think of even revolutionary moments in painting, the impact of the image on its surrounding world may seem hopelessly curtailed. Géricault's portraits of the mad did nothing to modify the juridical status or treatment of the insane; nor did the appearance of *Olympia* at the Salon of 1865 do much, so far as we can tell, to change the interesting nocturnal economy of Paris. Yet this is only a truth of logistics, of *administration* of the image. The danger is that this obvious truth of instrumental inadequacy conceals, makes it difficult to think through, a subtle and more important truth, of topology.

Instrumentally, an *Olympia* at the Salon of 1865 may do little to affect the status of prostitution; but the essential point is that its juxtaposition of Odalisque and Prostitute, or Géricault's elision of the social fixity of the portrait with the social placelessness of the insane, these collisions of discursive forms occur *within* the social formation: not as echoes or duplicates of prior events in the social base that are then expressed, limpidly, without distortion, on the surface of the canvas; but as signifying *work*, the effortful and unprecedented pulling away of discursive forms, away from their normal locations and into *this* painting, *this* image. To look for a result in the form of a change in the base, or in the political sphere, is once again to assume that it is only there, in those arbitrarily privileged zones, that 'real' change happens. If your politics are such that the only changes you recognise are those which take place in the economic sphere, and all the rest are mere swirlings in the cloud of superstructure, then you will not find a painting a particularly interesting or forceful instrument. And this will be because power is located exclusively in agencies other than discourse: in capital, in the factory, in the production and distribution of wealth. The only revolution and indeed the only change that will then be recognised is in those limited spheres privileged by the analysis. Either too narrow or too ambitious in its sense of social change, a dogmatic Historical Materialism will miss where the power *is* in discourse, and in painting. In fact it will be found in every act of looking, where the discursive form of the image meets the discourses brought to bear upon the image by the viewer, and effects a change; where in order to recognise the new discursive form that is the image, the existing boundaries of discourse, the categories and codes of recognition, must be moved, turned and overturned in order to recognise what this image is, that is at once Odalisque and Prostitute, socially fixed by the portrait and socially displaced as insanity. If power is thought of as vast, centralised, as a juggernaut, as panoply, then it will not be seen that power can also be microscopic and discrete, a matter of local moments of change, and that such change may take place whenever an image meets the existing discourses, and moves them over; or finds its viewer, and changes him or her. The power of painting is there, in the thousands of gazes caught by its surface, and the resultant turning, and the shifting, the redirecting of the discursive flow. Power not as a monolith, but as a swarm of points traversing social stratifications and individual persons.

These remarks on the 'swarm of points' lead to the last semiological position in this paper, which concerns the sign as *project*.

One might usefully draw a distinction between *classical* and *projective* models of sign activity. A 'classical' conception (e.g. Port Royal, Saussure) of the sign gives it two halves: a meaning, and the thing which carries the meaning. The meaning of a word may be, for example, the idea I have in my mind when I use that particular word. The idea exists in some degree of separation from the word itself; the idea is anterior to its expression. But it is a characteristic of signs that are given some permanent or notational form (a text, a painting, etc.) that the signs are able to travel away from the context of their making both in space and in time, without ceasing to be signs. Such objects as texts or paintings are structures governed by 'dissemination'. They enter contexts other than the context of their emergence. But even in that first context (for example, the Salon of 1865), the sign acquires its meaning from an interpreter. That is, its meaning comes *to* the sign *from* the place it projects itself forward to, or 'lands' in. Until it completes this projection, so the argument runs, it is not *yet* a sign, not even 'half' a sign. Which gives to writing about art a double mandate: it is both archival and hermeneutic.

The first of these is the mandate which governs most art history at the present time: to trace the painting back to its original context of production. Yet the context may now have to be defined in a new way. It cannot be thought of simply as the circumstances of patronage or commission (important though such factors most certainly are) nor as the conditions of original perception and its notation. Original context must be considered to be a much more global affair, consisting of the complex interaction among all the practices which make up the sphere of culture: the scientific, military, medical, intellectual and religious practices, the legal and political structures, the structures of class, sexuality and economic life, in the given society. It is here, in the interactive sphere, that one would locate the theoretical position of, for example, Mukarovsky, or the work of Svetlana Alpers and Michael Baxandall, among others.[5]

The second, hermeneutic mandate arises from the fact that the sign projects itself historically: it throws itself forward in space and time. Let us say that it survives into a much later period. Its interpretation will now be governed by two historical 'horizons', 'then' and 'now'; but the 'then' is only known as it arises within the 'now', and one must accept this fact – which is simply the fact of living in history. Signs are subject to historical process; their meaning can never escape historical determinations. This gives to thinking and writing about signs a necessary mandate to *go on* interpreting works of art beyond the context of their making. To insist that interpretation attempts exclusively to reconstruct a 'period' response amounts here to a negation of the sign's projective character. As Keith Moxey has put it,

> The focus of the 'intention' of the work of art assigns it a 'terminal' role in the life of culture, a location representing a synthesis of ideas current in the culture of the patron or patrons who commissioned it. It ignores the life of the work of art after it has entered a social context. By concentrating on the way in which the work of art 'reflects' the life of its times, the pre-occupation with 'intention' fails to recognise the function of the work of art in the development of cultural attitudes and therefore as an agent of social change.[6]

But if we open the work of art fully to the present, does this mean *anarchy* of interpretation? The question may be newer to art historians than it is to literary critics, who have faced the 'anarchy' issue several times (Wimsatt and Beardsley on 'intention'; Barthes, *Critique et vérité*; Derrida, *Of Grammatology*).[7] There seem to be about three positions: to separate 'original meaning' from 'subsequent interpretation', usually in order to privilege the former; to assume the position that 'dissemination' *is* anarchic (arguably Derrida's viewpoint); and to claim that anarchy of interpretation cannot arise, because interpretation is always bounded by a specific historical horizon, forms of life, and institutions of interpretation. However, the semiological approach is at this point not so much prescriptive as descriptive. It accounts for what we are already doing, rather than what we should be doing, when we interpret. If one chooses to separate 'original meaning' from 'subsequent interpretation', this is because one's historical horizon, forms of life, and institutions of interpretation enjoin one to do so; if we choose to dissolve the distinction between 'original meaning' and 'subsequent interpretation', it will be for the same reason. What we do and will do when we interpret is a matter, in other words, entirely in the domain of *pragmatics*.

10

Imaging

Teresa de Lauretis

Cinema has been studied as an apparatus of representation, an image machine developed to construct images or visions of social reality and the spectators' place in it. But, insofar as cinema is directly implicated in the production and reproduction of meanings, values, and ideology in *both* sociality and subjectivity, it should be better understood as a signifying practice, a work of semiosis: a work that produces effects of meaning and perception, self-images and subject positions for all those involved, makers and viewers; and thus a semiotic process in which the subject is continually engaged, represented, and inscribed in ideology.[1] The latter emphasis is quite consonant with the present concerns of theoretical feminism in its effort to articulate the relations of the female subject to ideology, representation, practice, and its need to reconceptualise women's position in the symbolic. But the current theories of the subject – Kristeva's as well as Lacan's – pose very serious difficulties for feminist theory. Part of the problem, as I have suggested, lies in their derivation from, and overwhelming dependence on, linguistics. It may well be, then, that part of the solution is to start elsewhere, which is not to say that we should ignore or discard a useful concept like signifying practice, but rather to propose that we rejoin it from another critical path.

If feminists have been so insistently engaged in practices of cinema, as film makers, critics, and theorists, it is because there the stakes are especially high. The representation of woman as image (spectacle, object to be looked at, vision of beauty – and the concurrent representation of the female body as the *locus* of sexuality, site of visual pleasure, or lure of the gaze) is so pervasive in our culture, well before and beyond the institution of cinema, that it necessarily constitutes a starting point for any understanding of sexual difference and its ideological effects in the construction of social subjects, its presence in all forms of subjectivity. Moreover, in our 'civilisation of the image', as Barthes has called it, cinema works most effectively as an *imaging* machine, which by producing images (of women or not of women) also tends to reproduce woman as image. The stakes for women in cinema, therefore, are very high, and our intervention most important at the theoretical level, if we are to obtain a conceptually rigorous and politically useful grasp of the

processes of imaging. In the context of the discussion of iconic signification, the feminist critique of representation has raised many questions
that require critical attention and further elaboration. In very general
terms, what are the conditions of presence of the image in cinema and
film? And vice versa, what are the conditions of presence of cinema and
film in imaging, in the production of a social imaginary?

More specifically, what is at stake, for film theory and for feminism, in
the notion of 'images of women', 'negative' images (literally, *clichés*), or
the alternative, 'positive' images? The notion circulates widely and has
acquired currency in private conversations as well as institutional discourses from film criticism to media shop talk, from academic courses in
women's studies to scholarly conferences and special journal issues.[2] Such
discussions of images of women rely on an often crude opposition of
positive and negative, which is not only uncomfortably close to popular
stereotypes such as the good guys versus the bad guys, or the nice girl
versus the bad woman, but also contains a less obvious and more risky
implication. For it assumes that images are directly absorbed by the viewers, that each image is immediately readable and meaningful in and of
itself, regardless of its context or of the circumstances of its production,
circulation, and reception. Viewers, in turn, are presumed to be at once
historically innocent and purely receptive, as if they too existed in the
world immune from other social practices and discourses, yet immediately susceptible to images, to a certain power of iconism, its truth or
reality effect. But this is not the case. And it is precisely the feminist
critique of representation that has conclusively demonstrated how any
image in our culture – let alone any image of woman – is placed within,
and read from, the encompassing context of patriarchal ideologies, whose
values and effects are social and subjective, aesthetic and affective, and
obviously permeate the entire social fabric and hence all social subjects,
women as well as men. Thus, since the historical innocence of women is
no longer a tenable critical category for feminism, we should rather think
of images as (potentially) productive of contradictions in both subjective
and social processes. This proposition leads to a second set of questions:
by what processes do images on the screen produce imaging on and off
screen, articulate meaning and desire, for the spectators? How are images
perceived? How do we *see*? How do we attribute meaning to what we see?
And do those meanings remain linked to images? What about language?
Or sound? What relations do language and sound bear to images? Do we
image as well as imagine, or are they the same thing? And then again we
must ask: what historical factors intervene in imaging? (Historical factors
might include social discourses, genre codification, audience expectations, but also unconscious production, memory, and fantasy.) Finally,
what are the 'productive relations' of imaging in film-making and film-
viewing, or spectatorship – productive of what? productive how?

These questions are by no means exhaustive of the intricate problematic of imaging. Moreover, they demand consideration of several areas of theoretical discourse that are indispensable in the study of cinematic signification and representation: semiotics, psychoanalysis, ideology, reception and perception theories.[3] In the following pages I will discuss some points at issue in the theoretical accounts of the image given by semiotics and by recent studies of perception; and in so doing I will attempt to outline the notion of imaging more precisely as the process of the articulation of meaning to images, the engagement of subjectivity in that process, and thus the mapping of a social vision into subjectivity. [...]

MAPPING

According to physiologist Colin Blakemore, our apparently unified view of the outside world is in fact produced by the interconnected operations of diverse neural processes. Not only are there different kinds of neuron or nerve cells in the brain and in the retina (the retina, the photosensitive layer at the back of the eye, is actually part of the cortex, composed of the same tissue and nerve cells); and not only do those nerve cells have different functions (for example, 'the main function of the nucleus is not to process visual information by transforming the messages from the eyes, but to filter the signals, depending on the activity of the other sense organs'),[4] but each neuron responds to a specific responsive field, and its action is inhibited or excited by the action of other, adjacent cortical cells. Different parts of the retina project through the optic nerves to different parts of the visual cortex and of the brain stem (the superior colliculus, in the lower part of the brain), producing two maps of the visual world or rather a discontinuous map in which are represented certain features of objects (edges and shapes, position, orientation). In other words, these interacting processes do not merely *record* a unified or preconstituted visual space, but actually constitute a discontinuous *map* of the external world. 'Map' is the term used by Blakemore: the activity of the optical and cortical cells constitutes, he says, 'a mapping of visual space on to the substance of the brain' (p. 14).

The perceptual apparatus, then, does not copy reality but symbolises it. This is supported by the fact that 'unnatural' stimulations of the retina or cortex (surgical, electrical, or manual) produce visual sensations; hence the familiar comic book truth that a blow on the head makes one see stars. This happens because 'the brain always assumes that a message from a particular sense organ is the result of the *expected* form of stimulation' (p. 17). The term 'expected' here implies that perception works by a set of learned responses, a cognitive pattern, a code; and further, that the principle of organisation or combination of sensory input is a kind of inference (it has been called 'unconscious inference').[5] The perceptual apparatus, moreover, is subject to adaptation or calibration, for expectations are readjusted on the basis of new stimuli or occurrences. Finally, perception is not merely patterned response but active anticipation. In the words of R. L. Gregory, perception is 'predictive': 'the study of perception shows that nothing is seen as "directly" as supposed in common sense.'[6] To perceive is to make a continuous series of educated guesses, on the basis of prior knowledges and expectations, however unconscious.

The term 'mapping', interestingly enough, is also used by Eco to define the process of semiosis, sign-making, the production of signs and meanings (without, to the best of my knowledge, any intended reference to Blakemore or psychophysiology). Mapping, for Eco, is the transformation of percepts into semantic units into expressions, a transformation that occurs by transferring – mapping – certain pertinent elements (features that have been recognised as pertinent) from one material continuum to another. The particular rules of articulation, the conditions of reproducibility or of invention, and the physical labour involved are the other parameters to be taken into account in Eco's classification of what he calls the modes of sign production. Eco's view of sign production, especially of the mode he calls invention, associating it with art and creativity, is from the perspective of the *maker* – the speaker, the artist, the producer of signs; it stems from his background in classical aesthetics as well as marxism. In *A Theory of Semiotics* he defines inventions as code-making, thus:

> We may define as invention a mode of production whereby the producer of the sign-function chooses a new material continuum not yet segmented for that purpose and proposes a new way of organising (of giving form to) it in order *to map* within it the formal pertinent elements of a content-type. Thus in invention we have a case of *ratio difficilis* realised within a heteromaterial expression; but since no previous convention exists to correlate the elements of the expression with the selected content, the sign producer must in some way *posit* this correlation so as to make it acceptable. In this sense inventions are radically different from recognition, choice, and replica.[7]

Inventions are radically different because, by establishing new codes, they are capable of transforming both the representation and the perception of reality, and thus eventually can change social reality. The perceptual model, on the contrary, is focused on the spectator, so to speak, rather than the film-maker. While Eco's model requires that, in order to change the world, one must produce new signs, which in turn will

produce new codes and different meanings or social values, the
other model says nothing about purposeful activity and rather stresses
adaptation to external events. But that adaptation is nonetheless a kind
of production – of sensation, cognition, memory, an ordering and
distribution of energy, a constant activity for survival, pleasure, self-
maintenance.

The notion of mapping common to these two models implies that
perception and signification are neither direct or simple reproduction
(copy, mimesis, reflection) nor inevitably predetermined by biology,
anatomy, or destiny; though they are socially determined and overdetermined. Put another way, what is called reproduction – as women well
know – is never simply natural or simply technical, never spontaneous,
automatic, without labour, without pain, without desire, without the
engagement of subjectivity. This is the case even for those signs that
Eco calls replicas, strictly coded signs for which the code is ready-made
and neither requires nor allows invention.[8] Since replicas, like all other
signs, are always produced in a communicational context, their (re)pro-
duction is still embedded in a speech act; it always occurs within a
process of enunciation and address that requires the mapping of other
elements or the making pertinent of other features, and that also involves
memory, expectations, decisions, pain, desire – in short, the whole discontinuous history of the subject. If, then, subjectivity is engaged in
semiosis at all levels, not just in visual pleasure but in all cognitive
processes, in turn semiosis (coded expectations, patterns of response,
assumptions, inferences, predictions, and, I would add, fantasy) is at
work in sensory perception, inscribed in the body – the human body
and the film body. Finally, the notion of mapping suggests an ongoing
but discontinuous process of perceiving-representing-meaning (I like to
call it 'imaging') that is neither linguistic (discrete, linear, syntagmatic, or
arbitrary) nor iconic (analogical, paradigmatic, or motivated), but both, or
perhaps neither. And in this imaging process are involved different codes
and modalities of semiotic production, as well as the semiotic production
of difference.

Difference. Inevitably that question comes back, we come back to the
question of imaging difference, the question of feminism. Which is not,
can no longer be, a matter of simple oppositions between negative and
positive images, iconic and verbal signification, imaginary and symbolic
processes, intuitive perception and intellectual cognition, and so forth.
Nor can it be simply a matter of reversing the hierarchy of value which
underlies each set, assigning dominance to one term over the other (as in
the feminine–masculine or female–male dichotomies). The fundamental proposition of feminism, that the personal is political, urges the displacement of all such oppositional terms, the crossing and recharting of
the space between them. No other course seems open if we are to

reconceptualise the relations that bind the social to the subjective. If we take up the notion of mapping, for instance, and allow it to act as a footbridge across the two distinct theoretical fields of psychophysiology and semiotics, we can envision a connection, a pathway between spheres of material existence, perception, and semiosis, which are usually thought of as self-contained and incommensurable.

Much the same way as classical semiology opposed iconic and verbal signs, perception and signification are usually considered distinct processes, often indeed opposed to one another as pertaining respectively to the sphere of subjectivity (feeling, affectivity, fantasy, pre-logical, pre-discursive, or primary processes) and to the sphere of sociality (rationality, communication, symbolisation, or secondary processes). Very few manifestations of culture, notably Art, are thought to partake of both. And even when a cultural form, such as cinema, clearly traverses both spheres, their presumed incommensurability dictates that questions of perception, identification, pleasure, or displeasure be accounted for in terms of individual idiosyncratic response or personal taste, and hence not publicly discussed; while a film's social import, its ultimate meaning, or its aesthetic qualities may be grasped, shared, taught, or debated 'objectively' in a generalised discourse. Thus, for example, even as the feminist critique of representation began with, and was developed from, the sheer displeasure of female spectators in the great majority of films, no other public discourse existed prior to it in which the question of displeasure in the 'image' of woman (and the attendant difficulties of identification) could be addressed. Thus, whenever displeasure was expressed, it would be inevitably dismissed as an exaggerated, over-sensitive, or hysterical reaction on the part of the individual woman. Such reactions appeared to violate the classic rule of aesthetic distance, and with it the artistic-social character of cinema, by an impingement of the subjective, the personal, the irrational. That the focus on 'positive' images of woman is now another formula in both film criticism and film-making is a measure of the social legitimation of a certain feminist discourse, and the consequent viability of its commercial and ideological exploitation (witness the recent crop of films like *The French Lieutenant's Woman, Tess, Gloria, Nine to Five, Rich and Famous, Personal Best, Tootsie*, etc.).

Feminist film theory, meanwhile, has gone well beyond the simple opposition of positive and negative images, and has indeed displaced the very terms of that opposition through a sustained critical attention to the hidden work of the apparatus.[9] It has shown, for instance, how narrativity works to anchor images to non-contradictory points of identification, so that the 'sexual difference' is ultimately reconfirmed and any ambiguity reconciled by narrative closure. The symptomatic reading of films as filmic texts has worked against such closure, seeking out the invisible subtext made of the gaps and excess in the narrative or visual texture of a film, and finding there, concurrent with the repression of the female's look, the signs of her elision from the text. Thus, it has been argued, it is the elision of woman that is represented in the film, rather than a positive or a negative image; and what the representation of woman *as* image, positive *or* negative, achieves is to deny women the status of subjects both on the screen and in the cinema. But even so an opposition is produced: the image and what the image hides (the elided woman), one visible and the other invisible, sound very much like a binary set. In short, we continue to face the difficulty of elaborating a new conceptual framework not founded on the dialectic logic of opposition, as all hegemonic discourses seem to be in Western culture. The notion of mapping and the theoretical bridge it sets up between perception and signification suggest a complex interaction and mutual implication, rather than opposition, between the spheres of subjectivity and sociality. It may be useful as a model, or at least a guiding concept in understanding the relations of imaging, the articulation of images to meanings in the cinema, as well as cinema's own role in mediating, binding, or indeed mapping the social into the subjective.

11

Desperately Seeking Difference: Jackie Stacey Considers Desire Between Women in Narrative Cinema

Jackie Stacey

During the last decade, feminist critics have developed an analysis of the constructions of sexual difference in dominant narrative cinema, drawing on psychoanalytic and post-structuralist theory. One of the main indictments of Hollywood film has been its passive positioning of the woman as sexual spectacle, as there 'to be looked at', and the active positioning of the male protagonist as bearer of the look. This pleasure has been identified as one of the central structures of dominant cinema, constructed in accordance with masculine desire. The question which has then arisen is that of the pleasure of the woman spectator. While this issue has hardly been addressed, the specifically homosexual pleasures of female spectatorship have been ignored completely. This article will attempt to suggest some of the theoretical reasons for this neglect.

THEORIES OF FEMININE SPECTATORSHIP: MASCULINISATION, MASOCHISM OR MARGINALITY

Laura Mulvey's 'Visual Pleasure and Narrative Cinema'[1] has been the springboard for much feminist film criticism during the last decade. Using psychoanalytic theory, Mulvey argued that the visual pleasures of Hollywood cinema are based on voyeuristic and fetishistic forms of looking. Because of the ways these looks are structured, the spectator necessarily identifies with the male protagonist in the narrative, and thus with his objectification of the female figure via the male gaze. The construction of woman as spectacle is built into the apparatus of dominant cinema, and the spectator position which is produced by the film narrative is necessarily a masculine one.

Mulvey maintained that visual pleasure in narrative film is built around two contradictory processes: the first involves objectification of the image and the second identification with it. The first process depends upon 'direct scopophilic contact with the female form displayed for [the spectator's] enjoyment'[2] and the spectator's look here is active and feels powerful. This form of pleasure requires the separation of the 'erotic identity of the subject from the object on the screen'.[3] This 'distance' between spectator and screen contributes to the voyeuristic pleasure of looking in on a private world. The second form of pleasure depends upon the opposite process, an identification with the image on the screen 'developed through narcissism and the constitution of the ego'.[4] The process of identification in the cinema, Mulvey argued, like the process of objectification, is structured by the narrative. It offers the spectator the pleasurable identification with the main male protagonist, and through him the power to indirectly possess the female character displayed as sexual object for his pleasure. The look of the male character moves the narrative forward and identification with it thus implies a sense of sharing in the power of his active look.

Two absences in Mulvey's argument have subsequently been addressed in film criticism. The first raises the question of the male figure as erotic object,[5] the second that of the feminine subject in the narrative, and, more specifically in relation to this article, women's active desire and the sexual aims of women in the audience in relationship to the female protagonist on the screen. As David Rodowick points out:

> her discussion of the female figure is restricted only to its function as masculine object-choice. In this manner, the place of the masculine is discussed as both the subject and object of the gaze: and the feminine is discussed only as an object which structures the masculine look according to its active (voyeuristic) and passive (fetishistic) forms. So where is the place of the feminine subject in this scenario?[6]

There are several possible ways of filling this theoretical gap. One would use a detailed textual analysis to demonstrate that different gendered spectator positions are produced by the film text, contradicting the unified masculine model of spectatorship. This would at least provide some space for an account of the feminine subject in the film text and in the cinema audience. The relationship of spectators to these feminine and masculine positions would then need to be explored further: do women necessarily take up a feminine and men a masculine spectator position?

Alternatively, we could accept a theory of the masculinisation of the spectator at a textual level, but argue that spectators bring different subjectivities to the film according to sexual difference,[7] and therefore respond differently to the visual pleasures offered in the text. I want to elaborate these two possibilities briefly, before moving on to discuss a third which offers a more flexible or mobile model of spectatorship and cinematic pleasure.

The first possibility is, then, arguing that the film text can be read and enjoyed from different gendered positions. This problematises the mono-lithic model of Hollywood cinema as an 'anthropomorphic male machine'[8] producing unified and masculinised spectators. It offers an explanation of women's pleasure in narrative cinema based on different processes of spectatorship, according to sexual difference. What this 'difference' signifies, however, in terms of cinematic pleasure, is highly contestable.

Raymond Bellour has explored the way the look is organised to create filmic discourse through detailed analyses of the system of enunciation in Hitchcock's work.[9] The mechanisms for eliminating the threat of sexual difference represented by the figure of the woman, he argues, are built into the apparatus of the cinema. Woman's desire only appears on the screen to be punished and controlled by assimilation to the desire of the male character. Bellour insists upon the masochistic nature of the woman spectator's pleasure in Hollywood film.

> I think that a woman can love, accept, and give positive value to these films only from her own masochism, and from a certain sadism that she can exercise in return on the masculine subject, within a system loaded with traps.[10]

Bellour, then, provides an account of the feminine subject and women's spectatorship which offers a different position from the masculine one set up by Mulvey. However, he fixes these positions within a rigid dicho-tomy which assumes a biologically determined equivalence between male/female and the masculine/feminine, sadistic/masochistic positions he believes to be set up by the cinematic apparatus. The apparatus here is seen as determining, controlling the meaning produced by a film text unproblematically.

> ... the resulting picture of the classical cinema is even more totalistic and deterministic than Mulvey's. Bellour sees it as a logically consist-ent, complete and closed system.[11]

The problem here is that Bellour's analysis, like those of many structural functionalists, leaves no room for subjectivity. The spectator is presumed to be an already fully constituted subject and is fixed by the text to a predetermined gender identification. There is no space for subjectivity to be seen as a process in which identification and object choice may be shifting, contradictory or precarious.

A second challenge to the model of the masculinised spectator set up
by Mulvey's 1975 essay comes from the work of Mary Ann Doane. She
draws on Freud's account of asymmetry in the development of masculinity and femininity to argue that women's pleasures are not motivated by
fetishistic and voyeuristic drives.

> For the female spectator there is a certain over-presence of the image –
> she **is** the image. Given the closeness of this relationship, the female
> spectator's desire can be described only in terms of a kind of narcissism
> – the female look demands a becoming. It thus appears to negate the
> very distance or gap specified...as the essential precondition for
> voyeurism.[12]

Feminist critics have frequently challenged the assumption that fetishism functions for women in the same way that it is supposed to for men.
Doane argues that the girl's understanding of the meaning of sexual
difference occurs simultaneously with seeing the boy's genitals; the
split between seeing and knowing, which enables the boy to disown the
difference which is necessary for fetishism, does not occur in girls.

> It is in the distance between the look and the threat that the boy's
> relation to the knowledge of sexual difference is formulated. The
> boy, unlike the girl in Freud's description, is capable of a re-vision...
> This gap between the visible and the knowable, the very possibility of
> disowning what is seen, prepares the ground for fetishism.[13]

This argument is useful in challenging the hegemony of the cinema
apparatus and in offering an account of visual pleasure which is neither
based on a phallic model, nor on the determinacy of the text. It allows for
an account of women's potential resistance to the dominant masculine
spectator position. However, it also sets women outside the problematic
pleasures of looking in the cinema, as if women do not have to negotiate
within patriarchal regimes. As Doane herself has pointed out:

> The feminist theorist is thus confronted with something of a double
> bind: she can continue to analyse and interpret various instances of the
> repression of woman, of her radical absence in the discourses of men –
> a pose which necessitates remaining within that very problematic
> herself, repeating its terms; or she can attempt to delineate a feminine
> specificity, always risking a recapitulation of patriarchal constructions
> and a naturalisation of 'woman'.[14]

In fact, this is a very familiar problem in feminist theory: how to argue
for a feminine specificity without falling into the trap of biological

essentialism. If we do argue that women differ from men in their relation to visual constructions of femininity, then further questions are generated for feminist film theory: do all women have the same relationship to images of themselves? Is there only one feminine spectator position? How do we account for diversity, contradiction or resistance within this category of feminine spectatorship?

The problem here is one which arises in relation to all cultural systems in which women have been defined as 'other' within patriarchal discourses: how can we express the extent of women's oppression without denying femininity any room to manoeuvre,[15] defining women as complete victims of patriarchy,[16] or as totally other to it?[17] Within the theories discussed so far, the female spectator is offered only the three rather frustrating options of masculinisation, masochism or marginality.

TOWARDS A MORE CONTRADICTORY MODEL OF SPECTATOR-SHIP

A different avenue of exploration would require a more complex and contradictory model of the relay of looks on the screen and between the audience and the diegetic characters.

> It might be better, as Barthes suggests, neither to destroy difference nor to valorise it, but to multiply and disperse differences, to move towards a world where differences would not be synonymous with exclusion.[18]

In her 1981 'Afterthoughts' on visual pleasure, Mulvey addresses many of the problems raised so far. In an attempt to develop a more 'mobile' position for the female spectator in the cinema, she turns to Freud's theories of the difficulties of attaining heterosexual femininity.[19] Required, unlike men, to relinquish the phallic activity and female object of infancy, women are argued to oscillate between masculine and feminine identifications. To demonstrate this oscillation between positions, Mulvey cites Pearl Chavez's ambivalence in *Duel in the Sun*, the splitting of her desire (to be Jesse's 'lady' or Lewt's tomboy lover), a splitting which also extends to the female spectator. Mulvey's revision is important for two reasons: it displaces the notions of the fixity of spectator positions produced by the text, and it focuses on the gaps and contradictions within patriarchal signification, thus opening up crucial questions of resistance and diversity. However, Mulvey maintains that fantasies of action 'can only find expression . . . through the metaphor of masculinity'. In order to identify with active desire, the female spectator must assume an (uncomfortably) masculine position:

...the female spectator's phantasy of masculinisation is always to some extent at cross purposes with itself, restless in its transvestite clothes.[20]

OPPRESSIVE DICHOTOMIES

Psychoanalytic accounts which theorise identification and object choice within a framework of linked binary oppositions (masculinity/femininity: activity/passivity) necessarily masculinise female homosexuality. Mary Ann Doane's reading of the first scene in the film *Caught* demonstrates the limitations of this psychoanalytic binarism perfectly.

The woman's sexuality, as spectator, must undergo a constant process of transformation. She must look, as if she were a man with the phallic power of the gaze, at a woman who would attract that gaze, in order to be that woman...The convolutions involved here are analogous to those described by Julia Kristeva as 'the double or triple twists of what we commonly call female homosexuality: "I am looking, as a man would, for a woman"; or else, "I submit myself, as if I were a man who thought he was a woman, to a woman who thinks she is a man".'[21]

Convolutions indeed. This insistence upon a gendered dualism of sexual desire maps homosexuality onto an assumed antithesis of masculinity and femininity. Such an asumption precludes a description of homosexual positionality without resorting to the manoeuvres cited by Doane. In arguing for a more complex model of cinematic spectatorship, I am suggesting that we need to separate gender identification from sexuality, too often conflated in the name of sexual difference.

In films where the woman is represented as sexual spectacle for the masculine gaze of the diegetic and the cinematic spectator, an identification with a masculine heterosexual desire is invited. The spectator's response can vary across a wide spectrum between outright acceptance and refusal. It has proved crucial for feminist film theorists to explore these variations. How might a woman's look at another woman, both within the diegesis and between spectator and character, compare with that of the male spectator?

This article considers the pleasures of two narrative films which develop around one woman's obsession with another woman, *All About Eve* (directed by Joseph Mankiewicz, 1950) and *Desperately Seeking Susan* (directed by Susan Seidelman, 1984). I shall argue that these films offer particular pleasures to the women in the audience which cannot simply be reduced to a masculine heterosexual equivalent. In so doing I am not claiming these films as 'lesbian films',[22] but rather using them to examine certain possibilities of pleasure.

I want to explore the representation of forms of desire and identification in these films in order to consider their implications for the pleasures of female spectatorship. My focus is on the relations between women on the screen, and between these representations and the women in the audience. Interestingly, the fascinations which structure both narratives are precisely about difference – forms of otherness between women characters which are not merely reducible to sexual difference, so often seen as the sole producer of desire itself.

THE INSCRIPTION OF ACTIVE FEMININE DESIRE

In *Alice Doesn't*, Teresa de Lauretis explores the function of the classic masculine Oedipal trajectory in dominant narrative. The subjects which motivate the narrative along the logic of the 'Oedipus', she argues, are necessarily masculine.

> However varied the conditions of the presence of the narrative form in fictional genres, rituals or social discourses, its movement seems to be that of a passage, a transformation predicated on the figure of the hero, a mythical subject...the **single** figure of the hero who crosses the boundary and penetrates the other space. In so doing, the hero, the mythical subject, is constructed as a human being and as male; he is the active principle of culture, the establisher of distinction, the creator of differences. Female is what is not susceptible to transformation, to life or death.[23]

De Lauretis then proceeds to outline the significance of this division between masculine and feminine within the textual narrative in terms of spectatorship.

> Therefore, to say that narrative is the production of Oedipus is to say that each reader – male or female – is constrained and defined within the two positions of a sexual difference thus conceived: male-hero-human, on the side of the subject; the female-obstacle-boundary-space, on the other.[24]

As de Lauretis herself acknowledges later in the chapter, this analysis leaves little space for either the question of the feminine subject in the narrative, or the pleasures of desire and identification of the women in the audience. In order to explore these questions more concretely, I want to discuss two texts – one a Hollywood production of 1950, the other a recent US 'independent' – whose central narrative concern is that of female desire. Both *All About Eve* and *Desperately Seeking Susan* have female protagonists whose desires and identifications move the narratives forward. In de Lauretis's terms, these texts construct not only a feminine object of desire in the narrative, but also a feminine subject of that desire.

All About Eve is particularly well suited to an analysis of these questions, as it is precisely about the pleasures and dangers of spectatorship for women. One of its central themes is the construction and reproduction of feminine identities, and the activity of looking is highlighted as an important part of these processes. The narrative concerns two women, a Broadway star and her most adoring spectator, Eve. In its course, we witness the transformation of Eve Butler (Anne Baxter) from spectator to star herself. The pleasures of spectatorship are emphasised by Eve's loyal attendance at every one of Margot Channing's (Bette Davis) performances. Its dangers are also made explicit as an intense rivalry develops between them. Eve emerges as a greedy and ambitious competitor, and Margot steps down from stardom into marriage, finally enabling her protegée to replace her as 'actress of the year' in a part written originally for Margot.

Eve's journey to stardom could be seen as the feminine equivalent to the masculine Oedipal trajectory described by de Lauretis above. Freud's later descriptions of the feminine Oedipal journey[25] contradict his previous symmetrical model wherein the girl's first love object is her father, as the boy's is his mother. In his later arguments, Freud also posited the mother as the girl's first love object. Her path to heterosexuality is therefore difficult and complex, since it requires her not only to relinquish her first object, like the boy, but to transform both its gender (female to male) and the aim (active to passive) directed at it. Up to this point, active desire towards another woman is an experience of all women, and its re-enactment in *All About Eve* may constitute one of the pleasures of spectatorship for the female viewer.

Eve is constantly referred to as innocent and childlike in the first half of the film and her transformation involves a process of maturation, of becoming a more confident adult. First she is passionately attached to Margot, but then she shifts her affection to Margot's lover Bill, attempting unsuccessfully to seduce him. Twice in the film she is shown interrupting their intimacy: during their farewell at the airport and then during their fierce argument about Margot's jealousy, shortly before Bill's welcome-home party. Eve's third object of desire, whom she actively pursues, is the married playwright, Lloyd Richards, husband to Margot's best friend. In both cases the stability of the older heterosexual couples, Margot and Bill, Karen and Lloyd, is threatened by the presence of the younger woman who completes the Oedipal triangle. Eve is finally punished for her desires by the patriarchal power of the aptly named Addison de Wit, who proves to be one step ahead of her manipulations.

The binary opposition between masculinity and femininity offers a limited framework for the discussion of Eve's fascination with Margot, which is articulated actively through an interplay of desire and identification during the film. In many ways, Margot is Eve's idealised object of desire. She follows Margot from city to city, never missing any of her performances. Her devotion to her favourite Broadway star is stressed at the very start of the film.

> **Karen**   But there are hundreds of plays on Broadway...
> **Eve**   Not with Margot Channing in them!

Margot is moved by Eve's representation of her 'tragic' past, and flattered by her adoration, so she decides to 'adopt' her.

> **Margot** (*voice over*)   We moved Eve's few pitiful possessions into my apartment. ... Eve became my sister, mother, lawyer, friend, psychiatrist and cop. The honeymoon was on!

Eve acts upon her desire to become more like her ideal. She begins to wear Margot's cast-off clothes, appearing in Margot's bedroom one morning in her old black suit. Birdie, Margot's personal assistant, responds suspiciously to Eve's behaviour.

> **Margot**   She thinks only of me.
> **Birdie**   She thinks only *about* you – like she's studying you – like you was a book, or a play, or a set of blueprints – how you walk, talk, eat, think, sleep.
> **Margot**   I'm sure that's very flattering, Birdie, and I'm sure there's nothing wrong with it.

The construction of Bette Davis as the desirable feminine ideal in this narrative has a double significance here. As well as being a 'great star' for Eve, she is clearly the same for the cinema audience. The film offers the fictional fulfilment of the spectator's dreams as well as Eve's, to be a star like Bette Davis, like Margot. Thus the identifications and desires of Eve, to some extent, narrativise a traditional pleasure of female spectatorship.

Margot is not only a star, she is also an extremely powerful woman who intimidates most of the male characters in the film. Her quick wit and disdain for conventional politeness, together with her flare for drama offstage as much as on, make her an attractive figure for Eve, an 'idealistic dreamy-eyed kid', as Bill describes her. It is this *difference* between the two women which motivates Eve, but which Eve also threatens. In trying to 'become as much like her ideal as possible', Eve almost replaces Margot in both her public and her private lives. She places a call to Bill on Margot's behalf, and captures his attention when he is on his way upstairs to see Margot before his coming home party. Margot begins to feel dispensable.

Margot   I could die right now and nobody would be confused. My inventory is all in shape and the merchandise all put away.

Yet even dressed in Margot's costume, having taken her role in the evening's performance, Eve cannot supplant her in the eyes of Bill, who rejects her attempt at seduction. The difference between the two women is repeatedly stressed and complete identification proves impossible.

All About Eve offers some unusual pleasures for a Hollywood film, since the active desire of a female character is articulated through looking at the female star. It is by watching Margot perform on the stage that Eve becomes intoxicated with her idol. The significance of active looking in the articulation of feminine desire is foregrounded at various points in the narrative. In one scene, we see Eve's devoted spectatorship in progress during one of Margot's performances. Eve watches Margot from the wings of the stage, and Margot bows to the applause of her audience. In the next scene the roles are reversed, and Margot discovers Eve on the empty stage bowing to an imaginary audience. Eve is holding up Margot's costume to sample the pleasures of stardom for herself. This process is then echoed in the closing scene of the film with Eve, now a Broadway star herself, and the newly introduced Phoebe, an adoring schoolgirl fan. The final shot shows Phoebe, having covertly donned Eve's bejewelled evening cloak, holding Eve's award and gazing at her reflection in the mirror. The reflected image, infinitely multiplied in the triptych of the glass, creates a spectacle of stardom that is the film's final shot, suggesting a perpetual regeneration of intra-feminine fascinations through the pleasure of looking.

THE DESIRE TO BE DESPERATE

Like *All About Eve, Desperately Seeking Susan* concerns a woman's obsession with another woman. But instead of being punished for acting upon her desires, like Eve, Roberta (Rosanna Arquette) acts upon her desires, if in a rather more haphazard way, and eventually her initiatives are rewarded with the realisation of her desires. Despite her classic feminine behaviour, forgetful, clumsy, unpunctual and indecisive, she succeeds in her quest to find Susan (Madonna).

Even at the very beginning of the film, when suburban housewife Roberta is represented at her most dependent and childlike, her actions propel the narrative movement. Having developed her own fantasy narrative about Susan by reading the personal advertisements, Roberta acts upon her desire to be 'desperate' and becomes entangled in Susan's life. She anonymously attends the romantic reunion of Susan and Jim, and then pursues Susan through the streets of Manhattan. When she loses sight of her quarry in a second-hand shop, she purchases the jacket which Susan has just exchanged. The key found in its pocket provides an excuse for direct contact, and Roberta uses the personals to initiate another meeting.

Not only is the narrative propelled structurally by Roberta's desire, but almost all the spectator sees of Susan at the beginning of the film is revealed through Roberta's fantasy. The narrativisation of her desires positions her as the central figure for spectator identification: through her desire we seek, and see, Susan. Thus, in the opening scenes, Susan is introduced by name when Roberta reads the personals aloud from under the dryer in the beauty salon. Immediately following Roberta's declaration 'I wish I was desperate', there is a cut to the first shot of Susan.

The cuts from the Glass' party to Susan's arrival in New York City work to the same effect. Repelled by her husband's TV commercial for his bathroom wares, Roberta leaves her guests and moves towards the window, as the ad's voice-over promises 'At Gary's Oasis, all your fantasies can come true'. Confronted with her own image in the reflection, she pushes it away by opening the window and looking out longingly onto Manhattan's skyline. The ensuing series of cuts between Roberta and the bridge across the river to the city link her desiring gaze to Susan's arrival there via the same bridge.

At certain points within *Desperately Seeking Susan*, Roberta explicitly becomes the bearer of the look. The best illustration of this transgression of traditional gender positionalities occurs in the scene in which she first catches sight of Susan. The shot sequence begins with Jim seeing Susan and is immediately followed with Roberta seeing her. It is, however, Roberta's point of view which is offered for the spectator's identification. Her look is specified by the use of the pay-slot telescope through which Roberta, and the spectator, see Susan.

In accordance with classic narrative cinema, the object of fascination in *Desperately Seeking Susan* is a woman – typically, a woman coded as a sexual spectacle. As a star Madonna's image is saturated in sexuality. In many ways she represents the '80s 'assertive style' of heterosexual spectacle, inviting masculine consumption. This is certainly emphasised by shots of Susan which reference classic pornographic poses and camera angles; for example, the shot of Susan lying on Roberta's bed reading her diary, which shows Susan lying on her back, wearing only a vest and a pair of shorts over her suspenders and lacy tights. (Although one could argue that the very next shot, from Susan's point of view, showing Gary upside down, subverts the conventional pornographic codes.) My aim is not to deny these meanings in *Desperately Seeking Susan*, in order to claim it as a 'progressive text', but to point to cinematic pleasures which may be available to the spectator *in addition* to those previously analysed by feminist film theory. Indeed, I believe such a project can only attempt to work within the highly contradictory constructions of femininity in mainstream films.

Susan is represented as puzzling and enigmatic to the protagonist, and to the spectator. The desire propelling the narrative is partly a desire to become more like her, but also a desire to know her, and to solve the riddle of her femininity. The protagonist begins to fulfil this desire by following the stranger, gathering clues about her identity and her life, such as her jacket, which, in turn, produces three other clues, a key, a photograph and a telephone number. The construction of her femininity as a riddle is emphasised by the series of intrigues and misunderstandings surrounding Susan's identity. The film partly relies on typical devices drawn from the mystery genre in constructing the protagonist's, and thus the spectator's, knowledge of Susan through a series of clues and coincidences. Thus, in some ways, Susan is positioned as the classic feminine enigma; she is, however, investigated by another woman.

One line of analysis might simply see Roberta as taking up the position of the masculine protagonist in expressing a desire to be 'desperate', which, after all, can be seen as identifying with Jim's position in relation to Susan, that of active desiring masculinity. Further legitimation for this reading could be seen in Jim's response to Roberta's advertisement to Susan in the personals. He automatically assumes it has been placed there by another man, perhaps a rival. How can we understand the construction of the female protagonist as the agent and articulator of desire for another woman in the narrative within existing psychoanalytic theories of sexual difference? The limitations of a dichotomy which offers only two significant categories for understanding the complex interplay of gender, sexual aim and object choice, are clearly demonstrated here.

DIFFERENCE AND DESIRE BETWEEN WOMEN

The difference which produces the narrative desire in *Desperately Seeking Susan* is not sexual difference, but the difference between two women in the film. It is the difference between suburban marriage and street credibility. Two sequences contrast the characters using smoking as a signifier of difference. The first occurs in Battery Park, where Roberta behaves awkwardly in the unfamiliar territory of public space. She is shown sitting on a park bench, knees tightly clenched, looking around nervously for Susan. Jim asks her for a light, to which she timidly replies that she does not smoke. The ensuing cut shows Susan, signalled by Jim's shout of recognition. Susan is sitting on the boat rail, striking a match on the bottom of her raised boot to light a cigarette.

Smoking is used again to emphasise difference in a subsequent sequence. This time, Roberta, having by now lost her memory and believing she may be Susan, lights a cigarette from Susan's box. Predictably, she chokes on the smoke, with the unfamiliarity of an adolescent novice. The next cut shows us Susan, in prison for attempting to skip her cab fare, taking a light from the prison matron and blowing the smoke defiantly straight back into her face. The contrast in their smoking ability is only one signifier of the characters' very different femininities. Roberta is represented as young, inexperienced and asexual, while Susan's behaviour and appearance are coded as sexually confident and provocative. Rhyming sequences are used to emphasise their differences even after Roberta has taken on her new identity as Susan. She ends up in the same prison cell, but her childlike acquiescence to authority contrasts with Susan's defiance of the law.

Susan transgresses conventional forms of feminine behaviour by appropriating public space for herself. She turns the public lavatory into her own private bathroom, drying her armpits with the hand blower, and changing her clothes in front of the mirror above the washbasins as if in her own bedroom. In the streets, Susan challenges the patronising offer of a free newspaper from a passerby by dropping the whole pile at his feet and taking only the top copy for herself. In contrast to Susan's supreme public confidence, Roberta is only capable in her own middle-class privacy. Arriving home after her day of city adventures, she manages to synchronise with a televised cooking show, catching up on its dinner preparations with confident dexterity in her familiar domestic environment.

As soon as Roberta becomes entangled in Susan's world, her respectable sexuality is thrown into question. First she is assumed to be having an affair, then she is arrested for suspected prostitution, and finally Gary asks her if she is a lesbian. When the two photographs of Roberta, one as a bride and one as a suspected prostitute, are laid down side by side at the police station, her apparent transformation from virgin to whore shocks her husband. The ironic effect of these largely misplaced accusations about Roberta's sexuality works partly in relation to Susan, who is represented as the epitome of opposition to acceptable bourgeois feminine sexuality. She avoids commitment, dependency or permanence in her relationships with men, and happily takes their money, while maintaining an intimate friendship with the woman who works at the Magic Box.

Roberta's desire is finally rewarded when she meets Susan in an almost farcical chase scene at that club during the chaotic film finale. Gary finds Roberta, Des finds 'Susan' (Roberta), Jim finds Susan, the villain finds the jewels (the earrings which Susan innocently pocketed earlier in the film), Susan and Roberta catch the villain, and Susan and Roberta find each other.... The last shot of the film is a front-page photograph of the two women hand in hand, triumphantly waving their reward cheque in return for the recovery of the priceless Nefertiti earrings. In the end, both women find what they were searching for throughout the narrative: Roberta has found Susan, and Susan has found enough money to finance many future escapades.

Roberta's desire to become more like her ideal – a more pleasingly co-ordinated, complete and attractive feminine image[26] – is offered temporary narrative fulfilment. However, the pleasures of this feminine desire cannot be collapsed into simple identification, since difference and otherness are continuously played upon, even when Roberta 'becomes' her idealised object. Both *Desperately Seeking Susan* and *All About Eve* tempt the woman spectator with the fictional fulfilment of becoming an ideal feminine other, while denying complete transformation by insisting upon differences between women. The rigid distinction between *either* desire *or* identification, so characteristic of psychoanalytic film theory, fails to address the construction of desires which involve a specific interplay of both processes.

12

The Oppositional Gaze: Black Female Spectators

bell hooks

When thinking about black female spectators, I remember being punished as a child for staring, for those hard intense direct looks children would give grown-ups, looks that were seen as confrontational, as gestures of resistance, challenges to authority. The 'gaze' has always been political in my life. Imagine the terror felt by the child who has come to understand through repeated punishments that one's gaze can be dangerous. The child who has learned so well to look the other way when necessary. Yet, when punished, the child is told by parents, 'Look at me when I talk to you'. Only, the child is afraid to look. Afraid to look, but fascinated by the gaze. There is power in looking.

Amazed the first time I read in history classes that white slave-owners (men, women, and children) punished enslaved black people for looking, I wondered how this traumatic relationship to the gaze had informed black parenting and black spectatorship. The politics of slavery, of racialised power relations, were such that the slaves were denied their right to gaze. Connecting this strategy of domination to that used by grown folks in southern black rural communities where I grew up, I was pained to think that there was no absolute difference between whites who had oppressed black people and ourselves. Years later, reading Michel Foucault, I thought again about these connections, about the ways power as domination reproduces itself in different locations employing similar apparatuses, strategies, and mechanisms of control. Since I knew as a child that the dominating power adults exercised over me and over my gaze was never so absolute that I did not dare to look, to sneak a peep, to stare dangerously, I knew that the slaves had looked. That all attempts to repress our/black peoples' right to gaze had produced in us an overwhelming longing to look, a rebellious desire, an oppositional gaze. By courageously looking, we defiantly declared: 'Not only will I stare. I want my look to change reality.' Even in the worse circumstances of domination, the ability to manipulate one's gaze in the face of structures of domination that would contain it, opens up the possibility of agency. In much of his work, Michel Foucault insists on describing domination in terms of 'relations of power' as part of an effort to challenge the assumption that 'power is a system of domination which controls everything and which leaves no room for freedom'. Emphatically stating that in all relations of power 'there is necessarily the possibility of resistance', he invites the critical thinker to search those margins, gaps, and locations on and through the body where agency can be found.

Stuart Hall calls for recognition of our agency as black spectators in his essay 'Cultural Identity and Cinematic Representation'. Speaking against the construction of white representations of blackness as totalising, Hall says of white presence: 'The error is not to conceptualise this "presence" in terms of power, but to locate that power as wholly external to us – as extrinsic force, whose influence can be thrown off like the serpent sheds its skin.' What Frantz Fanon reminds us, in *Black Skin, White Masks*, is how power is inside as well as outside:

> ...the movements, the attitudes, the glances of the Other fixed me there, in the sense in which a chemical solution is fixed by a dye. I was indignant; I demanded an explanation. Nothing happened. I burst apart. Now the fragments have been put together again by another self. This 'look', from – so to speak – the place of the Other, fixes us, not only in its violence, hostility and aggression, but in the ambivalence of its desire.

Spaces of agency exist for black people, wherein we can both interrogate the gaze of the Other but also look back, and at one another, naming what we see. The 'gaze' has been and is a site of resistance for colonised black people globally. Subordinates in relations of power learn experientially that there is a critical gaze, one that 'looks' to document, one that is oppositional. In resistance struggle, the power of the dominated to assert agency by claiming and cultivating 'awareness' politicises 'looking' relations – one learns to look a certain way in order to resist.

When most black people in the United States first had the opportunity to look at film and television, they did so fully aware that mass media was a system of knowledge and power reproducing and maintaining white supremacy. To stare at the television, or mainstream movies, to engage its images, was to engage its negation of black representation. It was the oppositional black gaze that responded to these looking relations by developing independent black cinema. Black viewers of mainstream cinema and television could chart the progress of political movements for racial equality *via* the construction of images, and did so. Within my family's southern black working-class home, located in a racially segregated neighbourhood, watching television was one way to develop critical spectatorship. Unless you went to work in the white world, across the tracks, you learned to look at white people by staring at them on the screen. Black looks, as they were constituted in the context of social movements for racial uplift, were interrogating gazes. We laughed at television shows like *Our Gang* and *Amos 'n' Andy*, at these white representations of blackness, but we also looked at them critically. Before racial integration, black viewers of movies and television experienced visual pleasure in a context where looking was also about contestation and confrontation.

Writing about black looking relations in 'Black British Cinema: Spectatorship and Identity Formation in Territories', Manthia Diawara identifies the power of the spectator: 'Every narration places the spectator in a position of agency; and race, class and sexual relations influence the way in which this subjecthood is filled by the spectator.' Of particular concern for him are moments of 'rupture' when the spectator resists 'complete identification with the film's discourse'. These ruptures define the relation between black spectators and dominant cinema prior to racial integration. Then, one's enjoyment of a film wherein representations of blackness were stereotypically degrading and dehumanising co-existed with a critical practice that restored presence where it was negated. Critical discussion of the film while it was in progress or at its conclusion maintained the distance between spectator and the image. Black films were also subject to critical interrogation. Since they came into being in part as a response to the failure of white-dominated cinema to represent blackness in a manner that did not reinforce white supremacy, they too were critiqued to see if images were seen as complicit with dominant cinematic practices.

Critical, interrogating black looks were mainly concerned with issues of race and racism, the way racial domination of blacks by whites overdetermined representation. They were rarely concerned with gender. As spectators, black men could repudiate the reproduction of racism in cinema and television, the negation of black presence, even as they could feel as though they were rebelling against white supremacy by daring to look, by engaging phallocentric politics of spectatorship. Given the real life public circumstances wherein black men were murdered/ lynched for looking at white womanhood, where the black male gaze was always subject to control and/or punishment by the powerful white Other, the private realm of television screens or dark theatres could unleash the repressed gaze. There they could 'look' at white womanhood without a structure of domination overseeing the gaze, interpreting, and punishing. That white supremacist structure that had murdered Emmet Till after interpreting his look as violation, as 'rape' of white womanhood, could not control black male responses to screen images. In their role as spectators, black men could enter an imaginative space of phallocentric power that mediated racial negation. This gendered relation to looking made the experience of the black male spectator radically different from

that of the black female spectator. Major early black male independent
film-makers represented black women in their films as objects of male
gaze. Whether looking through the camera or as spectators watching
films, whether mainstream cinema or 'race' movies such as those made
by Oscar Micheaux, the black male gaze had a different scope from that
of the black female.

Black women have written little about black female spectatorship,
about our moviegoing practices. A growing body of film theory and
criticism by black women has only begun to emerge. The prolonged
silence of black women as spectators and critics was a response to
absence, to cinematic negation. In 'The Technology of Gender', Teresa
de Lauretis, drawing on the work of Monique Wittig, calls attention to
'the power of discourses to "do violence" to people, a violence which is
material and physical, although produced by abstract and scientific discourses as well as the discourses of the mass media'. With the possible
exception of early race movies, black female spectators have had to
develop looking relations within a cinematic context that constructs our
presence as absence, that denies the 'body' of the black female so as to
perpetuate white supremacy and with it a phallocentric spectatorship
where the woman to be looked at and desired is 'white'. (Recent movies
do not conform to this paradigm but I am turning to the past with the
intent to chart the development of black female spectatorship.)

Talking with black women of all ages and classes, in different areas of
the United States, about their filmic looking relations, I hear again and
again ambivalent responses to cinema. Only a few of the black women I
talked with remembered the pleasure of race movies, and even those who
did, felt that pleasure interrupted and usurped by Hollywood. Most of
the black women I talked with were adamant that they never went to
movies expecting to see compelling representations of black femaleness.
They were all acutely aware of cinematic racism – its violent erasure of
black womanhood. In Anne Friedberg's essay 'A Denial of Difference:
Theories of Cinematic Identification' she stresses that 'identification can
only be made through recognition, and all recognition is itself an implicit
confirmation of the ideology of the status quo'. Even when representations of black women were present in film, our bodies and being were
there to serve – to enhance and maintain white womanhood as object of
the phallocentric gaze.

Commenting on Hollywood's characterisation of black women in *Girls
on Film*, Julie Burchill describes this absent presence:

Black women have been mothers without children (Mammies – who
can ever forget the sickening spectacle of Hattie MacDaniels waiting on
the simpering Vivien Leigh hand and foot and enquiring like a
ninny, 'What's ma lamb gonna wear?')...Lena Horne, the first black

performer signed to a long term contract with a major (MGM), looked gutless but was actually quite spirited. She seethed when Tallulah Bankhead complimented her on the paleness of her skin and the non-Negroidness of her features.

When black women actresses like Lena Horne appeared in mainstream cinema most white viewers were not aware that they were looking at black females unless the film was specifically coded as being about blacks. Burchill is one of the few white women film critics who has dared to examine the intersection of race and gender in relation to the construction of the category 'woman' in film as object of the phallocentric gaze. With characteristic wit she asserts: 'What does it say about racial purity that the best blondes have all been brunettes (Harlow, Monroe, Bardot)? I think it says that we are not as white as we think.' Burchill could easily have said 'we are not as white as we want to be', for clearly the obsession to have white women film stars be ultra-white was a cinematic practice that sought to maintain a distance, a separation between that image and the black female Other; it was a way to perpetuate white supremacy. Politics of race and gender were inscribed into mainstream cinematic narrative from *Birth of A Nation* on. As a seminal work, this film identified what the place and function of white womanhood would be in cinema. There was clearly no place for black women.

Remembering my past in relation to screen images of black womanhood, I wrote a short essay, 'Do you remember Sapphire?' which explored both the negation of black female representation in cinema and television and our rejection of these images. Identifying the character of 'Sapphire' from *Amos 'n' Andy* as that screen representation of black femaleness I first saw in childhood, I wrote:

> She was even then backdrop, foil. She was bitch – nag. She was there to soften images of black men, to make them seem vulnerable, easygoing, funny, and unthreatening to a white audience. She was there as man in drag, as castrating bitch, as someone to be lied to, someone to be tricked, someone the white and black audience could hate. Scapegoated on all sides. *She was not us.* We laughed with the black men, with the white people. We laughed at this black woman who was not us. And we did not even long to be there on the screen. How could we long to be there when our image, visually constructed, was so ugly. We did not long to be there. We did not long for her. We did not want our construction to be this hated black female thing – foil, backdrop. Her black female image was not the body of desire. There was nothing to see. She was not us.

Grown black women had a different response to Sapphire; they identified with her frustrations and her woes. They resented the way she was mocked. They resented the way these screen images could assault black womanhood, could name us bitches, nags. And in opposition they claimed Sapphire as their own, as the symbol of that angry part of themselves white folks and black men could not even begin to understand.

Conventional representations of black women have done violence to the image. Responding to this assault, many black women spectators shut out the image, looked the other way, accorded cinema no importance in their lives. Then there were those spectators whose gaze was that of desire and complicity. Assuming a posture of subordination, they submitted to cinema's capacity to seduce and betray. They were cinematically 'gaslighted'. Every black woman I spoke with who was/is an ardent moviegoer, a lover of the Hollywood film, testified that to experience fully the pleasure of that cinema they had to close down critique, analysis; they had to forget racism. And mostly they did not think about sexism. What was the nature then of this adoring black female gaze – this look that could bring pleasure in the midst of negation? In her first novel, *The Bluest Eye*, Toni Morrison constructs a portrait of the black female spectator; her gaze is the masochistic look of victimisation. Describing her looking relations, Miss Pauline Breedlove, a poor working woman, maid in the house of a prosperous white family, asserts:

> The onliest time I be happy seem like was when I was in the picture show. Every time I got, I went, I'd go early, before the show started. They's cut off the lights, and everything be black. Then the screen would light up, and I's move right on in them picture. White men taking such good care of they women, and they all dressed up in big clean houses with the bath tubs right in the same room with the toilet. Them pictures gave me a lot of pleasure.

To experience pleasure, Miss Pauline sitting in the dark must imagine herself transformed, turned into the white woman portrayed on the screen. After watching movies, feeling the pleasure, she says, 'But it made coming home hard'.

We come home to ourselves. Not all black women spectators submitted to that spectacle of regression through identification. Most of the women I talked with felt that they consciously resisted identification with films – that this tension made moviegoing less than pleasurable; at times it caused pain. As one black woman put, 'I could always get pleasure from movies as long as I did not look too deep'. For black female spectators who have 'looked too deep' the encounter with the screen hurt. That some of us chose to stop looking was a gesture of resistance, turning away was one way to protest, to reject negation. My pleasure in the screen ended abruptly when I and my sisters first watched *Imitation of*

Life. Writing about this experience in the 'Sapphire' piece, I addressed the movie directly, confessing:

> I had until now forgotten you, that screen image seen in adolescence, those images that made me stop looking. It was there in *Imitation of Life*, that comfortable mammy image. There was something familiar about this hard-working black woman who loved her daughter so much, loved her in a way that hurt. Indeed, as young southern black girls watching this film, Peola's mother reminded us of the hardworking, churchgoing, Big Mamas we knew and loved. Consequently, it was not this image that captured our gaze; we were fascinated by Peola.

Addressing her, I wrote:

> You were different. There was something scary in this image of young sexual sensual black beauty betrayed – that daughter who did not want to be confined by blackness, that 'tragic mulatto' who did not want to be negated. 'Just let me escape this image forever', she could have said. I will always remember that image. I remembered how we cried for her, for our unrealised desiring selves. She was tragic because there was no place in the cinema for her, no loving pictures. She too was absent image. It was better then, that we were absent, for when we were there it was humiliating, strange, sad. We cried all night for you, for the cinema that had no place for you. And like you, we stopped thinking it would one day be different.

When I returned to films as a young woman, after a long period of silence, I had developed an oppositional gaze. Not only would I not be hurt by the absence of black female presence, or the insertion of violating representation, I interrogated the work, cultivated a way to look past race and gender for aspects of content, form, language. Foreign films and US independent cinema were the primary locations of my filmic looking relations, even though I also watched Hollywood films.

From 'jump', black female spectators have gone to films with aware-ness of the way in which race and racism determined the visual construc-tion of gender. Whether it was *Birth of A Nation* or Shirley Temple shows, we knew that white womanhood was the racialised sexual difference occupying the place of stardom in mainstream narrative film. We assumed white women knew it too. Reading Laura Mulvey's provocative essay, 'Visual Pleasure and Narrative Cinema', from a standpoint that acknowledges race, one sees clearly why black women spectators not duped by mainstream cinema would develop an oppositional gaze. Plac-ing ourselves outside that pleasure in looking, Mulvey argues, was determined by a 'split between active/male and passive/female'. Black female spectators actively chose not to identify with the film's imaginary subject because such identification was disenabling.

Looking at films with an oppositional gaze, black women were able to critically assess the cinema's construction of white womanhood as object of phallocentric gaze and choose not to identify with either the victim or the perpetrator. Black female spectators, who refused to identify with white womanhood, who would not take on the phallocentric gaze of desire and possession, created a critical space where the binary opposition Mulvey posits of 'woman as image, man as bearer of the look' was continually deconstructed. As critical spectators, black women looked from a location that disrupted, one akin to that described by Annette Kuhn in *The Power of The Image*:

> . . . the acts of analysis, of deconstruction and of reading 'against the grain' offer an additional pleasure – the pleasure of resistance, of saying 'no': not to 'unsophisticated' enjoyment, by ourselves and others, of culturally dominant images, but to the structures of power which ask us to consume them uncritically and in highly circumscribed ways.

Mainstream feminist film criticism in no way acknowledges black female spectatorship. It does not even consider the possibility that women can construct an oppositional gaze via an understanding and awareness of the politics of race and racism. Feminist film theory rooted in an ahistorical psychoanalytic framework that privileges sexual difference actively suppresses recognition of race, re-enacting and mirroring the erasure of black womanhood that occurs in films, silencing any discussion of racial difference – of racialised sexual difference. Despite feminist critical interventions aimed at deconstructing the category 'woman' which highlight the significance of race, many feminist film critics continue to structure their discourse as though it speaks about 'women' when in actuality it speaks only about white women. It seems ironic that the cover of the recent anthology *Feminism and Film Theory* edited by Constance Penley has a graphic that is a reproduction of the photo of white actresses Rosalind Russell and Dorothy Arzner on the 1936 set of the film *Craig's Wife* yet there is no acknowledgment in any essay in this collection that the woman 'subject' under discussion is always white. Even though there are photos of black women from films reproduced in the text, there is no acknowledgment of racial difference.

It would be too simplistic to interpret this failure of insight solely as a gesture of racism. Importantly, it also speaks to the problem of structuring feminist film theory around a totalising narrative of woman as object whose image functions solely to reaffirm and reinscribe patriarchy. Mary Ann Doane addresses this issue in the essay 'Remembering Women: Psychical and Historical Construction in Film Theory':

This attachment to the figure of a degeneralisible Woman as the product of the apparatus indicates why, for many, feminist film theory seems to have reached an impasse, a certain blockage in its theorisation... In focusing upon the task of delineating in great detail the attributes of woman as effect of the apparatus, feminist film theory participates in the abstraction of women.

The concept 'Woman' effaces the difference between women in specific socio-historical contexts, between women defined precisely as historical subjects rather than as *a* psychic subject (or non-subject). Though Doane does not focus on race, her comments speak directly to the problem of its erasure. For it is only as one imagines 'woman' in the abstract, when woman becomes fiction or fantasy, can race not be seen as significant. Are we really to imagine that feminist theorists writing only about images of white women, who subsume this specific historical subject under the totalising category 'woman', do not 'see' the whiteness of the image? It may very well be that they engage in a process of denial that eliminates the necessity of revisioning conventional ways of thinking about psychoanalysis as a paradigm of analysis and the need to rethink a body of feminist film theory that is firmly rooted in a denial of the reality that sex/sexuality may not be the primary and/or exclusive signifier of difference. Doane's essay appears in a very recent anthology, *Psychoanalysis and Cinema*, edited by E. Ann Kaplan, where, once again, none of the theory presented acknowledges or discusses racial difference, with the exception of one essay, 'Not Speaking with Language, Speaking with No Language', which problematises notions of orientalism in its examination of Leslie Thornton's film *Adynata*. Yet in most of the essays, the theories espoused are rendered problematic if one includes race as a category of analysis.

Constructing feminist film theory along these lines enables the production of a discursive practice that need never theorise any aspect of black female representation or spectatorship. Yet the existence of black women within white supremacist culture problematises, and makes complex, the overall issue of female identity, representation, and spectatorship. If, as Friedberg suggests, 'identification is a process which commands the subject to be displaced by an other; it is a procedure which breaches the separation between self and other, and, in this way, replicates the very structure of patriarchy.' If identification 'demands sameness, necessitates similarity, disallows difference' – must we then surmise that many feminist film critics who are 'overidentified' with the mainstream cinematic apparatus produce theories that replicate its totalising agenda? Why is it that feminist film criticism, which has most claimed the terrain of woman's identity, representation, and subjectivity as its field of analysis, remains aggressively silent on the subject of blackness and specifically representations of black womanhood? Just as mainstream cinema has historically forced aware black female spectators not to look, much feminist film criticism disallows the possibility of a theoretical dialogue that might include black women's voices. It is difficult to talk when you feel no one is listening, when you feel as though a special jargon or narrative has been created that only the chosen can understand. No wonder then that black women have for the most part confined our critical commentary on film to conversations. And it must be reiterated that this gesture is a strategy that protects us from the violence perpetuated and advocated by discourses of mass media. A new focus on issues of race and representation in the field of film theory could critically intervene on the historical repression reproduced in some arenas of contemporary critical practice, making a discursive space for discussion of black female spectatorship possible.

When I asked a black woman in her twenties, an obsessive moviegoer, why she thought we had not written about black female spectatorship, she commented: 'We are afraid to talk about ourselves as spectators because we have been so abused by "the gaze".' An aspect of that abuse was the imposition of the assumption that black female looking relations were not important enough to theorise. Film theory as a critical 'turf' in the United States has been and continues to be influenced by and reflective of white racial domination. Since feminist film criticism was initially rooted in a women's liberation movement informed by racist practices, it did not open up the discursive terrain and make it more inclusive. Recently, even those white film theorists who include an analysis of race show no interest in black female spectatorship. In her introduction to the collection of essays *Visual and Other Pleasures*, Laura Mulvey describes her initial romantic absorption in Hollywood cinema, stating:

> Although this great, previously unquestioned and unanalysed love was put in crisis by the impact of feminism on my thought in the early 1970s, it also had an enormous influence on the development of my critical work and ideas and the debate within film culture with which I became preoccupied over the next fifteen years or so. Watched through eyes that were affected by the changing climate of consciousness, the movies lost their magic.

Watching movies from a feminist perspective, Mulvey arrived at that location of disaffection that is the starting point for many black women approaching cinema within the lived harsh reality of racism. Yet her account of being a part of a film culture whose roots rest on a founding relationship of adoration and love indicates how difficult it would have been to enter that world from 'jump' as a critical spectator whose gaze had been formed in opposition.

Given the context of class exploitation, and racist and sexist domination, it has only been through resistance, struggle, reading, and looking 'against the grain', that black women have been able to value our process of looking enough to publicly name it. Centrally, those black female spectators who attest to the oppositionality of their gaze deconstruct theories of female spectatorship that have relied heavily on the assumption that, as Doane suggests in her essay, 'Woman's Stake: Filming the Female Body', 'woman can only mimic man's relation to language, that is assume a position defined by the penis-phallus as the supreme arbiter of lack'. Identifying with neither the phallocentric gaze nor the construction of white womanhood as lack, critical black female spectators construct a theory of looking relations where cinematic visual delight is the pleasure of interrogation. Every black woman spectator I talked to, with rare exception, spoke of being 'on guard' at the movies. Talking about the way being a critical spectator of Hollywood films influenced her, black woman film-maker Julie Dash exclaims, 'I make films because I was such a spectator!' Looking at Hollywood cinema from a distance, from that critical politicised standpoint that did not want to be seduced by narratives reproducing her negation, Dash watched mainstream movies over and over again for the pleasure of deconstructing them. And of course there is that added delight if one happens, in the process of interrogation, to come across a narrative that invites the black female spectator to engage the text with no threat of violation.

Significantly, I began to write film criticism in response to the first Spike Lee movie, *She's Gotta Have It*, contesting Lee's replication of mainstream patriarchal cinematic practices that explicitly represents woman (in this instance black woman) as the object of a phallocentric gaze. Lee's investment in patriarchal filmic practices that mirror dominant patterns makes him the perfect black candidate for entrance to the Hollywood canon. His work mimics the cinematic construction of white womanhood as object, replacing her body as text on which to write male desire with the black female body. It is transference without transformation. Entering the discourse of film criticism from the politicised location of resistance, of not wanting, as a working-class black woman I interviewed stated, 'to see black women in the position white women have occupied in film forever', I began to think critically about black female spectatorship.

For years I went to independent and/or foreign films where I was the only black female present in the theatre. I often imagined that in every theatre in the United States there was another black woman watching the same film wondering why she was the only visible black female spectator. I remember trying to share with one of my five sisters the cinema I liked so much. She was 'enraged' that I brought her to a theatre where she would have to read subtitles. To her it was a violation of Hollywood notions of spectatorship, of coming to the movies to be entertained. When

I interviewed her to ask what had changed her mind over the years, led her to embrace this cinema, she connected it to coming to critical consciousness, saying, 'I learned that there was more to looking than I had been exposed to in ordinary (Hollywood) movies'. I shared that though most of the films I loved were all white, I could engage them because they did not have in their deep structure a subtext reproducing the narrative of white supremacy. Her response was to say that these films demystified 'whiteness', since the lives they depicted seemed less rooted in fantasies of escape. They were, she suggested, more like 'what we knew life to be, the deeper side of life as well'. Always more seduced and enchanted with Hollywood cinema than me, she stressed that unaware black female spectators must 'break out', no longer be imprisoned by images that enact a drama of our negation. Though she still sees Hollywood films, because 'they are a major influence in the culture' – she no longer feels duped or victimised.

Talking with black female spectators, looking at written discussions either in fiction or academic essays about black women, I noted the connection made between the realm of representation in mass media and the capacity of black women to construct ourselves as subjects in daily life. The extent to which black women feel devalued, objectified, dehumanised in this society determines the scope and texture of their looking relations. Those black women whose identities were constructed in resistance, by practices that oppose the dominant order, were most inclined to develop an oppositional gaze. Now that there is a growing interest in films produced by black women and those films have become more accessible to viewers, it is possible to talk about black female spectatorship in relation to that work. So far, most discussions of black spectatorship that I have come across focus on men. In 'Black Spectatorship: Problems of Identification and Resistance' Manthia Diawara suggests that 'the components of difference' among elements of sex, gender, and sexuality give rise to different readings of the same material, adding that these conditions produce a 'resisting' spectator. He focuses his critical discussion on black masculinity.

The recent publication of the anthology *The Female Gaze: Women as Viewers of Popular Culture* excited me, especially as it included an essay, 'Black Looks', by Jacqui Roach and Petal Felix that attempts to address black female spectatorship. The essay posed provocative questions that were not answered: Is there a black female gaze? How do black women relate to the gender politics of representation? Concluding, the authors assert that black females have 'our own reality, our own history, our own gaze – one which sees the world rather differently from "anyone else"'. Yet, they do not name/describe this experience of seeing 'rather differently'. The absence of definition and explanation suggests they are assuming an essentialist stance wherein it is presumed that black women, as victims of race and gender oppression, have an inherently different field of vision. Many black women do not 'see differently' precisely because their perceptions of reality are so profoundly colonised, shaped by dominant ways of knowing. As Trinh T. Minh-ha points out in 'Outside In, Inside Out': 'Subjectivity does not merely consist of talking about oneself...be this talking indulgent or critical.'

Critical black female spectatorship emerges as a site of resistance only when individual black women actively resist the imposition of dominant ways of knowing and looking. While every black woman I talked to was aware of racism, that awareness did not automatically correspond with politicisation, the development of an oppositional gaze. When it did, individual black women consciously named the process. Manthia Diawara's 'resisting spectatorship' is a term that does not adequately describe the terrain of black female spectatorship. We do more than resist. We create alternative texts that are not solely reactions. As critical spectators, black women participate in a broad range of looking relations, contest, resist, revision, interrogate, and invent on multiple levels. Certainly when I watch the work of black women film-makers Camille Billops, Kathleen Collins, Julie Dash, Ayoka Chenzira, Zeinabu Davis, I do not need to 'resist' the images even as I still choose to watch their work with a critical eye.

Black female critical thinkers concerned with creating space for the construction of radical black female subjectivity, and the way cultural production informs this possibility, fully acknowledge the importance of mass media, film in particular, as a powerful site for critical intervention. Certainly Julie Dash's film *Illusions* identifies the terrain of Hollywood cinema as a space of knowledge production that has enormous power. Yet, she also creates a filmic narrative wherein the black female protagonist subversively claims that space. Inverting the 'real-life' power structure, she offers the black female spectator representations that challenge stereotypical notions that place us outside the realm of filmic discursive practices. Within the film she uses the strategy of Hollywood suspense films to undermine those cinematic practices that deny black women a place in this structure. Problematising the question of 'racial' identity by depicting passing, suddenly it is the white male's capacity to gaze, define, and know that is called into question.

When Mary Ann Doane describes in 'Woman's Stake: Filming the Female Body' the way in which feminist film-making practice can elaborate 'a special syntax for a different articulation of the female body', she names a critical process that 'undoes the structure of the classical narrative through an insistence upon its repressions'. An eloquent description, this precisely names Dash's strategy in *Illusions* even though the film is not unproblematic and works within certain conventions that are not successfully challenged. For example, the film does not indicate whether the character Mignon will make Hollywood films that subvert and transform the genre or whether she will simply assimilate and perpetuate the norm. Still, subversively, *Illusions* problematises the issue of race and spectatorship. White people in the film are unable to 'see' that race informs their looking relations. Though she is passing to gain access to the machinery of cultural production represented by film, Mignon continually asserts her ties to black community. The bond between her and the young black woman singer Esther Jeeter is affirmed by caring gestures of affirmation, often expressed by eye-to-eye contact, the direct unmediated gaze of recognition. Ironically, it is the desiring objectifying sexualised white male gaze that threatens to penetrate her 'secrets' and disrupt her process. Metaphorically, Dash suggests the power of black women to make films will be threatened and undermined by that white male gaze that seeks to reinscribe the black female body in a narrative of voyeuristic pleasure where the only relevant opposition is male/female, and the only location for the female is as a victim. These tensions are not resolved by the narrative. It is not at all evident that Mignon will triumph over the white supremacist capitalist imperialist dominating 'gaze'.

Throughout *Illusions*, Mignon's power is affirmed by her contact with the younger black woman whom she nurtures and protects. It is this process of mirrored recognition that enables both black women to define their reality, apart from the reality imposed upon them by structures of domination. The shared gaze of the two women reinforces their solidarity. As the younger subject, Esther represents a potential audience for films that Mignon might produce, films wherein black females will be the narrative focus. Julie Dash's recent feature-length film *Daughters of the Dust* dares to place black females at the centre of its narrative. This focus caused critics (especially white males) to critique the film negatively or to express many reservations. Clearly, the impact of racism and sexism so overdetermine spectatorship – not only what we look at but who we identify with – that viewers who are not black females find it hard to empathise with the central characters in the movie. They are adrift without a white presence in the film.

Another representation of black females nurturing one another *via* recognition of their common struggle for subjectivity is depicted in Sankofa's collective work *Passion of Remembrance*. In the film, two black women friends, Louise and Maggie, are from the onset of the narrative struggling with the issue of subjectivity, of their place in progressive black liberation movements that have been sexist. They challenge old norms and want to replace them with new understandings of the complexity of black identity, and the need for liberation struggles that address that complexity. Dressing to go to a party, Louise and Maggie claim the 'gaze'. Looking at one another, staring in mirrors, they appear completely focused on their encounter with black femaleness. How they see themselves is most important, not how they will be stared at by others. Dancing to the tune 'Let's get Loose', they display their bodies not for a voyeuristic colonising gaze but for that look of recognition that affirms their subjectivity – that constitutes them as spectators. Mutually empowered they eagerly leave the privatised domain to confront the public. Disrupting conventional racist and sexist stereotypical representations of black female bodies, these scenes invite the audience to look differently. They act to critically intervene and transform conventional filmic practices, changing notions of spectatorship. *Illusions, Daughters of the Dust*, and *A Passion of Remembrance* employ a deconstructive filmic practice to undermine existing grand cinematic narratives even as they retheorise subjectivity in the realm of the visual. Without providing 'realistic' positive representations that emerge only as a response to the totalising nature of existing narratives, they offer points of radical departure. Opening up a space for the assertion of a critical black female spectatorship, they do not simply offer diverse representations, they imagine new transgressive possibilities for the formulation of identity.

In this sense they make explicit a critical practice that provides us with different ways to think about black female subjectivity and black female spectatorship. Cinematically, they provide new points of recognition, embodying Stuart Hall's vision of a critical practice that acknowledges that identity is constituted 'not outside but within representation', and invites us to see film 'not as a second-order mirror held up to reflect what already exists, but as that form of representation which is able to constitute us as new kinds of subjects, and thereby enable us to discover who we are'. It is this critical practice that enables production of feminist film theory that theorises black female spectatorship. Looking and looking back, black women involve ourselves in a process whereby we see our history as counter-memory, using it as a way to know the present and invent the future.

13

Of the Gaze as *Objet Petit a*

Jacques Lacan

I

I saw myself seeing myself, young Parque says somewhere. Certainly, this statement has rich and complex implications in relation to the theme developed in *La Jeune Parque*, that of femininity – but we haven't got there yet. We are dealing with the philosopher, who apprehends something that is one of the essential correlates of consciousness in its relation to representation, and which is designated as *I see myself seeing myself*. What evidence can we really attach to this formula? How is it that it remains, in fact, correlative with that fundamental mode to which we referred in the Cartesian *cogito*, by which the subject apprehends himself as thought?

What isolates this apprehension of thought by itself is a sort of doubt, which has been called methodological doubt, which concerns whatever might give support to thought in representation. How is it, then, that the *I see myself seeing myself* remains its envelope and base, and, perhaps more than one thinks, grounds its certainty? For, *I warm myself by warming myself* is a reference to the body as body – I feel that sensation of warmth which, from some point inside me, is diffused and locates me as body. Whereas in the *I see myself seeing myself*, there is no such sensation of being absorbed by vision.

Furthermore, the phenomenologists have succeeded in articulating with precision, and in the most disconcerting way, that it is quite clear that I see *outside*, that perception is not in me, that it is on the objects that it apprehends. And yet I apprehend the world in a perception that seems to concern the immanence of the *I see myself seeing myself*. The privilege of the subject seems to be established here from that bipolar reflexive relation by which, as soon as I perceive, my representations belong to me.

This is how the world is struck with a presumption of idealisation, of the suspicion of yielding me only my representations. Serious practice does not really weigh very heavy, but, on the other hand, the philosopher, the idealist, is placed there, as much in confrontation with himself as in confrontation with those who are listening to him, in an embarrassing position. How can one deny that nothing of the world appears to me except in my representations? This is the irreducible method of Bishop Berkeley, about whose subjective position much might be said – including something that may have eluded you in passing, namely, this *belong to me* aspect of representations, so reminiscent of property. When carried to the limit, the process of this meditation, of this reflecting reflection, goes so far as to reduce the subject apprehended by the Cartesian meditation to a power of annihilation.

The mode of my presence in the world is the subject in so far as by reducing itself solely to this certainty of being a subject, it becomes active annihilation. In fact, the process of the philosophical meditation throws the subject towards the transforming historical action, and, around this point, orders the configured modes of active self-consciousness through its metamorphoses in history. As for the meditation on being that reaches its culmination in the thought of Heidegger, it restores to being itself that power of annihilation – or at least poses the question of how it may be related to it.

This is also the point to which Maurice Merleau-Ponty leads us. But, if you refer to his text, you will see that it is at this point that he chooses to withdraw, in order to propose a return to the sources of intuition concerning the visible and the invisible, to come back to that which is prior to all reflection, thetic or non-thetic, in order to locate the emergence of vision itself. For him, it is a question of restoring – for, he tells us, it can only be a question of a reconstruction or a restoration, not of a path traversed in the opposite direction – of reconstituting the way by which, not from the body, but from something that he calls the flesh of the world, the original point of vision was able to emerge. It would seem that in this way one sees, in this unfinished work, the emergence of something like the search for an unnamed substance from which I, the seer, extract myself. From the toils (*rets*), or rays (*rais*), if you prefer, of an iridescence of which I am at first a part, I emerge as eye, assuming, in a way, emergence from what I would like to call the function of *seeingness* (*voyure*).

A wild odour emanates from it, providing a glimpse on the horizon of the hunt of Artemis – whose touch seems to be associated at this moment of tragic failure in which we lost him who speaks.

Yet is this really the way he wished to take? The traces that remain of the part to come from his meditation permit us to doubt it. The reference-points that are provided in it, more particularly for the strictly psycho-analytic unconscious, allow us to perceive that he may have been directed towards some search, original in relation to the philosophical tradition, towards that new dimension of meditation on the subject that analysis enables us to trace.

Personally, I cannot but be struck by certain of these notes, which are for me less enigmatic than they may seem to other readers, because they correspond very exactly to the schemata – with one of them, in particular – that I shall be dealing with here. Read, for example, the note concerning what he calls the turning inside-out of the finger of a glove, in as much as it seems to appear there – note the way in which the leather envelops the fur in a winter glove – that consciousness, in its illusion of *seeing itself seeing itself*, finds its basis in the inside-out structure of the gaze.

II

But what is the gaze?

I shall set out from this first point of annihilation in which is marked, in the field of the reduction of the subject, a break – which warns us of the need to introduce another reference, that which analysis assumes in reducing the privileges of the consciousness.

Psycho-analysis regards the consciousness as irremediably limited, and institutes it as a principle, not only of idealisation, but of *méconnaissance*, as – using a term that takes on new value by being referred to a visible domain – *scotoma*. The term was introduced into the psycho-analytic vocabulary by the French School. Is it simply a metaphor? We find here once again the ambiguity that affects anything that is inscribed in the register of the scopic drive.

For us, consciousness matters only in its relation to what, for propaedeutic reasons, I have tried to show you in the fiction of the incomplete text – on the basis of which it is a question of recentring the subject as speaking in the very lacunae of that in which, at first sight, it presents itself as speaking. But I am stating here only the relation of the preconscious to the unconscious. The dynamic that is attached to the consciousness as such, the attention the subject brings to his own text, remains up to this point, as Freud has stressed, outside theory and, strictly speaking, not yet articulated.

It is here that I propose that the interest the subject takes in his own split is bound up with that which determines it – namely, a privileged object, which has emerged from some primal separation, from some self-mutilation induced by the very approach of the real, whose name, in our algebra, is the *objet a*.

In the scopic relation, the object on which depends the phantasy from which the subject is suspended in an essential vacillation is the gaze. Its privilege – and also that by which the subject for so long has been misunderstood as being in its dependence – derives from its very structure.

Let us schematise at once what we mean. From the moment that this gaze appears, the subject tries to adapt himself to it, he becomes that punctiform object, that point of vanishing being with which the subject confuses his own failure. Furthermore, of all the objects in which the subject may recognise his dependence in the register of desire, the gaze is specified as unapprehensible. That is why it is, more than any other object, misunderstood (*méconnu*), and it is perhaps for this reason, too, that the subject manages, fortunately, to symbolise his own vanishing and punctiform bar (*trait*) in the illusion of the consciousness of *seeing onself see oneself*, in which the gaze is elided.

If, then, the gaze is that underside of consciousness, how shall we try to imagine it?

The expression is not inapt, for we can give body to the gaze. Sartre, in one of the most brilliant passages of *L'Etre et le Néant*, brings it into function in the dimension of the existence of others. Others would remain suspended in the same, partially de-realising, conditions that are, in Sartre's definition, those of objectivity, were it not for the gaze. The gaze, as conceived by Sartre, is the gaze by which I am surprised – surprised in so far as it changes all the perspectives, the lines of force, of my world, orders it, from the point of nothingness where I am, in a sort of radiated reticulation of the organisms. As the locus of the relation between me, the annihilating subject, and that which surrounds me, the gaze seems to possess such a privilege that it goes so far as to have me scotomised, I who look, the eye of him who sees me as object. In so far as I am under the gaze, Sartre writes, I no longer see the eye that looks at me and, if I see the eye, the gaze disappears.

Is this a correct phenomenological analysis? No. It is not true that, when I am under the gaze, when I solicit a gaze, when I obtain it, I do not see it as a gaze. Painters, above all, have grasped this gaze as such in the mask and I have only to remind you of Goya, for example, for you to realise this.

The gaze sees itself – to be precise, the gaze of which Sartre speaks, the gaze that surprises me and reduces me to shame, since this is the feeling he regards as the most dominant. The gaze I encounter – you can find this in Sartre's own writing – is, not a seen gaze, but a gaze imagined by me in the field of the Other.

If you turn to Sartre's own text, you will see that, far from speaking of the emergence of this gaze as of something that concerns the organ of sight, he refers to the sound of rustling leaves, suddenly heard while out hunting, to a footstep heard in a corridor. And when are these sounds heard? At the moment when he has presented himself in the action of looking through a keyhole. A gaze surprises him in the function of voyeur, disturbs him, overwhelms him and reduces him to a feeling of shame. The gaze in question is certainly the presence of others as such. But does this mean that originally it is in the relation of subject to subject, in the function of the existence of others as looking at me, that we apprehend what the gaze really is? Is it not clear that the gaze intervenes here only in as much as it is not the annihiliating subject, correlative of the world of objectivity, who feels himself surprised, but the subject sustaining himself in a function of desire?

It is not precisely because desire is established here in the domain of seeing that we can make it vanish?

III

We can apprehend this privilege of the gaze in the function of desire, by pouring ourselves, as it were, along the veins through which the domain of vision has been integrated into the field of desire.

It is not for nothing that it was at the very period when the Cartesian meditation inaugurated in all its purity the function of the subject that the dimension of optics that I shall distinguish here by calling 'geometral' or 'flat' (as opposed to perspective) optics was developed.

I shall illustrate for you, by one object among others, what seems to me exemplary in a function that so curiously attracted so much reflection at the time.

One reference, for those who would like to carry further what I tried to convey to you today, is Baltrusaïtis' book, *Anamorphoses*.

In my seminar, I have made great use of the function of anamorphosis, in so far as it is an exemplary structure. What does a simple, non-cylindrical anamorphosis consist of? Suppose there is a portrait on this flat piece of paper that I am holding. By chance, you see the blackboard, in an oblique position in relation to the piece of paper. Suppose that, by means of a series of ideal threads or lines, I reproduce on the oblique surface each point of the image drawn on my sheet of paper. You can easily imagine what the result would be – you would obtain a figure enlarged and distorted according to the lines of what may be called a perspective. One supposes that – if I take away that which has helped in the construction, namely, the image placed in my own visual field – the impression I will retain, while remaining in that place, will be more or less the same. At least, I will recognise the general outlines of the image – at best, I will have an identical impression.

I will now pass around something that dates from a hundred years earlier, from 1533, a reproduction of a painting that, I think, you all know – Hans Holbein's *The Ambassadors* (Plate 2). It will serve to refresh the memories of those who know the picture well. Those who do not should examine it attentively. I shall come back to it shortly.

Vision is ordered according to a mode that may generally be called the function of images. This function is defined by a point-by-point correspondence of two unities in space. Whatever optical intermediaries may be used to establish their relation, whether their image is virtual, or real,

Plate 2   The Ambassadors: Jean de Dinteville and Georges de Selve, by Hans Holbein the younger (1533).
Reproduced courtesy of the National Gallery Company Limited. Research by ISI

the point-by-point correspondence is essential. That which is of the mode of the image in the field of vision is therefore reducible to the simple schema that enables us to establish anamorphosis, that is to say, to the relation of an image, in so far as it is linked to a surface, with a certain point that we shall call the 'geometral' point. Anything that is determined by this method, in which the straight line plays its role of being the path of light, can be called an image.

Art is mingled with science here. Leonardo da Vinci is both a scientist, on account of his dioptric constructions, and an artist. Vitruvius's treatise on architecture is not far away. It is in Vignola and in Alberti that we find the progressive interrogation of the geometral laws of perspective, and it is around research on perspective that is centred a privileged interest for the domain of vision – whose relation with the institution of the Cartesian subject, which is itself a sort of geometral point, a point of perspective, we cannot fail to see. And, around the geometral perspective, the picture – this is a very important function to which we shall return – is organised in a way that is quite new in the history of painting.

I should now like to refer you to Diderot. The *Lettre sur les aveugles à l'usage de ceux qui voient* (Letter on the Blind for the use of those who see) will show you that this construction allows that which concerns vision to escape totally. For the geometral space of vision – even if we include those imaginary parts in the virtual space of the mirror, of which, as you know, I have spoken at length – is perfectly reconstructible, imaginable, by a blind man.

What is at issue in geometral perspective is simply the mapping of space, not sight. The blind man may perfectly well conceive that the field of space that he knows, and which he knows as real, may be perceived at a distance, and as a simultaneous act. For him, it is a question of apprehending a temporal function, instantaneity. In Descartes, dioptrics, the action of the eyes, is represented as the conjugated action of two sticks. The geometral dimension of vision does not exhaust, therefore, far from it, what the field of vision as such offers us as the original subjectifying relation.

This is why it is so important to acknowledge the inverted use of perspective in the structure of anamorphosis.

It was Dürer himself who invented the apparatus to establish perspective. Dürer's 'lucinda' is comparable to what, a little while ago, I placed between that blackboard and myself, namely, a certain image, or more exactly a canvas, a trellis that will be traversed by straight lines – which are not necessarily rays, but also threads – which will link each point that I have to see in the world to a point at which the canvas will, by this line, be traversed.

It was to establish a correct perspective image, therefore, that the *lucinda* was introduced. If I reverse its use, I will have the pleasure of obtaining not the restoration of the world that lies at the end, but the distortion, on another surface, of the image that I would have obtained on the first, and I will dwell, as on some delicious game, on this method that makes anything appear at will in a particular stretching.

I would ask you to believe that such an enchantment took place in its time. Baltrusaïtis' book will tell you of the furious polemics that these practices gave rise to, and which culminated in works of considerable length. The convent of the Minims, now destroyed, which once stood near the rue des Tournelles, carried on the very long wall of one of its galleries and representing as if by chance St John at Patmos a picture that had to be looked at through a hole, so that its distorting value could be appreciated to its full extent.

Distortion may lend itself – this was not the case for this particular fresco – to all the paranoiac ambiguities, and every possible use has been made of it, from Arcimboldi to Salvador Dali. I will go so far as to say that this fascination complements what geometral researches into perspective allow to escape from vision.

How is it that nobody has ever thought of connecting this with . . . the effect of an erection? Imagine a tattoo traced on the sexual organ *ad hoc* in the state of repose and assuming its, if I may say so, developed form in another state.

How can we not see here, immanent in the geometral dimension – a partial dimension in the field of the gaze, a dimension that has nothing to do with vision as such – something symbolic of the function of the lack, of the appearance of the phallic ghost?

Now, in *The Ambassadors* – I hope everyone has had time now to look at the reproduction – what do you see? What is this strange, suspended, oblique object in the foreground in front of these two figures?

The two figures are frozen, stiffened in their showy adornments. Between them is a series of objects that represent in the painting of the period the symbols of *vanitas*. At the same period, Cornelius Agrippa wrote his *De Vanitate scientiarum*, aimed as much at the arts as the sciences, and these objects are all symbolic of the sciences and arts as they were grouped at the time in the *trivium* and *quadrivium*. What, then, before this display of the domain of appearance in all its most fascinating forms, is this object, which from some angles appears to be flying through the air, at others to be tilted? You cannot know – for you turn away, thus escaping the fascination of the picture.

Begin by walking out of the room in which no doubt it has long held your attention. It is then that, turning round as you leave – as the author of the *Anamorphoses* describes it – you apprehend in this form . . . What? A skull.

This is not how it is presented at first – that figure, which the author compares to a cuttlebone and which for me suggests rather that loaf composed of two books which Dali was once pleased to place on the head of an old woman, chosen deliberately for her wretched, filthy appearance and, indeed, because she seems to be unaware of the fact, or, again, Dali's soft watches, whose signification is obviously less phallic than that of the object depicted in a flying position in the foreground of this picture.

All this shows that at the very heart of the period in which the subject emerged and geometral optics was an object of research, Holbein makes visible for us here something that is simply the subject as annihilated – annihilated in the form that is, strictly speaking, the imaged embodiment of the *minus-phi* $[(-\phi)]$ of castration, which for us, centres the whole organisation of the desires through the framework of the fundamental drives.

But it is further still that we must seek the function of vision. We shall then see emerging on the basis of vision, not the phallic symbol, the anamorphic ghost, but the gaze as such, in its pulsatile, dazzling and spread out function, as it is in this picture.

This picture is simply what any picture is, a trap for the gaze. In any picture, it is precisely in seeking the gaze in each of its points that you will see it disappear. I shall try to develop this further next time.

QUESTIONS AND ANSWERS

F. WAHL: *You have explained that the original apprehension of the gaze in the gaze of others, as described by Sartre, was not the fundamental experience of the gaze. I would like you to explain in greater detail what you have already sketched for us, the apprehension of the gaze in the direction of desire.*

LACAN: If one does not stress the dialectic of desire one does not understand why the gaze of others should disorganise the field of perception. It is because the subject in question is not that of the reflexive consciousness, but that of desire. One thinks it is a question of the geometral eye-point, whereas it is a question of a quite different eye – that which flies in the foreground of *The Ambassadors*.

WAHL: *But I don't understand how others will reappear in your discourse...*

LACAN: Look, the main thing is that I don't come a cropper!

WAHL: *I would also like to say that, when you speak of the subject and of the real, one is tempted, on first hearing, to consider the terms in themselves. But gradually one realises that they are to be understood in their relation to one another, and that they have a topological definition – subject and real are to be situated on either side of the split, in the resistance of the phantasy. The real is, in a way, an experience of resistance.*

LACAN: My discourse proceeds, in the following way: each term is sustained only in its topological relation with the others, and the subject of the *cogito* is treated in exactly the same way.

W A H L : *Is topology for you a method of discovery or of exposition?*

L A C A N : It is the mapping of the topology proper to our experience as analysts, which may later be taken in a metaphysical perspective. I think Merleau-Ponty was moving in this direction – see the second part of the book, his reference to the *Wolf Man* and to the finger of a glove.

P. K A U F M A N N : *You have provided us with a typical structure of the gaze, but you have said nothing of the dilation of light.*

L A C A N : I said that the gaze was not the eye, except in that flying form in which Holbein has the cheek to show me my own soft watch... Next time, I will talk about embodied light.

26 February 1964

14

Pornography, Nostalgia, Montage: A Triad of the Gaze

Slavoj Žižek

As it is ordinarily understood, *pornography* is the genre supposed to 'reveal all there is to reveal', to hide nothing, to register 'all' and offer it to our view. It is nevertheless precisely in pornographic cinema that the 'substance of enjoyment' perceived by the view from aside is *radically lost* – why? Let us recall the antinomic relation of gaze and eye as articulated by Lacan in *Seminar XI*: the eye viewing the object is on the side of the subject, while the gaze is on the side of the object. When I look at an object, the object is always already gazing at me, and from a point at which I cannot see it:

> In the scopic field, everything is articulated between two terms that act in an antinomic way – on the side of things, there is the gaze, that is to say, things look at me, and yet I see them. This is how one should understand those words, so strongly stressed, in the Gospel, *They have eyes that they might not see.* That they might not see what? Precisely, that things are looking at them.[1]

This antinomy of gaze and view is lost in pornography – why? Because pornography is inherently *perverse*; its perverse character lies not in the obvious fact that it 'goes all the way and shows us all the dirty details'; its perversity is, rather, to be conceived in a strictly formal way. In pornography, the spectator is forced a priori to occupy a perverse position. Instead of being on the side of the viewed object, the gaze falls into ourselves, the spectators, which is why the image we see on the screen contains no spot, no sublime-mysterious point from which it gazes at us. It is only we who gaze stupidly at the image that 'reveals all'. Contrary to the commonplace according to which, in pornography, the other (the person shown on the screen) is degraded to an object of our voyeuristic pleasure, we must stress that it is the spectator himself who effectively occupies the position of the object. The real subjects are the actors on the screen trying to rouse us sexually, while we, the spectators, are reduced to a paralysed object-gaze.[2]

Pornography thus misses, reduces the point of the object-gaze in the other. This miss has precisely the form of a missed, failed encounter. That is to say, in a 'normal', non-pornographic film, a love scene is always built around a certain insurmountable limit; 'all cannot be shown'. At a certain point the image is blurred, the camera moves off, the scene is interrupted, we never directly see 'that' (the penetration of sexual organs, etc.). In contrast to this limit of representability defining the 'normal' love story or melodrama, pornography goes beyond, it 'shows everything'. The paradox is, however, that by trespassing the limit, it always *goes too far*, i.e., it *misses* what remains concealed in a 'normal', non-pornographic love scene. To refer to the phrase from Brecht's *Threepenny Opera*: if you run too fast after happiness, you may overtake it and happiness may stay behind. If we proceed too hastily 'to the point', if we show 'the thing itself', we necessarily lose what we were after. The effect is extremely vulgar and depressing (as can be confirmed by anyone who has watched any hard-core movies). Pornography is thus just another variation on the paradox of Achilles and the tortoise that, according to Lacan, defines the relation of the subject to the object of his desire. Naturally, Achilles can easily outdistance the tortoise and leave it behind, but the point is that he cannot come up alongside it, he cannot rejoin it. The subject is always too slow or too quick, it can never keep pace with the object of its desire. The unattainable/forbidden object approached but never reached by the 'normal' love story – the sexual act – exists only as concealed, indicated, 'faked'. As soon as we 'show it', its charm is dispelled, we have 'gone too far'. Instead of the sublime Thing, we are stuck with vulgar, groaning fornication.

The consequence of this is that harmony, congruence between the filmic narrative (the unfolding of the story) and the immediate display of the sexual act, is structurally impossible: if we choose one, we necessarily lose the other. In other words, if we want to have a love story that 'takes', that moves us, we must not 'go all the way' and 'show it all' (the details of the sexual act), because as soon as we 'show it all', the story is no longer 'taken seriously' and starts to function only as a pretext for introducing acts of copulation. We can detect this gap via a kind of 'knowledge in the real', which determines the way actors behave in different film genres. The characters included in the diegetic reality always react as if they knew in which genre of film they were. If, for example, a door creaks in a horror film, the actor will react by turning his head anxiously toward it; if a door creaks in a family comedy, the same actor will shout at his small child not to sneak around the apartment. The same is true to an even greater extent of the 'porno' film: before we pass to the sexual activity, we need a short introduction – normally, a stupid plot serving as pretext for the actors to begin copulation (the housewife calls in a plumber, a new secretary reports to the manager, etc.) The point is that even in the manner in which they enact this introductory plot, the actors divulge that this is for them only a stupid although necessary formality that has to be gotten over with as quickly as possible so as to begin tackling the 'real thing'.[3]

The fantasy ideal of a perfect work of pornography would be precisely to preserve this impossible harmony, the balance between narration and explicit depiction of the sexual act, i.e., to avoid the necessary *vel* that condemns us to lose one of the two poles. Let us take an old-fashioned, nostalgic melodrama like *Out of Africa*, and let us assume that the film is precisely the one shown in cinemas, except for an additional ten minutes. When Robert Redford and Meryl Streep have their first love encounter, the scene – in this slightly longer version of the film – is not interrupted, the camera 'shows it all', details of their aroused sexual organs, penetration, orgasm, etc. Then, after the act, the story goes on as usual, we return to the film we all know. The problem is that such a movie is structurally impossible. Even if it were to be shot, it simply 'would not function'; the additional ten minutes would derail us, for the rest of the movie we would be unable to regain our balance and follow the narration with the usual disavowed belief in the diegetic reality. The sexual act would function as an intrusion of the real undermining the consistency of this diegetic reality.

Nostalgia

In pornography, the gaze *qua* object falls thus onto the subject-spectator, causing an effect of depressing desublimation. Which is why, to extract the gaze-object in its pure, formal status, we have to turn to pornography's opposite pole: nostalgia. Let us take what is probably today the most notorious case of nostalgic fascination in the domain of cinema: the American *film noir* of the 1940s. What, precisely, is so fascinating about this genre? It is clear that we can no longer identify with it. The most dramatic scenes from *Casablanca, Murder, My Sweet*, or *Out of the Past* provoke laughter today among spectators, but nevertheless, far from posing a threat to the genre's power of fascination, this kind of distance is its very condition. That is to say, what fascinates us is precisely a certain gaze, the gaze of the 'other', of the hypothetical, mythic spectator from the '40s who was supposedly still able to identify immediately with the universe of *film noir*. What we really see, when we watch a *film noir*, is this gaze of the other: we are fascinated by the gaze of the mythic 'naïve' spectator, the one who was 'still able to take it seriously', in other words, the one who 'believes in it' for us, in place of us. For that reason, our relation to a *film noir* is always divided, split between fascination and ironic distance: ironic distance toward its diegetic reality, fascination with the gaze.

This gaze-object appears in its purest form in a series of films in which the logic of nostalgia is brought to self-reference: *Body Heat, Driver, Shane*. As Fredric Jameson has already observed in his well-known article on postmodernism,[4] *Body Heat* reverses the usual nostalgic procedure in which the fragment of the past that serves as the object of nostalgia is extracted from its historic context, from its continuity, and inserted into a kind of mythic, eternal, timeless present. Here, in this *film noir* – a vague remake of *Double Indemnity*, which takes place in contemporary Florida – present time itself is viewed through the eyes of the *film noir* of the '40s. Instead of transposing a fragment of the past into a timeless, mythic present, we view the present itself as if it were part of the mythic past. If we do not take into consideration this 'gaze of the '40s', *Body Heat* remains simply a contemporary film about contemporary times and, as such, totally incomprehensible. Its whole power of fascination is bestowed upon it by the fact that it looks at the present with the eyes of the mythical past. The same dialectic of the gaze is at work in Walter Hill's *Driver*; its starting point is again the *film noir* of the '40s which, as such, *does not exist*. It started to exist only when it was discovered by French critics in the '50s (it is no accident that even in English, the term used to designate this genre is French: *film noir*). What was, in America itself, a series of low-budget B-productions of little critical prestige, was miraculously transformed, through the intervention of the French gaze, into a sublime object of art, a kind of film pendant to philosophical existentialism. Directors who had in America the status of skilled craftsmen, at best, became *auteurs*, each of them staging in his films a unique tragic vision of the universe. But the crucial fact is that this French view of *film noir* exerted a considerable influence on French film production, so that in France itself, a genre homologous to the American *film noir* was established; its most distinguished example is probably Jean-Pierre Melville's *Samurai*. Hill's *Driver* is a kind of remake of *Samurai*, an attempt to transpose the French gaze back onto America itself – a paradox of American film about America, it becomes incomprehensible: we must include the 'French gaze'.

Our last example is *Shane*, the classic western by George Stevens. As is well known, the end of the '40s witnessed the first great crisis of the western as a genre. Pure, simple westerns began to produce an effect of artificiality and mechanical routine, their formula was seemingly exhausted. Authors reacted to this crisis by overlaying westerns with elements of other genres. Thus we have *film noir* westerns (Raoul Welsh's *Pursued*, which achieves the almost impossible task of transposing into a western the dark universe of the *film noir*); musical comedy westerns (*Seven Brides for Seven Brothers*); psychological westerns (*The Gunfighter*, with Gregory Peck); historical epic westerns (the remake of *Cimarron*), etc. In the '50s, André Bazin baptised this new, 'reflected' genre the *meta-western*. The way *Shane* functions can be grasped only against the background of the 'meta-western', *Shane* is the paradox of a western, the 'meta-' dimension of which is the *western itself*. In other words, it is a western that implies a kind of nostalgic distance toward the universe of westerns: a western that functions, so to speak, as its own myth. To explain the effect produced by *Shane*, we must again refer to the function of the gaze. That is to say, if we remain on the commonsense level, if we do not include the dimension of the gaze, a simple and understandable question arises: if the meta-dimension of this western is the western itself, what accounts for the distance between the two levels? Why does the meta-western not simply overlap with the western itself? Why do we not have a western pure and simple? The answer is that, by means of a structural necessity, *Shane* belongs in the context of the meta-western: on the level of its immediate diegetic contents, it is of course a western pure and simple, one of the purest ever made. But the very form of its historical context determines that we perceive it as meta-western, i.e., precisely because, in its diegetic contents, it is pure western, the dimension 'beyond western' opened up by the historical context can be filled out only by the western itself. In other words, *Shane* is a pure western *at a time when pure westerns were no longer possible*, when the western was already perceived from a certain nostalgic distance, as a lost object. Which is why it is highly indicative that the story is told from a child's perspective (the perspective of a little boy, a member of a farming family defended against violent cattle breeders by Shane, a mythic hero appearing suddenly out of nowhere). The innocent, naïve gaze of the other that fascinates us in nostalgia is in the last resort always the gaze of a child.

In nostalgic, retrofilms, then, the logic of the gaze *qua* object appears as such. The real object of fascination is not the displayed scene but the gaze of the naïve 'other' absorbed, enchanted by it. In *Shane*, for example, we can be fascinated by the mysterious apparition of Shane only through the medium of the 'innocent' child's gaze, never immediately. Such a logic of fascination by which the subject sees in the object (in the image it views) its own gaze, i.e., by which, in the viewed image, it 'sees itself seeing', is defined by Lacan as the very illusion of perfect self-mirroring that characterises the Cartesian philosophical tradition of the subject of self-reflection.[5] But what happens here with the *antinomy* between eye and gaze? That is to say, the whole point of Lacan's argument is to oppose to the self-mirroring of philosophical subjectivity the irreducible discord between the gaze *qua* object and the subject's eye. Far from being the point of self-sufficient self-mirroring, the gaze *qua* object functions like a blot that blurs the transparency of the viewed image. I can never see properly, can never include in the totality of my field of vision, the point in the other from which it gazes back at me. Like the extended blot in

Holbein's *Ambassadors*, this point throws the harmony of my vision off balance.

The answer to our problem is clear: the function of the nostalgic object is precisely to *conceal* the antinomy between eye and gaze – i.e., the traumatic impact of the gaze *qua* object – by means of its power of fascination. In nostalgia, the gaze of the other is in a way domesticated, 'gentrified'; instead of the gaze erupting like a traumatic, disharmonious blot, we have the illusion of 'seeing ourselves seeing', of seeing the gaze itself. In a way, we could say that the function of fascination is precisely to blind us to the fact that the other is already gazing at us. In Kafka's parable 'The Door of the Law', the man from the country waiting at the entrance to the court is fascinated by the secret beyond the door he is forbidden to trespass. In the end, the power of fascination exerted by the court is dispelled. But how, exactly? Its power is lost when the door keeper tells him that this entrance was, from the very start, meant only for him. In other words, he tells the man from the country that the thing that fascinated him was, in a way, gazing back at him all along, addressing him. That is, the man's desire was from the very start 'part of the game'. The whole spectacle of the Door of the Law and the secret beyond it was staged only to capture his desire. If the power of fascination is to produce its effect, this fact must remain concealed. As soon as the subject becomes aware that the other gazes at him (that the door is meant only for him), the fascination is dispelled.

In his Bayreuth production of *Tristan und Isolde*, Jean-Pierre Ponelle introduced an extremely interesting change in Wagner's original plot, a change that precisely concerns the functioning of the gaze as object of fascination. In Wagner's libretto, the denouement simply resumes the mythic tradition. The wounded Tristan takes refuge in his castle in Cornwall and waits for Isolde to follow him. When, because of a misunderstanding concerning the colour of the sail of Isolde's vessel, he becomes convinced that Isolde will not arrive, he dies in agony. Whereupon Isolde arrives together with her lawful husband, King Marke, who is willing to forgive the sinful couple. It is, however, too late; Tristan is already dead. In esctatic agony, Isolde herself dies embracing the dead Tristan. What Ponelle did was simply to stage the last act as if the end of the 'real' action were Tristan's death. All that follows – the arrival of Isolde and Marke, Isolde's death – is just Tristan's mortal delirium. In reality, Isolde has simply broken the vow to her lover and returned, repentant, to her husband. The much-celebrated end of *Tristan und Isolde*, Isolde's love-death, appears thus as what it effectively is: the *masculine* fantasy of a finally accomplished sexual relationship by which the couple is forever united in mortal ecstasy, or, more precisely, in which the *woman* follows her man into death in an act of ecstatic self-abandonment.

But the crucial point for us is the way Ponelle staged this delirious apparition of Isolde. Because she appears to *Tristan*, we would expect her to stand *in front of* him and thus fascinate his gaze. In Ponelle's *mise-en-scène*, however, Tristan looks directly at us, the spectators in the hall, while the dazzlingly illuminated Isolde grows luxuriantly *behind* him, as that which is 'in him more than himself'. The object at which Tristan stares in fascination is thus literally *the gaze of the other* (embodied in us, the spectators), the gaze that sees Isolde, i.e., the gaze that sees not only Tristan but also his sublime other, that which is in him more than himself, the 'treasure', *agalma*, in him. At this point, Ponelle adroitly made use of the words sung by Isolde. Far from plunging into a kind of autistic trance, she continually addresses the gaze of the other: 'Friends! Do you see, can't you see, how he [Tristan] glitters more and more?' – that which 'glitters more and more' in him being of course *herself* as the illuminated apparition behind him.

If the function of nostalgic fascination is thus to conceal, to appease the disharmonious irruption of the gaze *qua* object, how is this gaze consequently *produced*? Which cinematic procedure opens up, hollows the void of the gaze *qua* object in the continuous flow of images? Our thesis is that this void constitutes the necessary leftover of *montage*, so that pornography, nostalgia, and montage form a kind of quasi-Hegelian 'triad' in relation to the status of the gaze *qua* object.

THE HITCHCOCKIAN CUT

Montage

Montage is usually conceived as a way of producing from fragments of the real – pieces of film, discontinuous individual shots – an effect of 'cinematic space', i.e., a specific cinematic reality. That is to say, it is universally acknowledged that 'cinematic space' is never a simple repetition or imitation of external, 'effective' reality, but an effect of montage. What is often overlooked, however, is the way this transformation of fragments of the real into cinematic reality produces, through a kind of structural necessity, a certain leftover, a surplus that is radically heterogeneous to cinematic reality but nonetheless implied by it, part of it.[6] That this surplus of the real is, in the last resort, precisely the gaze *qua* object, is best exemplified by the work of Hitchcock.

We have already pointed out that the fundamental constituent of the Hitchcockian universe is the so-called 'spot': the stain upon which reality revolves, passes over into the real, the mysterious detail that 'sticks out', that does not 'fit' into the symbolic network of reality and that, as such, indicates that 'something is amiss'. The fact that this spot ultimately coincides with the threatening gaze of the other is confirmed in an almost too obvious way by the famous tennis court scene from *Strangers on a Train*, in which Guy watches the crowd watching the game. The camera first gives us a long shot of the crowd; all heads turn alternately left and right, following the path of the ball, all except one, which stares with a fixed gaze into the camera, i.e., at Guy. The camera then quickly approaches this motionless head. It is Bruno, linked to Guy by a murderous pact. Here we have in pure, distilled form the stiff, motionless gaze, sticking out like a strange body and thus disturbing the harmony of the image by introducing a threatening dimension.

The function of the famous Hitchcockian 'tracking shot' is precisely to produce a spot: in the tracking shot, the camera moves from an establishing shot to a close-up of a detail that remains a blurred spot, the true form of which is accessible only to an anamorphotic 'view from aside'. The shot slowly isolates from its surroundings the element that cannot be integrated into the symbolic reality, that must remain a strange body if the depicted reality is to retain its consistency. But what interests us here is the fact that under certain conditions, montage *does* intervene in the tracking shot, i.e., the continuous approach of the camera is interrupted by cuts.

What, more precisely, are these conditions? Briefly, the tracking shot must be interrupted when it is 'subjective', when the camera shows us the subjective view of a person approaching the object-spot. That is to say, whenever, in a Hitchcock film, a hero, a person around whom the scene is structured, approaches an object, a thing, another person, anything that can become 'uncanny' (*unheimlich*) in the Freudian sense, Hitchcock as a rule alternates the 'objective' shot of this person in motion, his/her approach toward the uncanny Thing, with a subjective shot of what this person sees, i.e., with a subjective view of the Thing. This is, so to speak, the elementary procedure, the zero degree of Hitchcockian montage.

Let us take a few examples. When, toward the end of *Psycho*, Lilah climbs up the rise to the mysterious old house, the presumed home of 'Norman's mother', Hitchcock alternates the objective shot of Lilah climbing with her subjective view of the old house. He does the same in *The Birds*, in the famous scene analysed in detail by Raymond Bellour,[7] when Melanie, after crossing the bay in a small rented boat, approaches the house where Mitch's mother and sister live. Again, he alternates an objective shot of the uneasy Melanie, aware of intruding on the privacy of a home, with her subjective view of the mysteriously silent house.[8] Of innumerable other examples, let us mention merely a short, trivial scene between Marion and a car dealer in *Psycho*. Here, Hitchcock uses his montage procedure several times (when Marion approaches the car dealer; when, toward the end of the scene, a policeman approaches who has already stopped her on the highway the same morning, etc.).

By means of this purely formal procedure, an entirely trivial, everyday incident is given an uneasy, threatening dimension that cannot be sufficiently explained by its diegetic contents (i.e., by the fact that Marion is buying a new car with stolen money and thus fears exposure). Hitchcockian montage elevates an everyday, trivial object into a sublime Thing. By purely formal manipulation, it succeeds in bestowing on an ordinary object the aura of anxiety and uneasiness.[9]

In Hitchcockian montage, two kinds of shots are thus permitted and two forbidden. Permitted are the objective shot of the person approaching a Thing and the subjective shot presenting the Thing as the person sees it. Forbidden are the objective shot of the Thing, of the 'uncanny' object, and – above all – the subjective shot of the approaching person from the perspective of the 'uncanny' object itself. Let us refer again to the above-mentioned scene from *Psycho* depicting Lilah approaching the house on the top of the hill. It is crucial that Hitchcock shows the threatening Thing (the house) exclusively from the point of view of Lilah. If he were to have added a 'neutral' objective shot of the house, the whole mysterious effect would have been lost. We (the spectators) would have to endure a radical desublimation; we would suddenly become aware that there is nothing 'uncanny' in the house as such, that the house is – like the 'black house' in the Patricia Highsmith short story – just an ordinary old house. The effect of uneasiness would be radically 'psychologised'; we would say to ourselves, 'This is just an ordinary house; all the mystery and anxiety attached to it are just an effect of the heroine's psychic turmoil!'

The effect of 'uncanniness' would also be lost if Hitchcock had immediately added a shot 'subjectifying' the Thing, i.e., a subjective shot from inside the house. Let us imagine that as Lilah approached the house, there had been a trembling shot showing Lilah through the curtains of the house window, accompanied by the sound of hollow breathing, thus indicating that somebody was watching her from inside the house. Such a procedure (used regularly in standard thrillers) would, of course, intensify the strain. We would say to ourselves, 'This is terrible! There is somebody in the house (Norman's mother?) watching Lilah; she is in mortal danger without knowing it!' But such a subjectification would again suspend the status of the gaze *qua object*, reducing it to the subjective point of view of another diegetic personality. Sergei Eisenstein himself once risked such a direct subjectification, in a scene from *The Old and the New*, a film that celebrated the successes of the collectivisation of Soviet agriculture in the late '20s. It is a somewhat Lysenkoist scene demonstrating the way nature finds pleasure in subordinating itself to the new rules of collective farming, the way even cows and bulls mate more ardently once they are included in *kilkhozes*. In a quick tracking shot, the camera approaches a cow from behind, and in the next shot it becomes clear that this view of the camera was the view of a bull mounting a cow. Needless to say, the effect of this scene is so obscenely vulgar that it is almost nauseating. What we have here is a kind of Stalinist pornography.

It would be wiser, then, to turn away from this Stalinist obscenity to the Hollywood decency of Hitchcock. Let us return to the scene from *Psycho* in which Lilah approaches the house where 'Norman's mother' presumably lives. In what does its 'uncanny' dimension consist? Could we not best describe the effect of this scene by paraphrasing the words of Lacan: in a way, *it is already the house that gazes at Lilah*? Lilah sees the house, but nonetheless she cannot see it at the point from which it gazes back at her. Here the situation is the same as that which Lacan recollects from his youth and reports in *Seminar XI*: as a student on holiday, he joined a fishing expedition. Among the fishermen on the boat, there was a certain Petit-Jean who, pointing out an empty sardine can glittering in the sun, asked Lacan: '*You see the can? Do you see it? Well, it doesn't see you!*' Lacan's comment: 'If what Petit-Jean said to me, namely that the can did not see me, had any meaning, it was because in a sense, it was looking at me, all the same.' It was looking at him because, as Lacan explains, using a key notion of the Hitchcockian universe, 'I functioned somewhat like a spot in the picture'.[10] Among these uneducated fishermen earning their living with great difficulty, he was effectively out of place, 'the man who knew too much'.

15

Motherhood According to Giovanni Bellini

Julia Kristeva

THE MATERNAL BODY

Cells fuse, split, and proliferate; volumes grow, tissues stretch, and body fluids change rhythm, speeding up or slowing down. Within the body, growing as a graft, indomitable, there is an other. And no one is present, within that simultaneously dual and alien space, to signify what is going on. 'It happens, but I'm not there.' 'I cannot realise it, but it goes on.' Motherhood's impossible syllogism.

This becoming-a-mother, this gestation, can possibly be accounted for by means of only two discourses. There is *science*; but as an objective discourse, science is not concerned with the subject, the mother as site of her proceedings. There is *Christian theology* (especially canonical theology); but theology defines maternity only as an impossible elsewhere, a sacred beyond, a vessel of divinity, a spiritual tie with the ineffable godhead, and transcendence's ultimate support – necessarily virginal and committed to assumption. Such are the wiles of Christian reason (Christianity's still matchless rationalism, or at least its rationalising power, finally become clear); through the maternal body (in a state of virginity and 'dormition'[1] before Assumption), it thus establishes a sort of subject at the point where the subject and its speech split apart, fragment, and vanish. Lay humanism took over the configuration of that subject through the cult of the mother; tenderness, love, and seat of social conservation.

And yet, if we presume that *someone* exists throughout the process of cells, molecules, and atoms accumulating, dividing, and multiplying without any *identity* (biological or socio-symbolical) having been formed so far, are we not positing an animism that reflects the inherent psychosis of the speaking Being? So, if we suppose that a *mother* is the subject of gestation, in other words the *master* of a process that science, despite its effective devices, acknowledges it cannot now and perhaps never will be able to take away from her; if we suppose her to be *master* of a process that is prior to the social-symbolic-linguistic contract of the group, then

158

we acknowledge the risk of losing identity at the same time as we ward it off. We recognise on the one hand that biology jolts us by means of unsymbolised instinctual drives and that this phenomenon eludes social intercourse, the representation of pre-existing objects, and the contract of desire. On the other hand, we immediately deny it; we say there can be no escape, for mamma is there, she embodies this phenomenon; she warrants that *everything is,* and that it is representable. In a double-barrelled move, psychotic tendencies are acknowledged, but at the same time they are settled, quieted, and bestowed upon the mother in order to maintain the ultimate guarantee: symbolic coherence.

This move, however, also reveals, better than any mother ever could, that the maternal body is the place of a splitting, which, even though hypostatised by Christianity, nonetheless remains a constant factor of social reality. Through a body, destined to ensure reproduction of the species, the woman-subject, although under the sway of the paternal function (as symbolising, speaking subject and like all others), is more of a *filter* than anyone else – a thoroughfare, a threshold where 'nature' confronts 'culture'. To imagine that there is *someone* in that filter – such is the source of religious mystifications, the font that nourishes them: the fantasy of the so-called 'Phallic' Mother. Because if, on the contrary, there were no one on this threshold, if the mother were not, that is, if she were not phallic, then every speaker would be led to conceive of its Being in relation to some void, a nothingness asymmetrically opposed to this Being, a permanent threat against, first, its mastery, and ultimately, its stability.

The discourse of analysis proves that the *desire* for motherhood is without fail a desire to bear a child of the father (a child of her own father) who, as a result, is often assimilated to the baby itself and thus returned to its place as *devalorised man,* summoned only to accomplish his function, which is to originate and justify reproductive desire. Only through these phantasmatic nuptials can the father–daughter incest be carried out and the baby come to exist. At that, the incest is too far removed, bringing peace only to those who firmly adhere to the paternal symbolic axis. Otherwise, once the object is produced, once the fruit is detached, the ceremony loses its effect unless it be repeated forever.

And yet, through and with this desire, motherhood seems to be impelled *also* by a non-symbolic, non-paternal causality. Only Ferenczi, Freud, and, later, Marie Bonaparte, have spoken about this, evoking the biological destiny of each differentiated sex. Maternal compulsion, spasm of a memory belonging to the species that either binds together or splits apart to perpetuate itself, series of markers with no other significance than the eternal return of the life–death biological cycle. How can we verbalise this pre-linguistic, unrepresentable memory? Heraclitus' flux, Epicurus' atoms, the whirling dust of cabalic, Arab, and Indian mystics, and the stippled drawings of psychedelics – all seem better metaphors than the theories of Being, the logos, and its laws.

Such an excursion to the limits of primal regression can be phantasmatically experienced as the reunion of a woman–mother with the body of *her* mother. The body of her mother is always the same Master–Mother of instinctual drive, a ruler over psychosis, a subject of biology, but also, one toward which women aspire all the more passionately simply because it lacks a penis: that body cannot penetrate her as can a man when possessing his wife. By giving birth, the woman enters into contact with her mother; she becomes, she is her own mother; they are the same continuity differentiating itself. She thus actualises the homosexual facet of motherhood, through which a woman is simultaneously closer to her instinctual memory, more open to her own psychosis, and consequently, more negatory of the social, symbolic bond.

The symbolic paternal facet relieves feminine aphasia present within the desire to bear the father's child. It is an appeasement that turns into melancholy as soon as the child becomes an object, a gift to others, neither self nor part of the self, an object destined to be a subject, an other. Melancholy readjusts the paranoia that drives to action (often violent) and to discourse (essentially parental, object-oriented, and pragmatic discourse) the feminine, verbal scarcity so prevalent in our culture.

The homosexual-maternal facet is a whirl of words, a complete absence of meaning and seeing; it is feeling, displacement, rhythm, sound, flashes, and fantasied clinging to the maternal body as a screen against the plunge. Perversion slows down the schizophrenia that collapsing identities and the delights of the well-known and oft-solicited (by some women) pantheist fusion both brush up against.

Those afflicted or affected by psychosis have put up in its place the image of the Mother: for women, a paradise lost but seemingly close at hand, for men, a hidden god but constantly present through occult fantasy. And even psychoanalysts believe in it.

Yet, swaying between these two positions can only mean, for the woman involved, that she is within an 'enceinte' separating her from the world of everyone else.[2] Enclosed in this 'elsewhere', an 'enceinte' woman loses communital meaning, which suddenly appears to her as worthless, absurd, or at best, comic – a surface agitation severed from its impossible foundations. Oriental nothingness probably better sums up what, in the eyes of a Westerner, can only be regression. And yet it is jouissance, but like a negative of the one, tied to an object, that is borne by the unfailingly masculine libido. Here, alterity becomes nuance, contradiction becomes a variant, tension becomes passage, and discharge becomes peace. This tendency towards equalisation, which is seen as a regressive extinction of symbolic capabilities, does not, however, reduce differences; it resides within the smallest, most archaic, and most uncertain of differences. It is powerful sublimation and indwelling of the symbolic within instinctual drives. It affects this series of 'little differences – resemblances' (as the Chinese logicians of antiquity would say). Before founding society in the same stroke as signs and communication, they are the precondition of the latter's existence, as they constitute the living entity within its species, with its needs, its elementary apperceptions and communication, distinguishing between the instinctual drives of life and death. It affects primal repression. An ultimate danger for identity, but also supreme power of symbolic instance thus returning to matters of its concern. Sublimation here is both eroticising without residue and a disappearance of eroticism as it returns to its source.

The speaker reaches this limit, this requisite of sociality, only by virtue of a particular, discursive practice called 'art'. A woman also attains it (and in our society, *especially*) through the strange form of split symbolisation (threshold of language and instinctual drive, of the 'symbolic' and the 'semiotic') of which the act of giving birth consists. As the archaic process of socialisation, one might even say civilisation, it causes the childbearing woman to cathect, immediately and unwittingly, the physiological operations and instinctual drives dividing and multiplying her, first, in a biological, and finally, a social teleology. The maternal body slips away from the discursive hold and immediately conceals a cipher that must be taken into account biologically and socially. This ciphering of the species, however, this pre-and trans-symbolic memory, makes the mother mistress of neither begetting nor instinctual drive (such a fantasy underlies the cult of any ultimately feminine deity); it does make of the maternal body the stakes of a natural and 'objective' control, independent of any individual consciousness; it inscribes both biological operations and their instinctual echoes into this necessary and hazardous *programme* constituting every species. The maternal body is the module of a biosocial programme. Its jouissance, which is mute, is nothing more than a recording, on the screen of the pre-conscious, of both the messages that consciousness, in its analytical course, picks up from this ciphering process and their classifications as empty foundation, as a-subjective lining of our rational exchanges as social beings. If it is true that every national language has its own dream language and unconscious, then each of the sexes – a division so much more archaic and fundamental than the one into languages – would have its own unconscious wherein the biological and social programme of the species would be ciphered in confrontation with language, exposed to its influence, but independent from it. The symbolic destiny of the speaking animal, which is essential although it comes second, being superimposed upon the biological – this destiny *seals off* (and in women, in order to preserve the homology of the group, it *censures*) that archaic basis and the special jouissance it procures in being transferred to the symbolic. Privileged, 'psychotic' moments, or whatever induces them naturally, thus become necessary. Among such 'natural' inducements, maternity is needed for this sexual modality to surface, this fragile, secretly guarded and incommunicable modality, quickly stifled by standard palliatives (by virile and 'rational' censorship, or by the sentimentality of 'maternal' tenderness toward a substitute-object for everything). This process is quite rightly understood as the demand for a penis. Fantasy indeed has no other sign, no other way to imagine that the speaker is capable of reaching the Mother, and thus, of unsettling its own limits. And, as long as there is language-symbolism-paternity, there will never be any other way to represent, to objectify, and to explain this unsettling of the symbolic stratum, this nature/culture threshold, this instilling the subjectless biological programme into the very body of a symbolising subject, this event called motherhood.

In other words, from the point of view of social coherence, which is where legislators, grammarians, and even psychoanalysts have their seat; which is where every body is made homologous to a male speaking body, motherhood would be nothing more than a phallic attempt to reach the Mother who is presumed to exist at the very place where (social and biological) identity recedes. If it is true that idealist ideologies develop along these lines, urging women to satisfy this presumed demand and to maintain the ensuing order, then, on the other hand, any negation of this utilitarian, social, and symbolic aspect of motherhood plunges into regression – but a particular regression whose currently recognised manifestations lead to the hypostasis of blind substance, to the negation of symbolic position, and to a justification of this regression under the aegis of the same Phallic Mother-screen.

The language of art, too, follows (but differently and more closely) the other aspect of maternal jouissance, the sublimation taking place at the very moment of primal repression within the mother's body, arising perhaps unwittingly out of her marginal position. At the intersection of sign and rhythm, of representation and light, of the symbolic and the semiotic, the artist speaks from a place where she is not, where she knows not. He delineates what, in her, is a body rejoicing [*jouissant*]. The very existence of aesthetic practice makes clear that the Mother as subject is a delusion, just as the negation of the so-called poetic dimension of language leads one to believe in the existence of the Mother, and consequently, of transcendence. Because, through a symbiosis of meaning and non-meaning, of representation and interplay of differences, the artist lodges into language, and through his identification with the mother (fetishism or incest – we shall return to this problem), his own specific jouissance, thus traversing both sign and object. Thus, before all other speakers, he bears witness to what the unconscious (through the screen of the mother) records of those clashes that occur between the biological and social programmes of the species. This means that through and across secondary repression (founding of signs), aesthetic practice touches upon primal repression (founding biological series and the laws of the species). At the place where it obscurely succeeds within the maternal body, every artist tries his hand, but rarely with equal success:

Nevertheless, craftsmen of Western art reveal better than anyone else the artist's debt to the maternal body and/or motherhood's entry into symbolic existence – that is, translibidinal jouissance, eroticism taken over by the language of art. Not only is a considerable portion of pictorial art devoted to motherhood, but within this representation itself, from Byzantine iconography to Renaissance humanism and the worship of the body that it initiates, two attitudes toward the maternal body emerge, prefiguring two destinies within the very economy of Western representation. Leonardo Da Vinci and Giovanni Bellini seem to exemplify in the best fashion the opposition between these two attitudes. On the one hand, there is a tilting toward the body as fetish. On the other, a predominance of luminous, chromatic differences beyond and despite corporeal representation. Florence and Venice. Worship of the figurable, representable man; or integration of the image accomplished in its truth-likeness within the luminous serenity of the unrepresentable.

A unique biographical experience and an uncommon, historical intersection of pagan-matriarchal Orientalism with sacred Christianity and incipient humanism was perhaps needed for Bellini's brush to retain the traces of a marginal experience, through and across which a maternal body might recognise its own, otherwise inexpressible in our culture.

LEONARDO AND BELLINI: FETISH AND PRIMAL REPRESSION

Giovanni Bellini: 1430?–1516. Approximately two hundred and twenty paintings, basically on sacred topics, are attributed to him or to his school. He taught Giorgione and Titian, and founded the Venetian Renaissance, which came somewhat later than the Florentine but was more organically allied to its Byzantine sources and more attracted by the display of the feminine body than by the Grecian beauty of young boys. Bellini's work is a synthesis of Flemish landscape painting, iconography, and Mediterranean architectural manner. He also contributed a completely new element: the luminous density of colour (the initial technique of oil painting, which was already being mastered, of shadows and brightness that, more so than the discovery of perspective, introduced volume into the body and into the painting. Historians of art emphasise, in Bellini's manner, the effect; they often neglect what this manner implies as to pictorial experimentation, but worse, they also neglect to observe it down to the most minute details of the painting's surface.

We have almost no biographical details: a nearly perfect discretion. His father was the painter Jacopo Bellini; his brother, the painter Gentile Bellini. His brother-in-law was the painter Andrea Mantegna. He was the official painter for the Ducal Palace, but the paintings executed in that capacity were destroyed. He was married, but his wife Ginevra Bocheta died young, as did his son, and it is uncertain whether he married again. He was urged by Isabella d'Este to paint pagan motifs but he backed out, refusing to do so; finally, he complied only when assisted by his disciples. In 1506, Dürer called him the best of painters. The spoors of his life leave a discrete imprint, and then they disappear. Bellini himself left us no words, no subjective writings. We must read him through his painting.

Bellini's discretion stands in contrast to the profusion of information and biographical notes left behind by his younger contemporary, Leonardo Da Vinci (1452–1519). Relying on biographical evidence and on paintings as *narrative* as *Virgin and Child with St. Anne* and the *Mona Lisa*, Freud could maintain that Leonardo's 'artistic personality' was formed, first, by the precocious seduction he was supposed to have experienced at the hands of his mother (the vampire tail of his dreams would represent the tongue of his mother, passionately kissing the illegitimate child); second, by a double motherhood (taken from his mother, Leonardo was raised in his father's family by his stepmother, who had no children of her own); and finally, by the impressive authority of an office-holding father. The father finally triumphed over the drawing power of the mother, which determined the young man's interest in art, and near the end of his life, Leonardo turned toward the sciences. Thus, we have the typical configuration of a homosexual structure. Persuaded by precocious seduction and double motherhood of the existence of a maternal phallus, the painter never stopped looking for fetish equivalents in the bodies of young people, in his friendships with them, in his miserly worship of objects and money, and in his avoidance of all contact with and access to the feminine body. His was a forbidden mother because she was the primordial seducer, the limit of an archaic, infantile jouissance that must never be reproduced. She established the child's diffident narcissism and cult of the masculine body which he ceaselessly painted, even when a mother figures at the centre of the painting. Take for example Leonardo's Virgins: *Madonna with the Carnation* and *Virgin and Child with St. Anne*. There we find the enigmatic smile, identical with that of the Mona Lisa, herself furtively masculine; with naïve tenderness, face and torso impulsively turn toward the male infant, who remains the real focus of pictorial space and narrative interest. The maternal figure is completely absorbed with her baby; it is he that makes her exist. 'Baby is my goal, and I know it all' – such is the slogan of the mother as master. But when Narcissus is thus sheltered and dominated, he can become the privileged explorer of secondary repression. He goes in quest of fantasies that ensure any group's cohesion; he reveals the phallic influence operating over everyone's imaginary. Such an attitude incites pleasure, but it dramatically affects a desire that is impossible to satisfy by an abundance of objects, bodies, or behaviours, which ceaselessly excite and disappoint. As long as there is father, a magisterial Lord, an intimate of Power, Leonardo turns to his symbolic power, eclipsing maternal imprint; he stops the gap in repression and surges towards scientific knowledge rather than investigating through graphic arts the pleasure-anguish within unconscious formations.

Within the economy of representation, this kind of structure unfailingly entails a humanist realism. First, there is a fetishism of the body and an extreme refinement of the technique of representation by resemblance. Next comes the staging of psychological episodes centred in the desire for a body – his, a child's, or another's. Finally, all chromatic, luminous, and architectural experimentation, releasing, threatening, torturing, and gratifying the artist subject within its practice, undergoes a figuration wherein it is reduced to a simple, technical device, destined to give the effect of representable, desirable, fetishistic forms.

The fundamental traits of Renaissance painting emerge in such a vision, and they are supported by the story of Leonardo's life that was brought out by Freud. They can be found elsewhere, both earlier and later; but with him better than with others, both in his biography and his painting, causes and effects come together and determine beyond the details of his life and the themes of his paintings, the very *economy* of representation, regardless of its *referent*. It is no accident that the major segments of this economy, which was to determine Western man's vision for four centuries to come, are fitted into place by virtue of the themes of motherhood, the woman's body, or the mother (Mona Lisa and the Virgin). The artist, as servant of the maternal phallus, displays this always and everywhere unaccomplished art of reproducing bodies and spaces as graspable, masterable *objects*, within reach of his eye and hand. They are the eye and hand of a child, underage to be sure, but of one who is the universal and nonetheless complex-ridden centre confronting that other function, which carries the appropriation of objects to its limit: science. Body-objects, passion for objects, painting divided into form-objects, painting-objects: the series remains open to centuries of object-oriented and figurable libido, delighting in images and capitalising on artistic merchandise. Among this machine's resources figure the untouchable mother and her baby-object, just as they appear in the paintings of Leonardo, Raphael, and others.

Both Bellini's enigmatic biography and the technique of his paintings suggest a different interpretation. Are we in fact dealing with projections made possible by our uncertain knowledge? Perhaps. But they seem well supported by the paintings, a veritable proof of the deductions that biographical information only suggested.

Commentators are puzzled. According to Vasari, Bellini, son of Jacopo, died a nonagenarian in 1516, and thus should have been born in 1426. Yet, in 1429, Jacopo's wife Anna Rinversi recorded in her will the birth of a first-born son. If Giovanni was born before this date, he must have been either an illegitimate child or the son of Jacopo or Anna by a previous marriage. Other biographers insist that Vasari was wrong and that Giovanni was the youngest child, after Nicolosia (Mantegna's wife) and Gentile. This hypothesis is corroborated most convincingly by Giovanni's social standing in relation to Gentile, who held the position of Seigniorial painter before Giovanni; in some paintings, Giovanni appears third after Jacopo and Gentile. But that does not explain why Giovanni, unlike his brother and sister, was living alone in 1459, outside the paternal household, at San Lio in Venice. Nor does it explain – and this is most crucial – why Anna's last will, dated 25 November 1471, does not list him among the children heirs, Nicolosia and Gentile. So it seems that Anna Rinversi did not recognise herself as Giovanni's mother, giving credence to speculations concerning an illegitimate birth or obscure marriage.[3]

Such is the situation, the biographical outline, greeting the viewer who confronts the work of this painter of motherhood above all other topics. Indeed, he was the son of a father: he bore his father's name, worked in his studio, and carried on his painterly tradition. He was also a brother; Gentile let him have the position of Seigniorial painter when he left for Constantinople; Giovanni also finished some of Gentile's paintings. But the mother is absent – the mother has been lost. Was he precociously weaned from an illegitimate, abandoned, dead, or concealed genetrix? Does this point to the disavowal of a 'sin' committed beyond the law's purview and of which Giovanni was the result? Whatever the truth may be, Anna does not seem to have replaced the 'real' mother, as the honourable Leonardo's wife replaced Leonardo's real mother: Anna knew nothing of the painter of Madonnas. But even if we do remain incredulous in the face of biographical lack and commentators' perplexity, let us also behold the distance, if not hostility, separating the bodies of infant and mother in his paintings. Maternal space is there, nevertheless – fascinating, attracting, and puzzling. But we have no direct access to it. As if there were a maternal *function* that, unlike the mother's solicitude in Leonardo's paintings toward the baby-object of all desire, was merely ineffable jouissance, beyond discourse, beyond narrative, beyond psychology, beyond lived experience and biography – in short, beyond figuration. The faces of his Madonnas are turned away, intent on something else that draws their gaze to the side, up above, or nowhere in particular, but never centres it in the baby. Even though the hands clasp the child and bodies sometimes hug each other, the mother is only partially present (hands and torso), because, from the neck up, the maternal body not covered by draperies – head, face, and eyes – flees the painting, is gripped by something other than its object. And the painter as baby can never reach this elsewhere, this inaccessible peace coloured with melancholy, neither through the portrayed corporeal contact, nor by the distribution of coloured blocks outlining corporeal volumes. It rather seems as though he sensed a shattering, a loss of identity, a sweet jubilation where *she* is not; but without 'her' – without eyes or vision – an *infinitesimal division* of colour and space rhythmically produce a peculiar, serene joy. To touch the mother would be to possess this presumed jouissance and to make it visible. Who holds this jouissance? The folds of coloured surfaces, the juxtaposition of full tones, the limitless volume resolving into a contrast of 'hots' and 'colds' in an architecture of pure colour, the sudden brightness in turn opening up colour itself – a last control of vision, beyond its own density, toward dazzling light. *The Ecstasy of Saint Francis* best sums up this search for jouissance, less by its theme than by the architectonics of a mountain coloured in watery tones against which the saint stands, staggering; it could even be a Taoist painting. But the search appears wherever colour, constructed volume, and light break away from the theme (always banal, canonical, with no psychology, no elaborate individualisation), implying that they are the real, objectless goal of the painting.

Given Bellini's profusion of virginal images, we might be tempted to think that the absent, dead, and mute mother, situated beyond the law, determines that fascination, not as it is confronted with a woman-'body' or woman-'subject', but as it is confronted with the very *function* of jouissance. And yet, Giovanni Bellini could reach it only by following the spoors of the father who, unlike the mother, was always present in the real as well as the symbolic life of the painter. For it was from his father that Giovanni took his first lessons in spatial liberation and sacred painting. In fact, Jacopo, neither dignitary nor lawyer, fervently pursued architecture (see his drawings for *Jesus and the Doctors, Christ before Pilate, The Funeral of the Virgin*, etc., in the Louvre; all are monumental displays of Romanesque or Gothic architecture) and venerated conventional notions of Byzantine motherhood (cf. his *Madonna and Child* paintings in the Correr Museum). Yet the dull seriousness of his motherhood scenes cast him as blind to the mother; he paints her as if carried along by the momentum of Byzantine canon. (Jacopo's real fervour, through the influence of his son-in-law Mantegna, seemed to reside in architectural innovation.) Only his son Giovanni was able to awaken this mother, thus instilling a symbolic life less into the father's sexual object than into its undiscovered jouissance.

First, Giovanni wanted to surpass his father, within the very space of the lost-unrepresentable-forbidden jouissance of a hidden mother, seducing the child through a lack of being.

But then, and most importantly, Giovanni could share in this both maternal and paternal jouissance: he aspired to become the very space where father and mother meet, only to disappear as parental, psychological, and social figures; a space of fundamental unrepresentability toward which all glances nonetheless converge; a primal scene where genitality dissolves sexual identification beyond their given difference. This is how breaking through primal repression, as described earlier and evidenced by the psychological drama or its aesthetic sublimation, was to be spelled out within the individual's biographical matrix.

In any case, we have here a different configuration of artistic practice controlling a different economy of representation. Bellini penetrates through the being and language of the father to position himself in the place where the mother could have been reached. He thus makes evident this always-already-past conditional of the maternal function, which stands instead of the jouissance of both sexes. A kind of incest is then committed, a kind of possession of the mother, which provides motherhood, that mute border, with a language; although in doing so, he deprives it of any right to a real existence (there is nothing 'feminist' in Bellini's action), he does accord it a symbolic status. Unfailingly, the result of this attitude (mother-child representation, marketable painting, etc.) is a fetishised image, but one floating over a luminous background, evoking an 'inner experience' rather than a referential 'object'. This experience, detectable in Bellini's paintings, seems to demand a consuming of the heterosexual relationship. The converse, however, does not hold true; the heterosexuality of this particular economy refers only to the specific relationship between the subject and his identity – the possibility of going through sign, object, and object-libido in order to tap and semiotise even the most minute displacements in those instinctual pressures that mark the dividing line between the species and its language. The point is to reach the threshold of repression by means of the identification with motherhood (be it as heterosexuality or symbolic incest), to reach this threshold where maternal jouissance, alone impassable, is arrayed.

If we see this threshold in a painting, we no longer hear words or meanings; not even sounds. (But in order to see it, we need a relationship to the mother other than that of the fetishistic, object-libidio; we must also work intently upon primal repression, which is insurmountable – making the task as tempting as it is risky.) As in the saturnine skies of Dante's *Paradise*, the voice here is silent. It burst forth as a cry only after having gone through colours and luminous spaces, at the end of Canto XXI. Plunged into a loss of signs, a loss of the seducing figure (the compassionate or laughing mother), we finally come upon deliverance:

'And tell why the sweet symphony of Paradise
    Which below sounds so devoutly
    Is silent in this heaven.'
'Your hearing is mortal, like your vision,'
    He answered me, 'therefore there is no song here,
    For the same reason Beatrice has no smile.'[4]

In general, Bellini's paintings have a common denominator in *sacra conversazione*. It is there that the 'sacred' scene of the Western World has been knotted and arrested. It was soon to be replaced by humanism and rational knowledge, achieving the progress with which we are all familiar. But with what loss of jouissance! As such, it reappears only in the work of certain modern painters (Rothko, Matisse) who rediscovered the technique of eclipsing a figure in order to have colour produce volume. Bellini was their precursor, trapped as he was in an epoch fraught with divergent trends.

[...]

SPACES AND GLIMMERS

Saint Francis in Ecstasy (1480–1485, Frick Collection, New York) portrays the saint against a cascade of aquamarine volumes, almost entirely engulfed by their morning glow, fading into semi-darkness at lower right. On the left, near the top of the painting, diagonally across from pulpit, book, and skull of the lower right corner, there appears another space, where a landscape, a donkey, and a great deal of light suggest the divine presence. This unfolding of the painting's surface into two planes, each with its own volume, is typical of Bellini's work. Each volume bends, twists, breaks, and fragments itself separately, producing a sense of torment among the represented forms. Yet, they are also homogenised into a single luminous mass by the green hues of the foreground and the orange hues of the background. This splitting/laminating of the surface is heightened by, among other elements, curving and broken lines, winding into a green spiral (a hill) in the lower-left foreground. Yet another spiral balances the first, near the top centre, constituting the lower right angle of the backdrop. Consequently, the split/laminated surface of the painting, tormented by the luminous colour of each section, finds in its left half a spiral movement that surges upwards, in contrast to the verticality of rocks on the right. Graphic constructions that divide, covered with iridescent coloured masses that bind together this multiple surface: foreground/background, upper left-hand diagonal/lower right-hand diagonal, lower diagonal spiral on the left/centred diagonal spiral near the top, undulating left half/vertical right half. Perhaps the saint's ecstasy is precisely this union between the drawing's implacable fragmentation and a soft lining encompassing the fragments within two masses of luminous hues: green and orange. There is interplay among cutting traces, together with infinitesimal differentiations within one colour, seeking itself within its own range, up to the borders of its complementarity, until it becomes lost in pure light.

In the *Madonna with the Child Jesus, Saints Catherine and Magdalene* (1490, Academy Galleries, Venice), angular, bending space no longer arises out of the graphic carving out of the drawing. Here the painting's surface constitutes a vault, as did the Frari triptych. But while the triptych's sense of curvature is produced by the curved back wall and arched ceiling, here the cupola effect is produced by the dark colour becoming luminous. The outline of the robe covering head and rounded shoulders of the Virgin gives support to it, and the infant's upward gaze suggests it as well – one sees this at once. But the curvature is achieved essentially by the turning of the more saturated colours, filling the painting's forms and volumes, toward yellowish-white. The brick reds or purples of the saints' garments, Mary's bluish-green robe, the deep orange of their flesh and the rust-maroon tint of their hair deepen or fade with each fold, running through the spectrum, within their own hue, between two invisible limits, from black, where colour is extinguished, to bright yellow, where it dazzles. This treatment of colour as such is accentuated by an elliptical placement of blinding flashes – exposed flesh changing to yellowish-pink, as in the upper curves of the three women's heads and lower curve of their hands and the baby. The brown background is one of Bellini's fundamental discoveries. Saturated with black, green, and red, the compactness of this brown tint inverts into its opposite – a vague, liquid, invisible colour, a sparkling medium engendering and suspending bare brightness. The curved space, repeating the curves of a nude body, results from subdued colour moving across the limits of its scale to the two extremes of the spectrum. A high level of sublimation is reached at the very point where anguish appears – an anguish that nudity might otherwise have provoked and that we call eroticism.

In *The Sacred Allegory* (1490–1500, Uffizi, Florence), the tormented graphic nature of forms, fragmented by outlines but bound together by colour, is present in the background. That reminder of the graphic space of *Saint Francis in Ecstasy*, however, here becomes geometrical; more Greek, more rational in the painting's foreground, where a terrace railing opens up three sides of a rectangular volume in front of the viewer. The floor is broken up into red and black squares and hexagons, while the tree of life delineates three-fourths of its surface. Light here is not engendered, as in *Madonna with the Child Jesus, Saints Catherine and Magdalene* to create the impression of vaulted space; nor does it burst forth from a corner in order to spiral, twist, and harmonise at the same time, as it did in *Saint*

Francis in Ecstasy. It simply exists as an incandescence within the dominating orange that lights up the browns, reds, and whites, from right to left and merges into blue sky at the top centre of the painting – flight, hearth, and azure opening. Because of the dominance of variegated yellows, the wavelike or broken features of the many planes of the background, as well as the regular geometry of the foreground, open up on infinity. There are no bent surfaces and no domes. Pure luminosity bathes each figuration, including those that firmly mark the fragmented spaces, and thus allows blinding light to predominate through the yellows. It marks the limits of representation in and for which a few coloured-object elements condense – unfailingly, but so as to escape all the more easily – as reds, greens, blacks, and blues, in lieu of robes, trees, sky, mountains, human and animal figures. Now all figural representation appears as a mirage under a yellow, desert sun. This allegorical painting is said to represent Saint Bernard's commentary on the first fourteen verses of Psalm 84, the 'restoration of Israel'. As Grace, Truth, Justice, and Peace discuss humanity's salvation through the Incarnation, a finally non-threatening Yahweh himself appears, announcing the arrival of justice and peace. The three women in the painting incorporate three aspects of this *sacra converzatione*: on the left, Maria Aeterna represents Grace and Peace; on the right, a second figure represents a condensation of Truth and Justice; and on the throne, Mary assumes the place of the Father. If this interpretation of the painting is correct, we are in fact confronted with a both thematic and chromatic representation of harmony. Far from suppressing spatial or colour differences, such harmony distributes them within an open infinity as integration of the limits separating figures, drawings, and nuances in colour and as their endless bonding together. This is the sublimation of a totalising power, pushed to the limits of representability: form *and* colour.

16

Why Peter Eisenman Writes Such Good Books

Jacques Derrida

This title barely conceals a quotation from another, well known title. It lifts a fragment, or rather a person. By translating the title 'Why I write such good books' (*Warum ich so qute Bucher schreibe*) into the third person, by summoning Nietzsche's *Ecce Homo* to bear witness, I take it upon myself to clear Eisenman of all suspicion. It is not he who speaks, it is I. I who write. I who, using displacements, withdrawals, fragmentations, play with identities, with persons and their titles, with the integrity of their proper names. Has one the right to do this? But who will declare the right? And in whose name?

By abusing metonymy as well as pseudonymy, following Nietzsche's example, I propose to undertake many things – all at once, or one by one. But I will not reveal them all, and certainly not to begin with. Without giving away all the leads, the threads, I will reveal neither the route, nor the connections. Is this not the best condition for writing good texts? Whoever assumes from a simple reading of my title that I am going to diagnose the paranoia of some Nietzsche of modern architecture has mistaken the address.

First I propose to draw attention to the art with which Eisenman himself knows how to play with titles. We will take a few examples, among which, first of all, there are the titles of his books. They are made up of words. But what are words for an architect? Or books?

I also want to propose, with the allusion to *Ecce Homo*, that Eisenman is, in the realm of architecture, if you will, the most anti-Wagnerian creator of our time. What might be a Wagnerian architecture? Where would one find its remains or its disguised presence today? These questions will remain unanswered here. But isn't it true that questions of art or politics are worthy of being pondered, if not posed?

I propose to speak of music, of musical instruments in one of Eisenman's works in progress. It is unnecessary to recall the fact that *Ecce Homo* is above all a book on music, and not only in its last chapter, *Der Fall Wagner, Ein Musikanten-Problem*.

172

Finally, I propose to note that the architectural value, the very axiom of architecture that Eisenman begins by overturning, is the measure of man, that which proportions everything to a human, all too human, scale: *Menschliches, Allzumenschliches, Mit zwei Fortsetzungen*, to cite another chapter of *Ecce Homo*. Already at the entry to the labyrinth of *Moving Arrows, Eros, and Other Errors*, one can read: 'Architecture traditionally has been related to human scale.' For the 'metaphysics of scale' which Eisenman's 'scaling' attempts to destabilise is, first of all, a humanism or an anthropocentrism. It is a human, all too human, desire for 'presence' and 'origin'. Even in its theological dimensions, this architecture of originary presence returns to man under the law of representation and aesthetics: 'In destabilising presence and origin, the value that architecture gives to representation and the aesthetic object is also called into question' (ibid.).

We should not, however, simply conclude that such an architecture will be Nietzschean. We shall not borrow *themes* or rather the *philosophemes* from *Ecce Homo*, but rather some figures (or tropes), some staging and apostrophes, and then a lexicon, similar to those computerised palettes where colours may be summoned up by a keystroke before beginning to type. So, I take this phrase which in a moment you will read on the screen (I write on my computer and you well know that Nietzsche was one of the first writers to use a typewriter); it is from the beginning of *Ecce Homo*. It concerns a 'labyrinth', the labyrinth of knowledge, his very own, the most dangerous of all, to which some would wish to forbid entry: '*man wird niemals in dies Labyrinth verwegener Erkenntnisse eintreten*'; a little further on, there is a citation from *Zarathustra*, and then an allusion to those who hold 'an Ariadne's thread in a cowardly hand'. Between these two phrases, one may also lift the allusion to those bold searchers who 'embark on terrible seas' ('*auf furchtbare Meere*') and to those whose soul is lured by flutes toward all the dangerous whirlpools ('*deren Seele mit Floeten zu jedem Irrschlunde gelockt wird*'). In brief, let us agree that what we retain from the chapter 'Why I Write Such Good Books' in *Ecce Homo*, is only this: the seduction of music, the musical instrument, the sea or the abyss, and the labyrinth.

A strange introduction to architecture, you will say, and especially to that of Peter Eisenman. In which hand must the thread be held? And firmly or loosely?

It is true that this is doubtless not my subject. I would rather speak of meetings, and of what a particular *meeting* means, what takes *place* at the intersection of chance and programme, of the aleatory and the necessary.

When I met Peter Eisenman, I thought in my naïveté that *discourse* would be my realm and that architecture 'properly speaking' – places, spaces, drawing, the silent calculation, stones, the resistance of materials – would be his. Of course I was not so naïve; I knew that discourse and language did not count for nothing in the activity of architects and above all in Eisenman's. I even had reason to think that they were more important than the architects themselves realised. But I did not understand to what extent, and above all in what way, his architecture confronted the very conditions of discourse, grammar, and semantics. Nor did I then understand why Eisenman is a writer – which, far from distancing him from architecture and making him one of those 'theoreticians' (who, as those who do neither say, write more than they build), on the contrary opens a space in which two writings, the verbal and the architectural, are inscribed, the one within the other, outside the traditional hierarchies. That is to say, what Eisenman writes 'with words' is not limited to a so-called theoretical reflection on the architectural object, which attempts to define what this object has been or what it ought to be. Certainly this aspect is to be found in Eisenman, but there is still something else, something that does not simply develop as a metalanguage on (or about) a certain traditional authority of discourse in architecture. This may be characterised as another treatment of the word, of another 'poetics', if you like, which participates with full legitimacy in the invention of architecture without submitting it to the order of discourse.

Our meeting was indeed a chance for me. But the *aléa* – as with all encounters – must have been programmed within an unfathomable agenda which I will not take the risk of analysing here. Let us begin at the point when Bernard Tschumi proposed to both of us that we collaborate in the conception of what was called, by convention, a 'garden' in the Parc de La Villette, a rather strange garden in that it does not admit any vegetation, only liquids and solids, water and minerals. I will not elaborate here on my first contribution, which was a text on the Chora in Plato's *Timeaus*. The unfathomable enigma of what Plato says about the architect-demiurge, of the place, of the inscription which imprints in it (in the place) the images of paradigms, etc., all this seemed to me to merit a kind of architectural test, a rigorous challenge: a challenge at once rigorous and necessary, inevitably rigorous, to all the text's poetic, rhetorical, and political stakes, with all the difficulties of reading which have resisted centuries of interpretation. But once again, I do not wish to speak here of what happened on my side of the proposition that I put forward, even as I put myself forward with the greatest misgivings. What is important here is what came from the other side, from Peter Eisenman.

As things seemed to have begun with words and a book, I quickly had to accept the obvious. Eisenman does not only take great pleasure, jubilation, in playing with language, with languages, at the meeting, the crossing of many idioms, welcoming chances, attentive to risk, to transplants, to the slippings and derivations of the letter. He also takes this play seriously, if one can say this, and without giving himself the principal, inductive, role in a work that one hesitates to call properly or purely architectural, without setting up this play of the letter as a *determining origin* (such a thing never exists for Eisenman), he does not leave it *outside the work*. For him, words are not *exergues*.

I will cite only two examples.

After he had translated, or rather transferred and transformed certain motifs appropriated by himself and for himself from my Chora text in a first architectural project, a limitless palimpsest, with 'scaling', 'quarry', and 'labyrinth', I insisted, and Eisenman fully agreed, on the need to give our common work a title, and an inventive title at that, one which did not have as its sole function the gathering of collective meaning, the production of those effects of legitimising identification which one expects from titles in general. On the other hand, precisely because what we were making was not a garden (the category under which the administration of La Villette naïvely classified the space entrusted to us), but something else, a place yet without name, if not unnameable, it was necessary to give it a name, and with this naming make a new gesture, a supplementary element of the project itself, something other than a simple reference to a thing that would exist in any case without its name, outside the name.

Three conditions seemed to be required.

1. That this title would be as strong, as subsuming, and as economical of the work as possible. Such was the 'classic' and normally referential function of the title and the name.

2. That this title, while designating the work from outside, should also be part of the work, imprinting it from within with an indispensable motion, so that the letters of the name would participate in this way in the very body of the architecture.

3. That the verbal structure should maintain such a relationship to the *aléa* of meeting of such a kind that no semantic order could stop the play, or totalise it from a centre, an origin or a principle.

Choral Work, this was the title invented by Eisenman.

Even though it surfaced at a moment when long discussions had already given rise to the first 'drawings' and the principal schema of the work, this title seemed to have imposed itself all of a sudden: by chance, but also as the result of calculation. No arguing, no reservations were possible. The title was perfect.

1. It names in the most apt fashion, by means of the most efficient and *economic* reference, a work that in its own way interprets, in a dimension that is both discursive and architectural, a reading of the platonic *chora*. The name *chora* is carried over into song (choral) and even into choreography. With the final *l*, choral: *chora* becomes more liquid or more aerial, I do not dare to say, more feminine.

2. It becomes indissociable from a construction on which it imposes from within a new dimension: choreographic, musical and vocal at the

same time. Speech, even song, are thus inscribed in the work, taking their place within a rhythmic composition. To give way to, or to take place is, in either sense, to make an architectural event out of music, or rather out of a choir.

3. In addition to being a musical allusion – and even a choreographic one in Plato's *chora* – this title is more than a title. It also designs a signature, a plural signature, written by both of us in concert. Eisenman had just done what he said he was doing. The performance, the felicitous efficacy of the performative, consisted in inventing by himself the form of a signature that not only signed for both of us, but enunciated in itself the plurality of the choral signature, the cosignature or the counter-signature. He gives me his signature in the sense one says of someone giving to a collaborator the 'power' to sign in his place. The work becomes musical, an architecture for many voices, at once different and harmonised in their very alterity. This comprises a gift as precious as it is petrified, a coral (*corail*). As if water had naturally allied itself with minerals for this simulacrum of spontaneous creation in the unconscious depths of some shared or divided ocean. *Ecce Homo*: the abyss of depths without bottom, music, a hyperbolic labyrinth.

The law is at the same time respected and mocked because the commission that we had been given also prescribed this: only water and stone should be used for this pseudo-garden and above all, no vegetation. And this was what had been created with a single blow, with a wave of the magic wand, in two words, so close to silence: the magic wand is also the baton of an orchestra conductor. I still hear it now, like the masterpiece of a maker of fireworks, the explosion of a fire-cracker. And how could I not be reminded of the *Music for the Royal Fireworks*, of the chorale, of Corelli's influence, of that 'architectural sense' we always admire in Handel.

The elements are thus brought to light, exposed to the air: earth, water and fire – as in the *Timeaus*, at the moment of the formation of the *cosmos*. But it is impossible to assign an order, a hierarchy or principle of deduction or derivation to all the meanings that intersect as if from a chance meeting, in hardly more than ten letters, sealed, forged (coined) in the idiomatic forge (forgery) of a single language. The 'title' is condensed in the stamp, the seal or the initials of this countersignature (because this was also a way not to sign while signing), but at the same time, it opens up the whole to which it seems to belong. Thus there is no capital role to be played by this title, itself open to other interpretations or, one might say, other performances, other musicians, other choreographers, or even other voices. Totalisation is impossible.

We might draw out some other threads, other chords in this labyrinthine skein. Eisenman often refers to the labyrinth to describe the routes called for by certain of his works:

These superpositions appear in a labyrinth, which is located at the site of the castle of Juliet. Like the story of Romeo and Juliet, it is an analogic expression of the unresolved tension between fate and free will. Here the labyrinth, like the castle sites, becomes a palimpsest.

Like the work it names, the title *Choral Work* is at the same time palimpsest and labyrinth, a maze of superimposed structures (Plato's text, the reading of it that I have proposed in my text, the slaughterhouses of La Villette, Eisenman's project for Venice (Cannaregio) and Tschumi's 'Follies'). In French, in a phrase that remains untranslatable, one would say: the title *se donne carrière*. 'Carrière' means quarry. But 'se donner carrière' is also to give free rein, to appropriate a space with a certain joyful insolence. Literally, I understand it in the sense of 'carrière' which at once gives itself graciously, offering up its own resources, but belongs first and foremost to the very space it enriches. How can one *give* in this way? How can one, while drawing from it, enrich the totality of which it forms a part? What is this strange economy of the gift? In *Choral Work* and elsewhere, Eisenman plays the game of constituting a part of the whole 'en carrière' (as quarry), as a mine of materials to be displaced for the rest at the interior of the same ensemble. The quarry is at the same time inside and outside, the resources are included. And the structure of our title obeys the same law, it has the same form of potentiality, the same power: the dynamics of an immanent invention. Everything is found inside but it is almost unforeseeable.

For my second example, I must pluck another chord/string. This musical and choreographic architecture was going to point toward, as if it incorporated or cited them in itself, both a poetic genre, that is, the *lyric*, and the stringed instrument which corresponds to this genre – the lyre.

The title was already given and we had progressed in the preparation of *Choral Work*, when Eisenman suggested that I finally take an initiative that was not solely discursive, theoretical or 'philosophical' (I place this word between quotation marks because the reading of the *chora* that I propose perhaps no longer belongs to the realm of philosophical thought, but we will leave this aside). He wanted, with justification, our choir to be more than the simple aggregation of two soloists, a writer and an architect. If the architect signed and 'designated', de-signed with words, I should for my part project or design visible forms. On returning from New York, in the airplane, I wrote Eisenman a letter containing a design and its interpretation. Thinking of one of the most enigmatic (to my mind) passages in Plato's *Timeaus*, I wanted the figure of a sieve to be inscribed on, in, and within the *Choral Work* itself, as the memory of a synecdoche or an errant metonymy. It would be errant in the sense that no reprise would be possible in any totality of which it would figure only a detached piece: neither fragment nor ruin. For the *Timeaus*, in effect, utilises what one no doubt calls abusively a metaphor, that of the sieve, in order to describe the way in which the place (the chora) filters the 'types', the forces or seeds that have been impressed on it:

> The nurse of becoming was characterised by the qualities of water and fire, of earth and air, and by others that go with them, and its visual appearance was therefore varied; but as there was no homogeneity or balance in the forces that filled it, no part of it was in equilibrium, but it swayed unevenly under the impact of their motion, and in turn communicated its motion to them. And its contents were in constant process of movement and separation, rather like the contents of a winnowing basket or similar implement for cleaning corn, in which the solid and heavy stuff is sifted out and settles on one side, the light and insubstantial on another: so the four basic constituents were shaken by the receptacle, which acted as a kind of shaking implement. (*Timeaus* 52e–53a)[1]

This is not the place to explain why I have always found this passage to be provocative and fascinating by reason of the very resistance it offers to reading. This is of little importance here. As if to give a body to this fascination, I thus wrote this letter to Eisenman on the airplane, a fragment of which you will permit me to cite:

> You will recall what we envisaged when we were together at Yale: that in order to finish, I would 'write', so to speak, without a single word, a heterogeneous piece, without origin or apparent destination, as if it were a fragment arriving, without indicating any totality (lost or promised), in order to break the circle of reappropriation, the triad of the three sites (Eisenman–Derrida, Tschumi, La Villette); to break, in short, the totalisation, the still too-historical configuration, so that it would be open to a general decipherment. And nevertheless I thought that, without giving any assurance on this subject, that some detached and enigmatic metonymy, rebelling against the history of the three sites and even against the palimpsest, should 'recall' by chance if one encountered it, something, the most incomprehensible of all, of the *chora*. For myself, today, that which I find the most enigmatic, which resists and provokes the most, in the reading which I am undertaking of the *Timeaus* is (we can talk about this again later), the allusion to the figure of the *sieve* (*plokanon*, a work or braided cord, 52e), and to the *chora* as *sieve* (sieve, sift, I also love these English words). There is in the *Timeaus* a figural allusion which I do not know how to interpret and which nevertheless seems to me decisive. It speaks of something like movement, the shaking (*seiesthai, seien, seiomena*), the tremor in the course of which a selection of the forces or seeds *takes place*; a sorting

a filtering in the very place where, nevertheless, the place remains impassive, indeterminate, amorphous, etc. It seems to me that this passage in the *Timeaus* is as erratic, as difficult to integrate, as deprived of origin and of manifest *telos* as that piece we have imagined for our *Choral Work*.

Thus I propose the following approximate 'representation', 'materialisation', 'formation': in one or three examples (if there are three, then each with different scalings), a *gilded* metal object (there is gold in the passage from the *Timeaus*, on the *chora*, and in your Cannaregio project) to be planted obliquely in the earth. Neither vertical, nor horizontal, an extremely solid frame that would resemble at once a web, a sieve, or a grill (grid) and a stringed musical instrument (piano, harp, lyre?: strings, stringed instrument, vocal chord, etc.). As a grill,

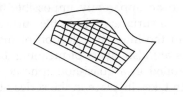

grid, etc., it would have a certain relationship with the *filter* (a telescope or a photographic acid bath, or a machine which has fallen from the sky having photographed or x-rayed – filtered – an aerial view). This would be both an interpretive and *selective* filter which would allow the reading and the sieving of the three sites and the three layers (Eisenman–Derrida, Tschumi, La Villette). As a stringed instrument, it would announce the concert and the multiple chorale, the *chora* of *Choral Work*.

I do not think that anything should be inscribed on this sculpture (for this is a sculpture), save perhaps the title, and a signature might figure somewhere (i.e. *Choral Work*, by ... 1986), as well as one or two Greek words (*plokanon, seiomena*, etc.). We should discuss this, among other things ... (30 May 1986)

One will note in this passage, the allusion to the filtering of a selective interpretation that evokes, in my letter, Nietzsche and a certain scene played out between Nietzsche and the pre-Socratics – those same figures that seem to haunt a given passage in the *Timeaus* (Democritus, for example).

So what does Eisenman do? He interprets in his turn, actively and selectively. He translates, transposes, transforms and appropriates my letter, rewriting it in *his* language, in his *languages*, both architectural structure (a structure that is already quite fixed): that of a lyre, lying down at an oblique angle. Then, in a change of scale, he re-inscribes it in its very interior, as a small lyre within a large one. He is not content to create a metonomy *en abyme*[2] at the bottom of the ocean where the coral is deposited in sediments, in order to outsmart the ruses of totalising reason. Among all the stringed instruments evoked in my letter (piano, harp, lyre) he chooses one, whose play he reinvents in his own language, English. And in inventing another architectural device, he transcribes this linguistic reinvention, one which is his, his own.

What then in fact happens? First he adds another justification and another dimension to the open title *Choral Work*, which then finds itself enriched and overdetermined. Then, on all the semantic and even formal strings/chords of the word 'lyre', which happens to be homographic in both French and English – we hear the resonance of different texts. These are added, superposed, superimposed one *within* the other, *on* or *under* the other according to an apparently impossible and unrepresentable topology seen through a surface; an invisible surface, certainly, but one which is audible from the internal reflection of many resonant layers. These resonant layers are also layers of meaning, but you immediately recognise what is implied in a quasi-homophonic way, in the English word *layer* which both takes its place in the series of layers I have noted and designates the totality.

The strata of this palimpsest, its 'layers' are thus bottomless, since, for the reasons I have given, they do not allow of totalisation.

Now, this structure of the non-totalisable palimpsest which draws from one of its elements the resources for the others (their *carrière* or quarry), and which makes an unrepresentable and unobjectifiable labyrinth out of this play of internal differences (scale without end, *scaling* without hierarchy): this is precisely the structure of *Choral Work*. Its structure of stone and metal, the superposition of layers (La Villette, the Eisenman–Derrida project, Tschumi's Follies, etc.) plunges into the abyss of the 'platonic' *chora*. 'Lyre', 'layers', would thus be a good title, over-title, or sub-title for *Choral Work*. And this title is inscribed *in* the work, like a piece of the very thing which it names. It says the truth of the work in the body of the work; it says the truth in a word which is many words, a kind of many-leaved book, but that is also the visible figure of a lyre, the visibility of an instrument which foments the invisible: music. And everything that 'lyric', in a word, may suggest.

But, for these same reasons, the truth of *Choral Work*, the truth which *lyre* or *layer* says and does and gives is not a truth: it is not presentable, representable, totalisable; it never shows itself. It gives rise to no revelation of presence, still less to an adequation. It is an irreducible inadequation which we have just evoked; and also a challenge to the *subjectile*. For all these layers of meaning and forms, of visibility and invisibility extend (lie, as in layers) *into* each other, *on*, or *under* each other, *in front* of or *behind* each other, but the truth of the relationship is never established, never stabilised in any judgement. It always causes something else to be said – allegorically – than that which is said. *In a word*, it causes one to lie. The truth of the work lies in this lying strength, this liar who accompanies all our representations (as Kant notes of the 'I think') but who also accompanies them as a lyre can accompany a choir.

Without equivalent and therefore without opposition. In this abyssal palimpsest, no truth can establish itself on any primitive or final presence of the meaning. In the labyrinth of this coral, the truth is the non-truth, the errance of one of those 'errors' which belong to the title of another labyrinth, another palimpsest, another 'quarry'. I have been speaking about this other for some time now without naming it directly. I speak of Romeo and Juliet, an entire story of names and contretemps about which I have also written elsewhere;[3] here, I speak of Eisenman's *Romeo and Juliet*, *Moving Arrows, Eros and Other Errors*. Have I not then lied? Have I not allegorically been speaking all this while about something other than that which you believed? Yes and no. The lie is without contrary, both absolute and null. It does not mislead in error, but in those 'moving errors' whose erring is at once finite and infinite, random and programmed. For this lie without contrary, there is no liar to be found. What remains 'is' the unfindable, something entirely different from a signatory, conscious and assured of its mastery, entirely different from a subject; rather an infinite series of subjectiles and countersignatories, you among them, ready to take, to pay or miss the pleasure given by the passing of Eros. Liar or lyre, this is the royal name, for the moment, one of the best names, by which to signify, that is, the homonym and the pseudonym, the multiple voice of this secret signatory, the encrypted title of *Choral Work*. But if I say that we owe this to language more than to Peter Eisenman, you will ask me 'which language?' There are so many. Do you mean the *meeting* of languages? An architecture which is at least tri-or quadrilingual, of polyglot stones or metals?

– But if I tell you that we owe this chance to Peter Eisenman, whose own name, as you know, embodies both stone and metal, will you believe me? Nevertheless, I tell you the truth. It is the truth of this man of iron, determined to break with the anthropomorphic scale, with 'man the measure of all things': he writes such good books! I swear it to you!

– This is of course what all the liars say; they would not be lying if they did not say that they were telling the truth.

– I see that you do not believe me; let us explain things in another way. What is it that I hoped to have shown, about the subject of the *Choral Work*, all the while proposing with the other hand an autobiographical description of my meeting with Peter Eisenman, in all of the languages which are at work within him? All of this in truth refers to two other works, the *Fin d'Ou T Hou S* and *Moving Arrows, Eros, and Other Errors*. That which Jeffrey Kipnis correctly analysed as 'the endless play of readings'[4] is equally valuable for these three works. Each of the three is at the same time bigger and smaller than the series, which no doubt also includes the project for Venice (Cannaregio) and several others. And I had to find an economic way of speaking about all three at once and in a few pages, those which were allowed me. Similarly, at La Villette, we had little space, a single space with which we had to work. We had already multiplied it or divided it by three within itself and we hoped to multiply it by three again in the future. For the moment we have to find a structure which multiplies within a given economy, *faisant flèche de tout bois* [literally, 'making an arrow out of any piece of wood,' i.e. making the best of one's resources], as we say in French, when meaning is displaced like an arrow, without ever being allowed to stop or collect itself, we will no longer oppose the errors which it provokes and which indeed are no longer lies, to the truth. Among *errors, eros,* and *arrows,* the transformation is endless, and the contamination at once inevitable and aleatory. None of Eisenman's three projects presides at the meeting. They intersect like arrows, making a generative force out of misreadings, misspellings, mispronunciations, a force which speaks of pleasure at the same time as procuring it. If I had enough time and enough space, I would analyse the stratagems with which Peter Eisenman plays, and what he has to do in his books, that is to say, in his constructions also, in order to fly like an arrow all the while avoiding being trapped by oppositions with which he nevertheless has to negotiate. The absence which he speaks of in *Moving Arrows . . .* is not opposed, and above all, is not dialectically opposed to presence. Linked as it is to the discontinuous structure of 'scaling', it is not a mere void. Determined by recursivity and by the internal-external difference of 'self-similarity', this absence 'produces', it 'is' (without being, nor being an origin or a productive cause) a *text*, better and something other than a 'good book'; more that a book, more than one; a text like 'an unending *transformation* of properties': 'Rather than an aesthetic object, the object becomes a text . . . ' That which overturns the opposition presence/absence, and thus an entire ontology, must nevertheless be advanced within the language that it transforms in this way, within which is inscribed that which this language literally contains *without* containing, is found imprinted. Eisenman's architecture marks this 'without' (which I prefer to write in English), with/without, within and out, etc. We are related to this 'without' of the language, by dominating it in order to play with it, and at the same time in order to be subjected to the law, its law which is the law *of* the language, of languages, in truth of all marks. We are in this sense at the same time both passive and active. And we could say something *analogous* on the subject of this active/passive opposition in the texts of Eisenman, something analogous as well on the subject of analogies. But one must also know how to stop an arrow. He too knows how to do it.

We might be tempted to speak here of an architectural *Witz*, of a new textual economy (and *oikos*, after all, *is* the house; Eisenman also builds houses), an economy in which we no longer have to exclude the invisible from the visible, to oppose the temporal and the spatial, discourse and architecture. Not that we confuse them, but we distribute them according to another hierarchy, a hier-archy without an 'arche', a memory without origin, a hierarchy without hierarchy.

What there is there (there is, *es gibt*) is something beyond *Witz*, as in beyond the pleasure principle, if at least we understand these two words, *Witz* and *plaisir* as implying the intractable law of saving and economy.

Finally, to raise the question of the book once more: there are those who would like sometimes to imply somewhat facilely, that the most innovative 'theoretician' architects write books instead of building. It should not be forgotten that those who hold to this dogma generally do neither one nor the other. Eisenman writes, in effect. But in order to break with the norms and the authority of the existing economy, he needed, by means of something which still resembled a book *effectively* to clear a new space in which this an-economy would be at the same time possible and, to a certain point, legitimised, negotiated. This negotiation takes place within time, and it needs time with the powers and the cultures of the moment. For beyond the economy, beyond the book, whose form still displays this encompassing mania of speech, he writes something else.

It is a *topos*: monuments have often been compared to books.[5] Eisenman's 'libretti' are, no doubt, no longer books. Nor are they at all 'good and beautiful'. They pass the test of calligraphy or of the *callistique*, that ancient name for the aesthetic. I would not say that they are, notwithstanding, sublime. In its very disproportionateness, the sublime is still a human measure.

Ecce Homo: end, the end of all, *la fin de tout*.

17

Las Meninas

Michel Foucault

I

The painter is standing a little back from his canvas (Plate 3). He is glancing at his model; perhaps he is considering whether to add some finishing touch, though it is also possible that the first stroke has not yet been made. The arm holding the brush is bent to the left, towards the palette; it is motionless, for an instant, between canvas and paints. The skilled hand is suspended in mid-air, arrested in rapt attention on the painter's gaze; and the gaze, in return, waits upon the arrested gesture. Between the fine point of the brush and the steely gaze, the scene is about to yield up its volume.

But not without a subtle system of feints. By standing back a little, the painter has placed himself to one side of the painting on which he is working. That is, for the spectator at present observing him he is to the right of his canvas, while the latter, the canvas, takes up the whole of the extreme left. And the canvas has its back turned to that spectator: he can see nothing of it but the reverse side, together with the huge frame on which it is stretched. The painter, on the other hand, is perfectly visible in his full height; or at any rate, he is not masked by the tall canvas which may soon absorb him, when, taking a step towards it again, he returns to his task; he has no doubt just appeared, at this very instant, before the eyes of the spectator, emerging from what is virtually a sort of vast cage projected backwards by the surface he is painting. Now he can be seen, caught in a moment of stillness, at the neutral centre of this oscillation. His dark torso and bright face are half-way between the visible and the invisible: emerging from that canvas beyond our view, he moves into our gaze; but when, in a moment, he makes a step to the right, removing himself from our gaze, he will be standing exactly in front of the canvas he is painting; he will enter that region where his painting, neglected for an instant, will, for him, become visible once more, free of shadow and free of reticence. As though the painter could not at the same time be seen on the picture where he is represented and also see that upon which he is representing something. He rules at the threshold of those two incompatible visibilities.

Plate 3   Diego Velázquez, *Las Meninas* (1656) Museo del Prado, Madrid. Reproduced courtesy of AKG, London, Museo del Prado

The painter is looking, his face turned slightly and his head leaning towards one shoulder. He is staring at a point to which, even though it is invisible, we, the spectators, can easily assign an object, since it is we, ourselves, who are that point: our bodies, our faces, our eyes. The spectacle he is observing is thus doubly invisible: first, because it is not represented within the space of the painting, and, second, because it is situated precisely in that blind point, in that essential hiding-place into which our gaze disappears from ourselves at the moment of our actual looking. And yet, how could we fail to see that invisibility, there in front of our eyes, since it has its own perceptible equivalent, its sealed-in figure, in the painting itself? We could, in effect, guess what it is the painter is looking at if it were possible for us to glance for a moment at the canvas he is working on; but all we can see of that canvas is its texture, the horizontal and vertical bars of the stretcher, and the obliquely rising foot of the easel. The tall, monotonous rectangle occupying the whole left portion of the real picture, and representing the back of the canvas within the picture, reconstitutes in the form of a surface the invisibility in depth of what the artist is observing: that space in which we are, and which we are. From the eyes of the painter to what he is observing there runs a compelling line that we, the onlookers, have no power of evading: it runs through the real picture and emerges from its surface to join the place from which we see the painter observing us; this dotted line reaches out to us ineluctably, and links us to the representation of the picture.

In appearance, this locus is a simple one; a matter of pure reciprocity: we are looking at a picture in which the painter is in turn looking out at us. A mere confrontation, eyes catching one another's glance, direct looks superimposing themselves upon one another as they cross. And yet this slender line of reciprocal visibility embraces a whole complex network of uncertainties, exchanges, and feints. The painter is turning his eyes towards us only in so far as we happen to occupy the same position as his subject. We, the spectators, are an additional factor. Though greeted by that gaze, we are also dismissed by it, replaced by that which was always there before we were: the model itself. But, inversely, the painter's gaze, addressed to the void confronting him outside the picture, accepts as many models as there are spectators; in this precise but neutral place, the observer and the observed take part in a ceaseless exchange. No gaze is stable, or rather, in the neutral furrow of the gaze piercing at a right angle through the canvas, subject and object, the spectator and the model, reverse their roles to infinity. And here the great canvas with its back to us on the extreme left of the picture exercises its second function: stubbornly invisible, it prevents the relation of these gazes from ever being discoverable or definitely established. The opaque fixity that it establishes on one side renders forever unstable the play of metamorphoses established in the centre between spectator and model. Because we can see only that reverse side, we do not know who we are, or what we are doing. Seen or seeing? The painter is observing a place which, from moment to moment, never ceases to change its content, its form, its face, its identity. But the attentive immobility of his eyes refers us back to another direction which they have often followed already, and which soon, there can be no doubt, they will take again: that of the motionless canvas upon which is being traced, has already been traced perhaps, for a long time and forever, a portrait that will never again be erased. So that the painter's sovereign gaze commands a virtual triangle whose outline defines this picture of a picture: at the top – the only visible corner – the painter's eyes; at one of the base angles, the invisible place occupied by the model; at the other base angle, the figure probably sketched out on the invisible surface of the canvas.

As soon as they place the spectator in the field of their gaze, the painter's eyes seize hold of him, force him to enter the picture, assign him a place at once privileged and inescapable, levy their luminous and visible tribute from him, and project it upon the inaccessible surface of the canvas within the picture. He sees his invisibility made visible to the painter and transposed into an image forever invisible to himself. A shock that is augmented and made more inevitable still by a marginal trap. At the extreme right, the picture is lit by a window represented in very sharp perspective; so sharp that we can see scarcely more than the embrasure; so that the flood of light streaming through it bathes at the same time, and with equal generosity, two neighbouring spaces, over-lapping but irreducible: the surface of the painting, together with the volume it represents (which is to say, the painter's studio, or the salon in which his easel is now set up), and, in front of that surface, the real volume occupied by the spectator (or again, the unreal site of the model). And as it passes through the room from right to left, this vast flood of golden light carries both the spectator towards the painter and the model towards the canvas; it is this light too, which, washing over the painter, makes him visible to the spectator and turns into golden lines, in the model's eyes, the frame of that enigmatic canvas on which his image, once transported there, is to be imprisoned. This extreme, partial, scar-cely indicated window frees a whole flow of daylight which serves as the common locus of the representation. It balances the invisible canvas on the other side of the picture: just as that canvas, by turning its back to the spectators, folds itself in against the picture representing it, and forms, by the superimposition of its reverse and visible side upon the surface of the picture depicting it, the ground, inaccessible to us, on which there shim-mers the Image *par excellence*, so does the window, a pure aperture, establish a space as manifest as the other is hidden; as much the common ground of painter, figures, models, and spectators, as the other is solitary (for no one is looking at it, not even the painter). From the right, there streams in through an invisible window the pure volume of a light that renders all representation visible; to the left extends the surface that conceals, on the other side of its all too visible woven texture, the repre-sentation it bears. The light, by flooding the scene (I mean the room as well as the canvas, the room represented on the canvas, and the room in which the canvas stands), envelops the figures and the spectators and carries them with it, under the painter's gaze, towards the place where his brush will represent them. But that place is concealed from us. We are observing ourselves being observed by the painter, and made visible to his eyes by the same light that enables us to see him. And just as we are about to apprehend ourselves, transcribed by his hand as though in a mirror, we find that we can in fact apprehend nothing of that mirror but its lustreless back. The other side of a psyche.

Now, as it happens, exactly opposite the spectators – ourselves – on the wall forming the far end of the room, Velázquez has represented a series of pictures; and we see that among all those hanging canvases there is one that shines with particular brightness. Its frame is wider and darker than those of the others; yet there is a fine white line around its inner edge diffusing over its whole surface a light whose source is not easy to determine; for it comes from nowhere, unless it be from a space within itself. In this strange light, two silhouettes are apparent, while above them, and a little behind them, is a heavy purple curtain. The other pictures reveal little more than a few paler patches buried in a darkness without depth. This particular one, on the other hand, opens onto a perspective of space in which recognisable forms recede from us in a light that belongs only to itself. Among all these elements intended to provide representations, while impeding them, hiding them, concealing them because of their position or their distance from us, this is the only one that fulfils its function in all honesty and enables us to see what it is supposed to show. Despite its distance from us, despite the shadows all around it. But it isn't a picture: it is a mirror. It offers us at last that enchantment of the double that until now has been denied us, not only by the distant paintings but also by the light in the foreground with its ironic canvas.

Of all the representations represented in the picture this is the only one visible; but no one is looking at it. Upright beside his canvas, his attention entirely taken up by his model, the painter is unable to see this looking-glass shining so softly behind him. The other figures in the picture are also, for the most part, turned to face what must be taking place in front – towards the bright invisibility bordering the canvas, towards that balcony of light where their eyes can gaze at those who are gazing back at them, and not towards that dark recess which marks the far end of the room in which they are represented. There are, it is true, some heads turned away from us in profile: but not one of them is turned far enough to see, at the back of the room, that solitary mirror, that tiny glowing rectangle which is nothing other than visibility, yet without any gaze able to grasp it, to render it actual, and to enjoy the suddenly ripe fruit of the spectacle it offers.

It must be admitted that this indifference is equalled only by the mirror's own. It is reflecting nothing, in fact, of all that is there in the same space as itself: neither the painter with his back to it, nor the figures in the centre of the room. It is not the visible it reflects, in those bright depths. In Dutch painting it was traditional for mirrors to play a duplicating role: they repeated the original contents of the picture, only inside an unreal, modified, contracted, concave space. One saw in them the same things as one saw in the first instance in the painting, but decomposed and recomposed according to a different law. Here, the mirror is saying nothing that has already been said before. Yet its position is more or less completely central: its upper edge is exactly on an imaginary line running half-way between the top and the bottom of the painting, it hangs right in the middle of the far wall (or at least in the middle of the portion we can see); it ought, therefore, to be governed by the same lines of perspective as the picture itself; we might well expect the same studio, the same painter, the same canvas to be arranged within it according to an identical space; it could be the perfect duplication.

In fact, it shows us nothing of what is represented in the picture itself. Its motionless gaze extends out in front of the picture, into that necessarily invisible region which forms its exterior face, to apprehend the figures arranged in that space. Instead of surrounding visible objects, this mirror cuts straight through the whole field of the representation, ignoring all it might apprehend within that field, and restores visibility to that which resides outside all view. But the invisibility that it overcomes in this way is not the invisibility of what is hidden: it does not make its way around any obstacle, it is not distorting any perspective, it is addressing itself to what is invisible both because of the picture's structure and because of its existence as painting. What it is reflecting is that which all the figures within the painting are looking at so fixedly, or at least those who are looking straight ahead; it is therefore what the spectator would be able to see if the painting extended further forward, if its bottom edge were brought lower until it included the figures the painter is using as models. But it is also, since the picture does stop there, displaying only the painter and his studio, what is exterior to the picture, in so far as it is a picture – in other words, a rectangular fragment of lines and colours intended to represent something to the eyes of any possible spectator. At the far end of the room, ignored by all, the unexpected mirror holds in its glow the figures that the painter is looking at (the painter in his represented, objective reality, the reality of the painter at his work); but also the figures that are looking at the painter (in that material reality which the lines and the colours have laid out upon the canvas). These two groups of figures are both equally inaccessible, but in different ways: the first because of an effect of composition peculiar to the painting; the second because of the law that presides over the very existence of all pictures in general. Here, the action of representation consists in bringing one of these two forms of invisibility into the place of the other, in an unstable superimposition – and in rendering them both, at the same moment, at the other extremity of the picture – at that pole which is the very height of its representation: that of a reflected depth in the far recess of the painting's depth. The mirror provides a metathesis of visibility that affects both the space represented in the picture and its nature as representation; it allows us to see, in the centre of the canvas, what in the painting is of necessity doubly invisible.

A strangely literal, though inverted, application of the advice given, so it is said, to his pupil by the old Pachero when the former was working in his studio in Seville: 'The image should stand out from the frame.'

II

But perhaps it is time to give a name at last to that image which appears in the depths of the mirror, and which the painter is contemplating in front of the picture. Perhaps it would be better, once and for all, to determine the identities of all the figures presented or indicated here, so as to avoid embroiling ourselves forever in those vague, rather abstract designations, so constantly prone to misunderstanding and duplication, 'the painter', 'the characters', 'the models', 'the spectators', 'the images'. Rather than pursue to infinity a language inevitably inadequate to the visible fact, it would be better to say that Velázquez composed a picture; that in this picture he represented himself, in his studio or in a room of the Escurial, in the act of painting two figures whom the Infanta Margarita has come there to watch, together with an entourage of duennas, maids of honour, courtiers, and dwarfs; that we can attribute names to this group of people with great precision: tradition recognises that here we have Doña Maria Agustina Sarmiente, over there Nieto, in the foreground Nicolaso Pertusato, an Italian jester. We could then add that the two personages serving as models to the painter are not visible, at least directly; but that we can see them in a mirror; and that they are, without any doubt, King Philip IV and his wife, Mariana.

These proper names would form useful landmarks and avoid ambiguous designations; they would tell us in any case what the painter is looking at, and the majority of the characters in the picture along with him. But the relation of language to painting is an infinite relation. It is not that words are imperfect, or that, when confronted by the visible, they prove insuperably inadequate. Neither can be reduced to the other's terms: it is in vain that we say what we see; what we see never resides in what we say. And it is in vain that we attempt to show, by the use of images, metaphors, or similes, what we are saying; the space where they achieve their splendour is not that deployed by our eyes but that defined by the sequential elements of syntax. And the proper name, in this particular context, is merely an artifice: it gives us a finger to point with, in other words, to pass surreptitiously from the space where one speaks to the space where one looks; in other words, to fold one over the other as though they were equivalents. But if one wishes to keep the relation of language to vision open, if one wishes to treat their incompatibility as a starting-point for speech instead of as an obstacle to be avoided, so as to stay as close as possible to both, then one must erase those proper names and preserve the infinity of the task. It is perhaps through the medium of this grey, anonymous language, always over-meticulous and repetitive because too broad, that the painting may, little by little, release its illuminations.

We must therefore pretend not to know who is to be reflected in the depths of that mirror, and interrogate that reflection in its own terms.

First, it is the reverse of the great canvas represented on the left. The reverse, or rather the right side, since it displays in full face what the canvas, by its position, is hiding from us. Furthermore, it is both in opposition to the window and a reinforcement of it. Like the window, it provides a ground which is common to the painting and to what lies outside it. But the window operates by the continuous movement of an effusion which, flowing from right to left, unites the attentive figures, the painter, and the canvas, with the spectacle they are observing; whereas the mirror, on the other hand, by means of a violent, instantaneous movement, a movement of pure surprise, leaps out from the picture in order to reach that which is observed yet invisible in front of it, and then, at the far end of its fictitious depth, to render it visible yet indifferent to every gaze. The compelling tracer line, joining the reflection to that which it is reflecting, cuts perpendicularly through the lateral flood of light. Lastly – and this is the mirror's third function – it stands adjacent to a doorway which forms an opening, like the mirror itself, in the far wall of the room. This doorway too forms a bright and sharply defined rectangle whose soft light does not shine through into the room. It would be nothing but a gilded panel if it were not recessed out from the room by means of one leaf of a carved door, the curve of a curtain, and the shadows of several steps. Beyond the steps, a corridor begins; but instead of losing itself in obscurity, it is dissipated in a yellow dazzle where the light, without coming in, whirls around on itself in dynamic repose. Against this background, at once near and limitless, a man stands out in full-length silhouette; he is seen in profile; with one hand he is holding back the weight of a curtain; his feet are placed on different steps; one knee is bent. He may be about to enter the room; or he may be merely observing what is going on inside it, content to surprise those within without being seen himself. Like the mirror, his eyes are directed towards the other side of the scene; nor is anyone paying any more attention to him than to the mirror. We do not know where he has come from: it could be that by following uncertain corridors he has just made his way around the outside of the room in which these characters are collected and the painter is at work; perhaps he too, a short while ago, was there in the forefront of the scene, in the invisible region still being contemplated by all those eyes in the picture. Like the images perceived in the looking-glass, it is possible that he too is an emissary from that evident yet hidden space. Even so, there is a difference: he is there in flesh and blood; he has appeared from the outside, on the threshold of the area represented; he is indubitable – not a probable reflection but an irruption. The mirror, by making visible, beyond even the walls of the studio itself, what is happening in front of the picture, creates, in its sagittal dimension, an oscillation between the interior and the exterior. One foot only on the lower step, his body entirely in profile, the ambiguous visitor is coming in and going out at the same time, like a pendulum caught at the bottom of its swing. He repeats on the spot, but in the dark reality of his body, the instantaneous movement of those images flashing across the room, plunging into the mirror, being reflected there, and springing out from it again like visible, new, and identical species. Pale, minuscule, those silhouetted figures in the mirror are challenged by the tall, solid stature of the man appearing in the doorway.

But we must move down again from the back of the picture towards the front of the stage; we must leave that periphery whose volute we have just been following. Starting from the painter's gaze, which constitutes an off-centre centre to the left, we perceive first of all the back of the canvas, then the paintings hung on the wall, with the mirror in their centre, then the open doorway, then more pictures, of which, because of the sharpness of the perspective, we can see no more than the edges of the frames, and finally, at the extreme right, the window, or rather the groove in the wall from which the light is pouring. This spiral shell presents us with the entire cycle of representation: the gaze, the palette and brush, the canvas innocent of signs (these are the material tools of representation), the paintings, the reflections, the real man (the completed representation, but as it were freed from its illusory or truthful contents, which are juxtaposed to it); then the representation dissolves again: we can see only the frames, and the light that is flooding the pictures from outside, but that they, in return, must reconstitute in their own kind, as though it were coming from elsewhere, passing through their dark wooden frames. And we do, in fact, see this light on the painting, apparently welling out from the crack of the frame; and from there it moves over to touch the brow, the cheekbones, the eyes, the gaze of the painter, who is holding a palette in one hand and in the other a fine brush... And so the spiral is closed, or rather, by means of that light, is opened.

This opening is not, like the one in the back wall, made by pulling back a door; it is the whole breadth of the picture itself, and the looks that pass across it are not those of a distant visitor. The frieze that occupies the foreground and the middle ground of the picture represents – if we include the painter – eight characters. Five of these, their heads more or less bent, turned or inclined, are looking straight out at right angles to the surface of the picture. The centre of the group is occupied by the little Infanta, with her flared pink and grey dress. The princess is turning her head towards the right side of the picture, while her torso and the big panniers of her dress slant away slightly towards the left; but her gaze is directed absolutely straight towards the spectator standing in front of the painting. A vertical line dividing the canvas into two equal halves would pass between the child's eyes. Her face is a third of the total height of the picture above the lower frame. So that here, beyond all question, resides the principal theme of the composition; this is the very object of this painting. As though to prove this and to emphasise it even more, Veláz-quez has made use of a traditional visual device: beside the principal figure he has placed a secondary one, kneeling and looking in towards the central one. Like a donor in prayer, like an angel greeting the Virgin, a maid of honour on her knees is stretching out her hands towards the princess. Her face stands out in perfect profile against the background. It is at the same height as that of the child. This attendant is looking at the princess and only at the princess. A little to the right, there stands another maid of honour, also turned towards the Infanta, leaning slightly over her, but with her eyes clearly directed towards the front, towards the same spot already being gazed at by the painter and the princess. Lastly, two other groups made up of two figures each: one of these groups is further away; the other, made up of the two dwarfs, is right in the foreground. One character in each of these pairs is looking straight out, the other to the left or the right. Because of their positions and their size, these two groups correspond and themselves form a pair: behind, the courtiers (the woman, to the left, looks to the right); in front, the dwarfs (the boy, who is at the extreme right, looks in towards the centre of the picture). This group of characters, arranged in this manner, can be taken to constitute, according to the way one looks at the picture and the centre of reference chosen, two different figures. The first would be a large X: the top left-hand point of this X would be the painter's eyes; the top right-hand one, the male courtier's eyes; at the bottom left-hand corner there is the corner of the canvas represented with its back towards us (or, more exactly, the foot of the easel); at the bottom right-hand corner, the dwarf (his foot on the dog's back). Where these two lines intersect, at the centre of the X, are the eyes of the Infanta. The second figure would be more that of a vast curve, its two ends determined by the painter on the left and the male courtier on the right – both these extremities occurring high up in the picture and set back from its surface; the centre of the curve, much nearer to us, would coincide with the princess's face and the look her maid of honour is directing towards her. This curve describes a shallow hollow across the centre of the picture which at once contains and sets off the position of the mirror at the back.

There are thus two centres around which the picture may be organised, according to whether the fluttering attention of the spectator decides to settle in this place or in that. The princess is, standing upright in the centre of a St Andrew's cross, which is revolving around her with its eddies of courtiers, maids of honour, animals, and fools. But this pivoting movement is frozen. Frozen by a spectacle that would be absolutely invisible if those same characters, suddenly motionless, were not offering us, as though in the hollow of a goblet, the possibility of seeing in the depths of a mirror the unforeseen double of what they are observing. In depth, it is the princess who is superimposed on the mirror; vertically, it is the reflection that is superimposed on the face. But, because of the perspective, they are very close to one another. Moreover, from each of them there springs an ineluctable line: the line issuing from the mirror crosses the whole of the depth represented (and even more, since the mirror forms a hole in the back wall and brings a further space into being behind it); the other line is shorter: it comes from the child's eyes and crosses only the foreground. These two sagittal lines converge at a very sharp angle, and the point where they meet, springing out from the painted surface, occurs in front of the picture, more or less exactly at the spot from which we are observing it. It is an uncertain point because we cannot see it; yet it is an inevitable and perfectly defined point too, since it is determined by those two dominating figures and confirmed further by other, adjacent dotted lines which also have their origin inside the picture and emerge from it in a similar fashion.

What is there, then, we ask at last, in that place which is completely inaccessible because it is exterior to the picture, yet is prescribed by all the lines of its composition? What is the spectacle, what are the faces that are reflected first of all in the depths of the Infanta's eyes, then in the courtiers' and the painter's, and finally in the distant glow of the mirror? But the question immediately becomes a double one: the face reflected in the mirror is also the face that is contemplating it; what all the figures in the picture are looking at are the two figures to whose eyes they too present a scene to be observed. The entire picture is looking out at a scene for which it is itself a scene. A condition of pure reciprocity manifested by the observing and observed mirror, the two stages of which are uncoupled at the two lower corners of the picture: on the left the canvas with its back to us, by means of which the exterior point is made into pure spectacle; to the right the dog lying on the floor, the only element in the picture that is neither looking at anything nor moving, because it is not intended, with its deep reliefs and the light playing on its silky hair, to be anything but an object to be seen.

Our first glance at the painting told us what it is that creates this spectacle-as-observation. It is the two sovereigns. One can sense their presence already in the respectful gaze of the figures in the picture, in the

astonishment of the child and the dwarfs. We recognise them, at the far
end of the picture, in the two tiny silhouettes gleaming out from the
looking-glass. In the midst of all those attentive faces, all those richly
dressed bodies, they are the palest, the most unreal, the most compro-
mised of all the painting's images: a movement, a little light, would be
sufficient to eclipse them. Of all these figures represented before us, they
are also the most ignored, since no one is paying the slightest attention to
that reflection which has slipped into the room behind them all, silently
occupying its unsuspected space; in so far as they are visible, they are the
frailest and the most distant form of all reality. Inversely, in so far as they
stand outside the picture and are therefore withdrawn from it in an
essential invisibility, they provide the centre around which the entire
representation is ordered: it is they who are being faced, it is towards
them that everyone is turned, it is to their eyes that the princess is being
presented in her holiday clothes; from the canvas with its back to us to
the Infanta, and from the Infanta to the dwarf playing on the extreme
right, there runs a curve (or again, the lower fork of the X opens) that
orders the whole arrangement of the picture to their gaze and thus makes
apparent the true centre of the composition, to which the Infanta's gaze
and the image in the mirror are both finally subject.

In the realm of the anecdote, this centre is symbolically sovereign, since
it is occupied by King Philip IV and his wife. But it is so above all because
of the triple function it fulfils in relation to the picture. For in it there
occurs an exact superimposition of the model's gaze as it is being painted,
of the spectator's as he contemplates the painting, and of the painter's as
he is composing his picture (not the one represented, but the one in front
of us which we are discussing). These three 'observing' functions come
together in a point exterior to the picture: that is, an ideal point in relation
to what is represented, but a perfectly real one too, since it is also the
starting-point that makes the representation possible. Within that reality
itself, it cannot not be invisible. And yet, that reality is projected within
the picture – projected and diffracted in three forms which correspond to
the three functions of that ideal and real point. They are: on the left, the
painter with his palette in his hand (a self-portrait of Velázquez); to the
right, the visitor, one foot on the step, ready to enter the room; he is
taking in the scene from the back, but he can see the royal couple, who are
the spectacle itself, from the front; and lastly, in the centre, the reflection
of the king and the queen, richly dressed, motionless, in the attitude of
patient models.

A reflection that shows us quite simply, and in shadow, what all those
in the foreground are looking at. It restores, as if by magic, what is lacking
in every gaze: in the painter's, the model, which his represented double is
duplicating over there in the picture; in the king's, his portrait, which is
being finished off on that slope of the canvas that he cannot perceive from

where he stands; in that of the spectator, the real centre of the scene, whose place he himself has taken as though by usurpation. But perhaps this generosity on the part of the mirror is feigned; perhaps it is hiding as much as and even more than it reveals. That space where the king and his wife hold sway belongs equally well to the artist and to the spectator: in the depths of the mirror there could also appear – there ought to appear – the anonymous face of the passer-by and that of Velázquez. For the function of that reflection is to draw into the interior of the picture what is intimately foreign to it: the gaze which has organised it and the gaze for which it is displayed. But because they are present within the picture, to the right and to the left, the artist and the visitor cannot be given a place in the mirror: just as the king appears in the depths of the looking-glass precisely because he does not belong to the picture.

In the great volute that runs around the perimeter of the studio, from the gaze of the painter, with his motionless hand and palette, right round to the finished paintings, representation came into being, reached completion, only to dissolve once more into the light; the cycle was complete. The lines that run through the depth of the picture, on the other hand, are not complete; they all lack a segment of their trajectories. This gap is caused by the absence of the king – an absence that is an artifice on the part of the painter. But this artifice both conceals and indicates another vacancy which is, on the contrary, immediate: that of the painter and the spectator when they are looking at or composing the picture. It may be that, in this picture, as in all the representations of which it is, as it were, the manifest essence, the profound invisibility of what one sees is inseparable from the invisibility of the person seeing – despite all mirrors, reflections, imitations, and portraits. Around the scene are arranged all the signs and successive forms of representation; but the double relation of the representation to its model and to its sovereign, to its author as well as to the person to whom it is being offered, this relation is necessarily interrupted. It can never be present without some residuum, even in a representation that offers itself as a spectacle. In the depth that traverses the picture, hollowing it into a fictitious recess and projecting it forward in front of itself, it is not possible for the pure felicity of the image ever to present in a full light both the master who is representing and the sovereign who is being represented.

Perhaps there exists, in this painting by Velázquez, the representation as it were, of Classical representation, and the definition of the space it opens up to us. And, indeed, representation undertakes to represent itself here in all its elements, with its images, the eyes to which it is offered, the faces it makes visible, the gestures that call it into being. But there, in the midst of this dispersion which it is simultaneously grouping together and spreading out before us, indicated compellingly from every side, is an essential void: the necessary disappearance of that which is its foundation – of the person it resembles and the person in whose eyes it is only a resemblance. This very subject – which is the same – has been elided. And representation, freed finally from the relation that was impeding it, can offer itself as representation in its pure form.

18

Aesthetic Illusion and Virtual Reality

Jean Baudrillard

There is always a camera hidden somewhere. It may be a real one – we may be filmed without knowing it. We may also be invited to replay our own life on a television network. Anyway, *the virtual camera is in our head*, and our whole life has taken on a video dimension. We might believe that we exist in the original, but today this original has become an exception for the happy few. Our own reality doesn't exist any more. We are exposed to the instantaneous retransmission of all our facts and gestures on a channel. We would have experienced this before as police control. Today it is just like an advertising promotion.

Thus it is irrelevant to get upset with talk shows or reality shows, and to criticise them as such. For they are only a spectacular version, and so an innocent one, of the transformation of life itself, of everyday life, into virtual reality. We don't need the media to reflect our problems in real time – *each existence is telepresent to itself.*

TV and the media have left their mediatised space in order to invest 'real' life from the inside, infiltrating it exactly like a virus in a normal cell.

We don't need digital gloves or a digital suit. As we are, we are moving around in the world as in a synthetic image. We have swallowed our microphones and headsets, producing intense interference effects, due to the short-circuit of life and its technical diffusion. We have interiorised our own prosthetic image and become the professional showmen of our own lives. Compared with this, the reality shows are only side-effects, and moreover mystifying, because in indicting them as manipulation, the critics assume that there is somewhere an original form of life, and that reality shows would be no more than its parody and simulation (Disneyland).

This criticism is over, as is every Situationist criticism of the 'spectacle' and the concept of 'spectacle', as also in substance all criticism of 'alienation'. Unfortunately, I would add. Because the human abstraction of the spectacle was never hopeless; it always offered the chance of disalienation. Whereas the operation of the world in real time, its unconditional

198

realisation, is really without alternative. Radicality has changed, and all negative criticism, surviving itself, actually helps its object to survive. For instance, the critic of religion and of its official manifestation misses the fact that religion is in practice far more realised in many other forms – irreligious, profane, political or cultural – where it is less easily recognisable as such.

It is the same thing with the virtual. Current criticism engaging with new techniques, new images, masks the fact that its concept has been distilled throughout real life, in homoeopathic doses, beyond detection. And if the level of reality decreases from day to day, it's because the medium itself has passed into life, and become a common ritual of transparency. It is the same for the virtual: all this digital, numerical and electronic equipment is only the epiphenomenon of the virtualisation of human beings in their core. If this can overwhelm people's fantasy to such a degree, it is because we are already, not in some other world, but in this very life, in a state of photosynthesis. If we can today produce a virtual clone to replace Richard Bohringer, it is because he has already replicated himself, he has already become his own clone.

But anyway the reality show can be used as a micromodel for the analysis of all virtual reality. Whether it's the immediacy of information on all screens, the telepresence, or presence on TV, in all actings and happenings, it is always a question of 'real time' – of the collapse of the real and its double. Live your life in real time (live and die directly on the screen). Think in real time (your thinking is immediately transferred on the printer). Make your revolution in real time (not in the street, but in the broadcasting studio). Live your love and passion in real time (by videotaping each other).

This conversion of the mediatised into the immediatised, that is, into an immediate catalytic operation of the real by the screen, this immediatic revolution is already implied in McLuhan's formula 'The Medium is the Message', which has never been analysed in all its consequences. McLuhan remains the prophetic theoretician of this collapse of the medium and the message, and thus in some way the prophet of the vanishing process of information and communication (whose significance he emphasised at the same time!). 'The Medium is the Message' remains as the *Mene Tekel Epharsim* of the communication era, its password and the sign of its end.

But there is another predecessor for all technologies of the virtual: it is the ready-made. Again, for example, the reality show: all those human beings, literally extracted from their real life to play out their AIDS or conjugal psychodrama on the TV screen have their prototype in the bottle rack of Duchamp. The artist extracted the bottle rack from the real world in the same way, displaced it on another level to confer on it an undefinable hyperreality. A paradoxical acting-out, putting an end to the bottle rack as a real object, to art as the invention of another scene and to the artist as the protagonist of another world. To all aesthetic idealisation Duchamp opposes a violent desublimation of art and of the real by their instantaneous short-circuit. Extrematisation of the two forms: the bottle rack, ex-inscribed from its context, from its idea, from its function, becomes more real than the real (hyperreal), and more art than art (it enters into the transaesthetics of banality, of insignificance, of nullity, where today the pure and indifferent form of art is to be seen).

Any object, any individual, any situation today could be a virtual ready-made. For all of them might be described in much the same way as Duchamp implicitly categorises his ready-made object: 'It exists, I met it!' This is the only label for existence. Graffiti – another form of ready-made – says nothing other than: 'I exist, here I am, my name is so and so'. The pure and minimal form of identity: 'I exist, I met myself'. The ready-made always seems like these stuffed animals, vitrified as if they were alive, hypnotised in the pure form of appearance – 'naturalised'. But I would say that today art in general also looks like a naturalised species, vitrified in its pure formal essence.

Duchamp's coup has since been repeated indefinitely, not only in the field of art, but in all individual and social functions, especially in the mediasphere. The last phase being precisely the reality show, where everybody is invited to present themselves as they are, key in hand, and to play their live show on the screen (with all its obscene connotations), just as the ready-made object plays its hyperrealistic role on the screen of the museum.

All these mediatic events relate to this crucial phase in the world of information and communication – a phase that art, politics and production have known before. The drama of the mediatic class is that it is starving on the other side of the screen, in front of an indifferent consuming mass, in front of the tele-absence of the masses. Any form of tele-presence will be good enough to exorcise this tele-absence. Just as it was a vital necessity for capital to have workers and producers transformed into active consumers, and even into direct stockholders in the capitalist economy (this doesn't change anything in business, the strategy being as always to remove the tablecloth without changing the organisation of the table), the telespectator has to be transferred not in front of the screen where he is staying anyway, passively escaping his responsibility as citizen, but on the screen, on the other side of the screen. In short, he must undergo the same conversion as Duchamp's bottle rack, when it was transferred to the other side of art, thus creating a definitive ambiguity between art and the real world. Today art is nothing more than this paradoxical confusion of the two. And information too is nothing more than the paradoxical confusion of the event and the medium, including all forms of intoxication and mystification connected to it.

So we have all become ready-mades. Objects transposed to the other side of the screen, mediumised (we don't even enjoy the good old status of passive spectator any more), hypostasised as if transfigured *in situ*, on the spot, by aesthetic or mediatic decision, transfigured in their specific habits and ways of life, as living museum exhibits. Thus we become cloned to our own image by high definition, and dedicated by involution into our own image to mediatic stupefaction, just as the ready-made is dedicated to aesthetic stupefaction. And just as Duchamp's acting-out opens on an overall aestheticisation, where any piece of junk will be promoted to a piece of art, and any piece of art demoted to a piece of junk – so this immediatic conversion opens on to a universal virtuality, that is to say the radical actualisation of reality through its acting-out in real time.

All cultural spaces are involved. For example, some new museums, following a sort of Disneyland processing, try to put people not so much in front of the painting – which is not interactive enough and even suspect as pure spectacular consumption – but into the painting. Insinuated audiovisually into the virtual reality of the *Déjeuner sur l'herbe*, people will enjoy it in real time, feeling and tasting the whole Impressionist context, and eventually interacting with the picture. The masses usually prefer passive roles, and avoid representation. This must change, and they must be made interactive partners. It is not a question of free speaking or free acting – just break their resistance and destroy their immunities.

It is a question of life and death. When the indifference of the masses becomes dangerous for the political or cultural class, then interactive strategies must be invented to exhort a response at any price. In fact, the interactive mass is still a mass, with all the characteristics of a mass, simply reflecting itself on both sides of the screen. But the screen is not a mirror, and, while there was some magic in passing beyond the mirror, there is no magic at all in passing beyond the screen. It's impossible anyway – there is no other side of the screen. No depth – just a surface. No hidden face – just an interface.

Besides, the masses were not without an answer. Their answer was silence, the silence of the silent majorities. This challenge of silence is now cancelled when people are forced to ask their own questions, when they are assigned to speech. If they had some questions, these would never be autonomous but would surely be programmed in a schedule. But even this implication *en trompe l'oeil* doesn't save media and information from inertia, from proliferating fatal inertia. Mass media or micromedia, directive or interactive, the chain reaction of the images is the same. It is simply materialised in real time and in everybody's head.

Now what exactly is at stake in this hegemonic trend towards virtuality? What is the idea of the virtual? It would seem to be the radical

actualisation, the unconditional realisation, of the world, the transformation of all our acts, of all historical events, of all material substance and
energy into pure information. The ideal would be the resolution of the
world by the actualisation of all facts and data.

This is the theme of Arthur C. Clarke's fable about the names of God. In
this fable, the monks of Tibet devote themselves to the fastidious work of
transcribing the 99 billion names of God, after which the world will be
accomplished, and it will end. Exhausted by this everlasting spelling of
the names of God, they call IBM computer experts who complete the
work in a few months. This offers a perfect allegory of the completion of
the world in real time by the operation of the virtual. Unfortunately this is
also the end of the world in real time. For with this virtual countdown of
the names of God, the great promise of the end was realised; and the
technicians of IBM, who left the site after work (and didn't believe of
course in the prophecy), saw the stars in the sky fading and vanishing
one by one.

Maybe it is an allegory of our technical transfiguration of the world: its
accelerated end, its anticipated resolution – the final score of modern
millenarianism, but without hope of salvation, revelation, or even apo-
calypse. Simply accelerating the process of declining (in the double sense
of the word) towards a pure and simple disappearance. The human
species would be invested, without knowing it, with the task of programming, by exhausting all its possibilities, the code *for the automatic disappearance of the world*.

Rather than the ideal transformation of the world, the ultimate end of
this transfiguration would be that of building a perfectly autonomous
world from which we can retire and remove ourselves. In order for us to
step out of it, the world must be brought to completion. As long as we
stay here as alien beings, the world cannot be perfect. And to be perfect it
must be constructed and artificial, because there is no perfection in the
natural state. The human being itself is a dangerous imperfection. If we
want to achieve this sort of immortality, we must also treat ourselves as
artefacts and get out of ourselves in order to move on an artificial orbit,
where we can revolve eternally.

We all dream of an *ex-nihilo* creation, of a world emerging and moving
without our intervention. We dream of perfect autonomous beings who,
far from acting against our will as in the fable, *The Sorcerer's Apprentice*,
would meet our desire to escape our own will, and realise the world as
a self-fulfilling prophecy. So we dream of perfect computers, of auto-
programming artificial intelligence. But if we allow artificial beings to
become intelligent, and even more intelligent than we are, we don't allow
them to have their own will. We don't allow them what God finally
allowed us – the intelligence of evil. We cannot bear real challenge from
another species; and if we concede intelligence to other beings, then this

intelligence must still be the manifestation of our desire. While God permitted us to raise such questions about our own liberty, we don't allow artificial beings to raise such questions about themselves. No liberty, no will, no desire, no sexuality. We want them complex, creative, interactive, but without spirit. By the way, it seems that these 'intelligent' machines have found, if not the way to transgression and freedom, at least the byways to accident and catastrophe. It seems that they have an evil genius for dysfunctions, electronic viruses and other perverse effects, which save them – and us, in the same way – from perfection and from reaching the limit of their possibilities.

The perfect crime would be to build a world-machine without defect, and to leave it without traces. But it never succeeds. We leave traces everywhere – viruses, lapses, germs, catastrophes – signs of defect, or imperfection, which are like our species' signature in the heart of an artificial world.

All forms of high technology illustrate the fact that behind its doubles and its prostheses, its biological clones and its virtual images, the human species is secretly fomenting its disappearance. For example, the video cassette recorder connected to the TV: it sees the film in your place. Were it not for this technical possibility of devolution, of a vicarious accomplishment, we would have felt obliged to see it for ourselves. For we always feel a little responsible for films we haven't seen, for desires we haven't realised, for people we haven't answered, for crimes we haven't committed, for money we haven't spent. All this generates a mass of deferred possibilities, and the idea that a machine is there that can deal with these possibilities, can stock them, filter them (an answer-machine, a memory bank), and progressively absorb and reabsorb them, is very comforting. All these machines can be called virtual, since they are the medium of virtual pleasure, the abstract pleasure of the image, which is often good enough for our happiness. Most of these machines are used for delusion, for the elusion of communication ('Leave a message . . .'), for absolving face-to-face relations and social responsibilities. They don't really lead to action, they substitute for it most of the time. So with the film on the video cassette recorder: maybe I'll see this film later, but maybe I won't do it at all. Am I sure I really want to see it anyway? But the machine must work. Thus the consumption of the machine converges with the consumption of the desire.

All these machines are wonderful. They give us a sort of freedom. They help us to get free from the machine itself, since they interconnect one with another and function in a loop. They help us to get free from our own will and from our own production. What a relief all at once to see twenty pages erased by a caprice of the word processor (or by an error of the user, which amounts to the same thing). They would never have had such a value if they hadn't been given the chance to disappear! What the computer gives to you, too easily perhaps, it takes away just as easily. Everything is in order. The technological equation amounts to zero. We always hear about negative perverse effects. But here the technique assumes a positive (homoeopathic) perverse effect. The integrated circuit reverses itself, performing in some way *the automatic writing of the world*.

Now let us consider some different aspects of this virtual achievement, of this automatic writing of the world. High definition. High fidelity. Real time. Genetic codes. Artificial intelligence.

In high definition, the (electronic, numerical or synthesised) image is nothing more than the emanation of the digital code that generated it. It has nothing more to do with representation, and even less with aesthetic illusion. All illusion is abolished by technical perfection. It is the same with the three-dimensional image: it is a pure disillusion, since the magic of the image lies simply in the subtraction of one dimension from the real world. In the hologram's perfection of the virtual image, all parts are microscopically identical to the whole, generating a fractal deconstruction of the image, which is supplanted by its own pure luminous definition.

High fidelity. Disappearance of the music by excess of fidelity, by the promiscuity of the music and its absolute technical model. Holographic music, holophonic, stereophonic, as if it had swallowed its own genetic code before expelling it as an artificial synthesis – clinical music, sterile, purged of all noise.

Real time. The equivalent of high definition for the image. Simultaneity of the event and its diffusion in information. Instant proximity of oneself and one's actions at a distance. Telepresence: you can manage your business *in situ* at the other end of the world, by the medium of your electronic clone. Like the space of the image in high definition, each moment in real time is microscopically coded, microscopically isolated, in a closed and integrated circuit. As in the hologram, each parcel of time concentrates the total information relative to the event, as if we could control the event from all sides at once. No distance, no memory, no continuity, no death: the extreme 'reality of time' is in fact extreme virtuality. All the suspense, all the unforeseeability, of time is over.

Genetic coding. What is at stake here is the simulation of a perfect human being, of a body of high definition, through the controlled engineering and dispatching of the genome. The construction of a virtual body outperforming the original – plastic genetic surgery. The genetic code itself, the DNA, which concentrates the whole definition of any living being in a minimal space and a minimal formula, is the ideal type of virtuality.

Last, but not least: artificial intelligence. Something like an artificial brain-recording, adapted to an artificial environment. Thinking almost instantaneously inscribed on the screen, in direct interaction with data, software and memories – intelligence in real time. Thinking becomes a high definition operation, suppressing all distance, all ambiguity, all enigmatic eventualities, suppressing the very illusion of thought. Just as the illusion of the image disappears into its virtual reality, just as the illusion of the body disappears into its genetic inscription, just as the illusion of the world disappears into its technical artefacts, so the natural intelligence of the world disappears into its artificial intelligence. There is no trace in all of this of the world as a game, as a fake, as a machination, as a crime, and not as a logical mechanism, or a reflex cybernetic machine, with the human brain as mirror and model.

Artificial intelligence is everything except artificial. It is definitive 'realthinking' (as we speak of *realpolitik*), fully materialised by the interaction of all virtualities of analysis and computing. We could even say that artificial intelligence goes beyond itself through too high a definition of the real, through a delirious sophistication of data and operations – but this is only the consequence of the fact that artificial intelligence is a matter of the hyperrealisation of thinking, of the objective processing of thinking.

There is not the slightest sense here of illusion, artifice, seduction, or a more subtle game of thought. For thought is neither a mechanism of higher functions nor a range of operational reflexes. It is a rhetoric of forms, of moving illusions and appearances. It reacts positively to the illusion of the world, and negatively to its reality. It plays off appearances against reality, turning the illusion of the world against the world itself. The thinking machine masters only the computing process. It doesn't rule over appearances, and its function, like that of all other cybernetic and virtual machines, is to destroy this essential illusion by counterfeiting the world in real time.

Curiously, all the above traits rely upon paradoxes. 'Real time' is in fact a purely virtual time. 'Artificial intelligence' is nothing like artificial. 'Virtual reality' is at the antipodes of the real world. As for 'high definition', it is synonymous with the *highest dilution* of reality. The highest definition of the medium corresponds to the lowest definition of the message. The highest definition of information corresponds to the lowest definition of the event. The highest definition of sex (in pornography) corresponds to the lowest definition of desire. The highest definition of language (as computer coding) corresponds to the lowest definition of sense. The highest definition of the other (as computer coding), corresponds to the lowest definition of exchange and alterity. Everywhere high definition corresponds to a world where referential substance is scarcely to be found any more.

Such are the stakes involved in the virtual realisation of the world. And we must take it as irreversible. This logic leads to the end, to the final solution, or resolution. Once performed, it would be the equivalent of a perfect crime. While the other crime, the 'original' crime, is never perfect, and always leaves traces – we as living and mortal beings are a living trace of this criminal imperfection – future extermination, which would result from the absolute determination of the world and of its elements, would leave no traces at all. We would not even have the choice or chance to die, to really die. We would have been kidnapped and disintegrated in real time and virtual reality long before the stars go out.

Artificial intelligence, tele-sensoriality, virtual reality and so on – all this is the end of illusion. The illusion of the world – not its analytical countdown – the wild illusion of passion, of thinking, the aesthetic illusion of the scene, the psychic and moral illusion of the other, of good and evil (of evil especially, perhaps), of true and false, the wild illusion of death, or of living at any price – all this is volatilised in psychosensorial telereality, in all these sophisticated technologies which transfer us to the virtual, to the contrary of illusion: to radical disillusion.

Fortunately, all this is impossible. High definition is 'virtually' unrealisable, in its attempt to produce images, sounds, information, bodies in microvision, in stereoscopy, as you have never seen them, as you will never see them. Unrealisable also is the fantasy of artificial intelligence. It is too intelligent, too operational to be true – this brain-becoming of the world, this world-becoming of the brain, as it has never functioned, without a body, autonomised, inhuman – a brain of high definition outlining a universe of high definition. Something like an ethical and technical purification. It will never succeed, fortunately. Not that we trust in human nature or in a future enlightenment, but because there is in fact no place for both natural and artificial intelligence. There is no place for both the illusion of the world and a virtual programming of the world. There is no place for both the world and its double.

When the virtual operation of the world is finished, when all the names of God have been spelled out – which is the same basic fantasy as the declining of the human genome or the worldwide declining of all data and information – then we too shall see the stars fading away.

Summaries and Notes

1. JULIA THOMAS: INTRODUCTION

Notes

1. James L. Watson (ed.), Preface, *Golden Arches East: McDonald's in East Asia* (Stanford, CA, 1997), p. v.
2. Jacques Lacan, *The Four Fundamental Concepts of Psycho-Analysis*, ed. Jacques-Alain Miller, trans. Alan Sheridan (1973) (Harmondsworth, 1994), p. 95.
3. Jacques Lacan, 'The Mirror Stage as Formative of the Function of the I as Revealed in Psychoanalytic Experience', *Ecrits: A Selection*, trans. Alan Sheridan (London, 1977), pp. 1–7.
4. John Berger, *Ways of Seeing* (London, 1972), pp. 83–112.
5. Ferdinand de Saussure, *Course in General Linguistics*, ed. Charles Bally and Albert Sechehaye, trans. Wade Baskin (1915) (New York and London, 1959).
6. Jacques Derrida, 'Why Peter Eisenman Writes Such Good Books', p. 174.
7. Ibid., p. 174.
8. W. J. T. Mitchell, *Iconology: Image, Text, Ideology* (Chicago and London, 1986), p. 56. Cited in David Summers, 'Real Metaphor: Towards a Redefinition of the "Conceptual" Image', *Visual Theory: Painting and Interpretation*, ed. Norman Bryson, Michael Ann Holly and Keith Moxey (Cambridge, 1991), pp. 231–59, p. 234.
9. Bryson et al. (eds), *Visual Theory*, p. 1.
10. Richard Wollheim, 'What the Spectator Sees', *Visual Theory*, pp. 101–50, p. 103.
11. Summers, 'Real Metaphor', p. 234.
12. Louis Althusser, 'Ideology and Ideological State Apparatuses', *Lenin and Philosophy and Other Essays*, trans. Ben Brewster (1968) (London, 1977), p. 11.
13. Edward W. Said, Orientalism: Western Conceptions of the Orient (Harmondsworth, 1978).
14. Luce Irigaray, *Speculum of the Other Woman*, trans. Gillian C. Gill (Ithaca, NY, 1985), p. 50.
15. Laura Mulvey, 'Visual Pleasure and Narrative Cinema', *Visual and Other Pleasures* (London, 1989), pp. 14–26.
16. Jacqueline Rose, *Sexuality in the Field of Vision* (London, 1986).
17. Derrida, 'Why Peter Eisenman Writes Such Good Books', p. 183.

2. RICHARD L. GREGORY, 'PERSPECTIVE'

(From *Eye and Brain: the Psychology of Seeing* (London, 1966), pp. 136–7, 160–76.)

Summary

Since the Renaissance perspective has come to seem the obvious way of viewing things, a representation of how we really see. Richard L. Gregory denaturalises this mechanism, suggesting that it is culturally determined: people in different societies do not see perspective, or even optical illusions, which rely on perspectival cues of distance and size, in the same way. An awareness of perspective, then, depends on experience and knowledge: it is learned and conventional rather than innate. Moreover, according to Gregory, not even people in Western society actually see in a way that accords with geometrical perspective, for the brain works alongside the eye in perception, utilising its knowledge of the relative size and distance of objects in order to scale the retinal image and compensate for the changes that occur with viewing distance. Thus, we are able to judge the size of distant things and, in effect, see them as the size they would be if they were nearer to us.

3.　KOBENA MERCER, 'MONSTER METAPHORS: NOTES ON MICHAEL JACKSON'S *THRILLER*'

(From *Welcome to the Jungle: New Positions in Black Cultural Studies*
(New York and London, 1994), pp. 33–51. Originally published in *Screen*,
27, 1 (January–February, 1986.)

Summary

Contemporary culture is fascinated by, and inundated with, images of the 'superstar', but how does this image function, and why is it so appealing? Kobena Mercer sets out to answer such questions by analysing the music video for Michael Jackson's *Thriller*. He argues that the image of Jackson is disparate from his real personality: there is no individual behind this mask, only a cultural construct. Nor is what 'Michael Jackson' represents stable or fixed. Rather, the video plays with his gender and race in a way that exposes such categories as shifting and unstable. In his discussion Mercer suggests that the pop video is not a neutral form of entertainment but relies on other visual and narrative conventions for its meanings, including, in this instance, the codes of the horror genre. *Thriller* is also significant for the spectatorial roles that it establishes, with the girl, who watches the horror movie, mirroring the fans who watch the video itself.

Notes

1. Roland Barthes, 'The Grain of the Voice', *Image–Music–Text* (London, 1977), p. 188.
2. Robert Johnson, 'The Michael Jackson Nobody Knows', *Ebony* (December 1984).
3. Nelson George, *The Michael Jackson Story* (London, 1984), p. 106.
4. On music video, see Michael Boodro, 'Rock Videos: Another World', *ZG*, 5 (1984); Dessa Fox, 'The Video Virus', *New Musical Express* (4 May 1985); Dave Laing, 'Music Video: Industrial Product – Cultural Form', *Screen*, 26, 2 (March–April 1985), 78–83.
5. Laing, 1985 ibid., 81.
6. Quoted in Andy Warhol and Bob Calacello, 'Michael Jackson', *Interview* (October 1982).
7. George, *The Michael Jackson Story*, p. 108.
8. Lyrics from *The Great Songs of Michael Jackson* (London, 1984).
9. Ian Chambers, *Urban Rhythms: Pop Music and Popular Culture* (London, 1985), p. 148.
10. See ibid., p. 143, and Richard Dyer, 'In Defence of Disco', *Gay Left*, 8.

11. Philip Brophy, 'Horrality – the Textuality of Contemporary Horror Films', *Screen*, 27:1 (1986), 2–13, 5.
12. Ibid., 3–5.
13. On the horror genre in cinema history, see S. S. Prawer, *Caligari's Children: The Film as Tale of Terror* (London and New York, 1980).
14. The 'Thriller' video is generally available as part of *The Making of Michael Jackson's Thriller*, Warner Home Video, 1984.
15. Stephen Neale, *Genre* (London, 1980), pp. 21, 56, 62.
16. Prawer, *Caligari's Children*, p. 15.
17. The 'fantasy of being a pop star's girlfriend' is examined in Dave Rimmer, *Like Punk Never Happened: Culture Club and the New Pop* (London, 1985), p. 112. Personal modes of enunciation in pop music are discussed in Alan Durant, *Conditions of Music* (London, 1984), pp. 201–6.
18. One of Freud's most famous patients, the Wolf Man, makes clear the connections between animals and sexuality. The Wolf Man's dream also reads like a horror film:

    'I dreamt that it was night and that I was lying on my bed. Suddenly the window opened of its own accord, and I was terrified to see some white wolves were sitting on the big walnut tree in front of the window.'

    Muriel Gardiner, *The Wolf Man and Sigmund Freud* (London, 1973), p. 173. Freud's reading suggests that the anxiety in the dream manifests a fear of castration for a repressed homosexual desire. My thanks to Mandy Merck for drawing out this last point.
19. Jacobson quoted in George, *The Michael Jackson Story*, pp. 83–4.
20. The notion of 'cryptonymy' as a name for unconscious meanings is developed in Nicholas Abraham and Maria Torok's rereading of Freud's Wolf Man. See Peggy Kamuf, 'Abraham's Wake', *Diacritics*, 9, 1 (Spring 1979), 32–43.
21. Neale, *Genre*, p. 45.
22. Geoff Brown, *Michael Jackson: Body and Soul* (London, 1984), p. 10.
23. Roland Barthes, *Mythologies* (1957) (London, 1973).
24. On stereotypes of black men in popular culture see, Donald Bogle, *Toms, Coons, Mulatoes, Mammies and Bucks: An Interpretive History of Blacks in American Films* (New York, 1973); Jim Pines, *Blacks in Film* (London, 1975); and Isaac Julien, *The Other Look*, unpublished BA dissertation, St. Martins School of Art, 1984.
25. Susan Sontag, *A Susan Sontag Reader*, ed. Elizabeth Hardwick (New York, 1983), p. 105.
26. Quoted in Gerri Hirshey, *Nowhere to Run: The Story of Soul Music* (London and New York, 1984), pp. 3–22.
27. Barthes, 'The Grain of the Voice', p. 181.

4.   ROSALIND COWARD, 'THE LOOK'

(From *Female Desire: Women's Sexuality Today* (London, 1984), pp. 75–82.)

Summary

Rosalind Coward discusses the implications for female sexuality of a society saturated with visual images and obsessed with looking. Starting from the premise that to look is not an innocent activity, but one that confers power according to gender, she analyses the way in which woman is positioned as the object of the male gaze. According to Coward, 'woman' does not signify a natural or essential identity but one that is constituted by visuality and dependent on ideas of beauty, immaturity and passivity. The male spectator is empowered by such images of women because they allow him to keep his distance and control, but for a woman, this ideal female image is more ambivalent and often results in low self-esteem and feelings of failure. Coward's argument is not simply defeatist, however, for by exposing the fact that looking and being looked at are culturally determined and involve gender and power relations, she undermines the naturalness of such relations and opens up the possibility for change.

Notes

1. For a summary of ideas about cinema as a voyeuristic activity, see J. Ellis, *Visible Fictions* (London, 1982).
2. See S. Freud, *On Narcissism*, in Standard Edition, Vol XIV.
3. Ibid., p. 89.

5.   SUSAN SONTAG, 'IN PLATO'S CAVE'
(From *On Photography* (Harmondsworth, 1977), pp. 3–24.)

Summary

'In Plato's Cave' is the first of six essays that make up Susan Sontag's book, *On Photography*. In this extract she analyses the place of photography in contemporary culture, from the role of the individual photographer and the psychological and sexual implications of picture-taking, to the camera's function in society, and how photographs are viewed and collected. Running through her argument is the suggestion that a photograph is not a direct representation of reality: hence the allusion to Plato's Cave. Plato describes how people trapped in a cave and unable to look behind them would mistake the shadows that they could see for reality itself. According to Sontag, society similarly views the photograph not as an illusion or 'shadow' but as a transparent and innocent mirror of the world, thereby ignoring the fact that this visual representation is always governed by ideologies, which involve value judgements about what is worth viewing or, indeed, what *can* be viewed, as well as artistic conventions of light, shade and positioning. Moreover, the photograph does not so much reflect an event as construct it: even the idea of what constitutes a significant historical occurrence is increasingly dependent on how photogenic it is. Sontag's discussion suggests the omnipresence of photography in society but she concludes by focusing on its limitations, the fact that it has no power on its own but is reliant for its meanings on its cultural and ideological context.

6.   ROLAND BARTHES, 'CAMERA LUCIDA: REFLECTIONS ON PHOTOGRAPHY'
(From *Camera Lucida: Reflections on Photography*, trans. Richard Howard (London, 1981), pp. 67–82. Originally published as *La Chambre Claire* (Paris, 1980).)

Summary

How can one discuss photography? What theoretical tools, if any, can be used to describe it? Are there meanings that are common to all photographs, or is the essence of the genre best captured in individual images? These are the questions that Roland Barthes poses in *Camera Lucida*, but there are no simple answers. The extract here sways between the poignancy of autobiography and the rigour of criticism, and this shift in the mode of address suggests the text's resistance to any reductive system or unified theory. The Winter Garden photograph that is discussed is a paradigm for these contradictions: it allows for an analysis of the medium of photography as a whole but is also startlingly unique. This particular image enables Barthes to suggest that the photograph achieves its effects by hiding its own materiality and appearing as its subject matter. It authenticates the people and objects that it represents by standing as proof that they were once present before the lens, that they really existed. But although this certification seems to suggest the reality and animation of the objects represented, photographs actually have the converse effect and, in their immobility and stasis, attest to the passing of time, anticipating, or pointing back, to the death of what they depict.

7. WALTER BENJAMIN 'THE WORK OF ART IN THE AGE OF MECHANICAL REPRODUCTION'

(Extract from *Illuminations*, ed. Hannah Arendt, trans. Harry Zohn (London, 1968), pp. 211–27. 'The Work of Art in the Age of Mechanical Reproduction' was originally published in German in *Zeitschrift für Social-forschung*, V, 1, 1936.)

Summary

First published in 1936, this essay takes contemporary Marxist ideas as its starting-point and analyses visual art in terms of its mode of production. According to Walter Benjamin, the meanings of traditional art forms and the public's reception of and relation to them are irrevocably changed by the emergence of technologies that allow them to be mechanically reproduced. This reproduction renders obsolete the originality and uniqueness of the work (what Benjamin calls its 'aura') and removes it from its historical and spatial location. Mechanical reproduction not only affects one's reaction to, and criticism of, art, which can no longer be assessed in terms of its authenticity and autonomy, but inaugurates different types of art that are specifically designed for reproduction and exhibition rather than for a ritualistic function. The archetypes of this new mechanically reproduced art are film and photography. In film the 'aura' of the stage actor is subsumed under an image that is technically produced by camera angles, cutting, and editing. Among the ideas raised in this essay is the notion that the reproducibility of art has a social and political impetus: the desire to bring objects closer to the spectator and to render them more 'equal' in status. Benjamin also anticipates later critics in his contention that perception is as much culturally determined as natural, and that changes in perception lead to concomitant transformations in society.

Notes

1. Quoted from Paul Valéry, *Aesthetics*, 'The Conquest of Ubiquity', trans. Ralph Manheim (New York, 1964), p. 225.
2. Of course, the history of a work of art encompasses more than this. The history of the 'Mona Lisa', for instance, encompasses the kind and number of its copies made in the seventeenth, eighteenth and nineteenth centuries.

3. Precisely because authenticity is not reproducible, the intensive penetration of certain (mechanical) processes of reproduction was instrumental in differentiating and grading authenticity. To develop such differentiations was an important function of the trade in works of art. The invention of the woodcut may be said to have struck at the root of the quality of authenticity even before its late flowering. To be sure, at the time of its origin a medieval picture of the Madonna could not yet be said to be 'authentic'. It became 'authentic' only during the succeeding centuries and perhaps most strikingly so during the last one.

4. The poorest provincial staging of *Faust* is superior to a Faust film in that, ideally, it competes with the first performance at Weimar. Before the screen it is unprofitable to remember traditional contents which might come to mind before the stage – for instance, that Goethe's friend Johann Heinrich Merck is hidden in Mephisto, and the like.

5. Abel Gance, 'Le Temps de l'image est venu', *L'Art cinématographique*, Vol. 2 (Paris, 1927), pp. 94f.

6. To satisfy the human interest of the masses may mean to have one's social function removed from the field of vision. Nothing guarantees that a portraitist of today, when painting a famous surgeon at the breakfast table in the midst of his family, depicts his social function more precisely than a painter of the seventeenth century who portrayed his medical doctors as representing this profession, like Rembrandt in his 'Anatomy Lesson'.

7. The definition of the aura as a 'unique phenomenon of a distance however close it may be' represents nothing but the formulation of the cult value of the work of art in categories of space and time perception. Distance is the opposite of closeness. The essentially distant object is the unapproachable one. Unapproachability is indeed a major quality of the cult image. True to its nature, it remains 'distant, however close it may be'. The closeness which one may gain from its subject matter does not impair the distance which it retains in its appearance.

8. To the extent to which the cult value of the painting is secularised the ideas of its fundamental uniqueness lose distinctness. In the imagination of the beholder the uniqueness of the phenomena which hold sway in the cult image is more and more displaced by the empirical uniqueness of the creator or of his creative achievement. To be sure, never completely so; the concept of authenticity always transcends mere genuineness. (This is particularly apparent in the collector who always retains some traces of the fetishist and who, by owning the work of art, shares in its ritual power.) Nevertheless, the function of the concept of authenticity remains determinate in the evaluation of art; with the secularisation of art, authenticity displaces the cult value of the work.

9. In the case of films, mechanical reproduction is not, as with literature and painting, an external condition for mass distribution. Mechanical reproduction is inherent in the very technique of film production. This technique not only permits in the most direct way but virtually causes mass distribution. It enforces distribution because the production of a film is so expensive that an individual who, for instance, might afford to buy a painting no longer can afford to buy a film. In 1927 it was calculated that a major film, in order to pay its way, had to reach an audience of nine million. With the sound film, to be sure, a setback in its international distribution occurred at first: audiences became limited by language barriers. This coincided with the Fascist emphasis on national interests. It is more important to focus on this connection with Fascism than on this setback, which was soon minimised by synchronisation.

The simultaneity of both phenomena is attributable to the depression. The same disturbances which, on a larger scale, led to an attempt to maintain the existing property structure by sheer force led the endangered film capital to speed up the development of the sound film. The introduction of the sound film brought about a temporary relief, not only because it again brought the masses into the theatres but also because it merged new capital from the electrical industry with that of the film industry. Thus, viewed from the outside, the sound film promoted national interests, but seen from the inside it helped to internationalise film production even more than previously.

10. This polarity cannot come into its own in the aesthetics of Idealism. Its idea of beauty comprises these polar opposites without differentiating between them and consequently excludes their polarity. Yet in Hegel this polarity announces itself as clearly as possible within the limits of Idealism. We quote from his *Philosophy of History:*

> Images were known of old. Piety at an early time required them for worship, but it could do without *beautiful* images. These might even be disturbing. In every beautiful painting there is also something nonspiritual, merely external, but its spirit speaks to man through its beauty. Worshipping, conversely, is concerned with the work as an object, for it is but a spiritless stupor of the soul...Fine art has arisen...in the church..., although it has already gone beyond its principle as art.

Likewise, the following passage from *The Philosophy of Fine Art* indicates that Hegel sensed a problem here.

> We are beyond the stage of reverence for works of art as divine and objects deserving our worship. The impression they produce is one of a more reflective kind, and the emotions they arouse require a higher test...
> (G. W. F. Hegel, *The Philosophy of Fine Art*, trans.,
> with notes, by F. P. B. Osmaston,
> Vol. 1 (London, 1920), p. 12.

The transition from the first kind of artistic reception to the second characterises the history of artistic reception in general. Apart from that, a certain oscillation between these two polar modes of reception can be demonstrated for each work of art. Take the Sistine Madonna. Since Hubert Grimme's research it has been known that the Madonna originally was painted for the purpose of exhibition. Grimme's research was inspired by the question: What is the purpose of the moulding in the foreground of the painting which the two cupids lean upon? How, Grimme asked further, did Raphael come to furnish the sky with two draperies? Research proved that the Madonna had been commissioned for the public lying-in-state of Pope Sixtus. The Popes lay in state in a certain side chapel of St Peter's. On that occasion Raphael's picture had been fastened in a nichelike background of the chapel, supported by the coffin. In this picture Raphael portrays the Madonna approaching the papal coffin in clouds from the background of the niche, which was demarcated by green drapes. At the obsequies of Sixtus a pre-eminent exhibition value of Raphael's picture was taken advantage of. Some time later it was placed on the high altar in the church of the Black Friars at Piacenza. The reason for this exile is to be found in the Roman rites which forbid the use of paintings exhibited at obsequies as cult objects on the high altar. This regulation devalued Raphael's picture to some degree. In order to obtain an adequate price nevertheless, the Papalcy resolved to add to the bargain the tacit toleration of the picture above the high altar. To avoid attention the picture was given to the monks of the far-off provincial town.

11. Bertolt Brecht, on a different level, engaged in analogous reflections: 'If the concept of "work of art" can no longer be applied to the thing that emerges once the work is transformed into a commodity, we have to eliminate this concept with cautious care but without fear, lest we liquidate the function of the very thing as well. For it has to go through this phase without mental reservation, and not as noncommittal deviation from the straight path; rather, what happens here with the work of art will change it fundamentally and erase its past to such an extent that should the old concept be taken up again – and it will, why not? – it will no longer stir any memory of the thing it once designated.'

12. Abel Gance, *L'Art cinématographiquè*, pp. 100–1.

13. Séverin-Mars, quoted by ibid., p. 100.

14. Alexandre Arnoux, *Cinéma pris* (1929), p. 28.

15. Franz Werfel, 'Ein Sommernachtstraum, Ein Film von Shakespeare und Reinhardt', *Neues Wiener Journal*, cited in *Lu*, 15 (November 1935).

16. 'The film...provides – or could provide – useful insight into the details of human actions...Character is never used as a source of motivation; the inner life of the persons never supplies the principal cause of the plot and seldom is its main result.' (Bertolt Brecht, *Versuche*, 'Der Dreigroschenprozess', p. 268.) The expansion of the field of the testable which mechanical equipment brings about for the actor corresponds to the extraordinary expansion of the field of the testable brought about for the individual through economic conditions. Thus, vocational aptitude tests become constantly more important. What matters in these tests are segmental performances of the individual. The film shot and the vocational aptitude test are taken before a committee of experts. The camera director in the studio occupies a place identical with that of the examiner during aptitude tests.

17. Luigi Pirandello, *Si Gira*, quoted by Léon Pierre-Quint, 'Signification du cinéma', *L'Art cinématographiquè*, pp. 14–15.

18. Rudolf Arnheim, *Film als Kunst* (Berlin, 1932), pp. 176 f. In this context certain seemingly unimportant details in which the film director deviates from stage practices gain in interest. Such is the attempt to let the actor play without make-up, as made among others by Dreyer in his *Jeanne d'Arc*. Dreyer spent months seeking the forty actors who constitute the Inquisitors' tribunal. The search for these actors resembled that for stage properties that are hard to come by. Dreyer made every effort to avoid resemblances of age, build, and physiognomy. If the actor thus becomes a stage property, this latter, on the other hand, frequently functions as actor. At least it is not unusual for the film to assign a role to the stage property. Instead of choosing at random from a great wealth of examples, let us concentrate on a particularly convincing one. A clock that is working will always be a disturbance on the stage. There it cannot be permitted its function of measuring time. Even in a naturalistic play, astronomical time would clash with theatrical time. Under these circumstances it is highly revealing that the film can, whenever appropriate, use time as measured by a clock. From this more than from many other touches it may clearly be recognised that under certain circumstances each and every prop in a film may assume important functions. From here it is but one step to Pudovkin's statement that 'the playing of an actor which is connected with an object and is built around it...is always one of the strongest methods of

cinematic construction.' (W. Pudovkin, *Filmregie und Filmmanuskript* (Berlin, 1928), p. 126.) The film is the first art form capable of demonstrating how matter plays tricks on man. Hence, films can be an excellent means of materialistic representation.

19. The change noted here in the method of exhibition caused by mechanical reproduction applies to politics as well. The present crisis of the bourgeois democracies comprises a crisis of the conditions which determine the public presentation of the rulers. Democracies exhibit a member of government directly and personally before the nation's representatives. Parliament is his public. Since the innovations of camera and recording equipment make it possible for the orator to become audible and visible to an unlimited number of persons, the presentation of the man of politics before camera and recording equipment becomes paramount. Parliaments, as much as theatres, are deserted. Radio and film not only affect the function of the professional actor but likewise the function of those who also exhibit themselves before this mechanical equipment, those who govern. Though their tasks may be different, the change affects equally the actor and the ruler. The trend is toward establishing controllable and transferable skills under certain social conditions. This results in a new selection, a selection before the equipment from which the star and the dictator emerge victorious.

20. The privileged character of the respective techniques is lost. Aldous Huxley writes:

> Advances in technology have led...to vulgarity...Process reproduction and the rotary press have made possible the indefinite multiplication of writing and pictures. Universal education and relatively high wages have created an enormous public who know how to read and can afford to buy reading and pictorial matter. A great industry has been called into existence in order to supply these commodities. Now, artistic talent is a very rare phenomenon; whence it follows...that, at every epoch and in all countries, most art has been bad. But the proportion of trash in this total artistic output is greater now than at any other period. That it must be so is a matter of simple arithmetic. The population of Western Europe has a little more than doubled during the last century. But the amount of reading – and seeing – matter has increased, I should imagine, at least twenty and possibly fifty or even a hundred times. If there were n men of talent in a population of x millions, there will presumably be 2n men of talent among 2x millions. The situation may be summed up thus. For every page of print and pictures published a century ago, twenty or perhaps even a hundred pages are published today. But for every man of talent then living, there are now only two men of talent. It may be of course that, thanks to universal education, many potential talents which in the past would have been stillborn are now enabled to realise themselves. Let us assume, then, that there are now three or even four men of talent to every one of earlier times. It still remains true to say that the consumption of reading – and seeing – matter has far outstripped the natural production of gifted writers and draughtsmen. It is the same with hearing-matter. Prosperity, the gramophone and the radio have created an audience of hearers who consume an amount of hearing-matter that has increased out of all proportion to the increase of population and the consequent natural increase of talented musicians. It follows from all this that in all the arts the output of trash is both absolutely and relatively greater than it was in the past; and that it must remain greater for just so long as the world continues to consume the

present inordinate quantities of reading-matter, seeing-matter, and hear-
ing-matter.

(Aldous Huxley, *Beyond the Mexique Bay. A Traveller's Journal*
(London, 1949), pp. 274 ff. First published in 1934)

This mode of observation is obviously not progressive.
21. The boldness of the cameraman is indeed comparable to that of the
surgeon. Luc Durtain lists among specific technical sleights of hand those
'which are required in surgery in the case of certain difficult operations.
I choose as an example a case of oto-rhinolaryngology;...the so-called
endonasal perspective procedure; or I refer to the acrobatic tricks of larynx
surgery which have to be performed following the reversed picture in the
laryngoscope. I might also speak of ear surgery which suggests the precision
work of watchmakers. What range of the most subtle muscular acrobatics is
required from the man who wants to repair or save the human body! We have
only to think of the couching of a cataract where there is virtually a debate of
steel with nearly fluid tissue, or of the major abdominal operations (laparo-
tomy).'

8.   MICHEL FOUCAULT, 'PANOPTICISM'

(From *Discipline and Punish: The Birth of the Prison*, trans. Alan Sheridan
(Harmondsworth, 1991), pp. 195–209. *Discipline and Punish* was originally
published as *Surveiller et punir: Naissance de la prison* (Paris, 1975).)

Summary

Michel Foucault uses the examples of a seventeenth-century plague-stricken town
and Jeremy Bentham's plans for the Panopticon to suggest how control is
exercised, and power relations constituted, in terms of the visual: through
surveillance and the arrangement of space. In the Panopticon, a prison building
in which individual cells circle a central watch-tower, the inmates' subordination
is achieved because they can be seen but are unable to see others or to ascertain
whether they are actually being observed at all. The Panopticon, therefore,
structures power relations according to one's ability or inability to look and in
terms of the roles of spectacle or spectator. Foucault's idea of power, however, is
particularly complex: although it is hierarchical, it is not stable or monolithic, nor
can it be gained by any one person. Rather, the power of the gaze is inaugurated
by the machinery of surveillance itself, in the institutions and the subject-
positions that it constructs. Moreover, although the examples used here are
historically specific, Foucault emphasises that they are models for a mechanism
that functions throughout society today, and in schools and hospitals as well as
prisons.

Notes

1. Archives militaires de Vincennes, A 1,516 91 sc. Pièce. This regulation is
   broadly similar to a whole series of others that date from the same period
   and earlier.
2. Jeremy Bentham, *The Works of Jeremy Bentham*, ed. John Bowring, vol. IV
   (London, 1843), pp. 60–4. [Hereafter cited as *P* with page nos in parentheses.]

3. In the *Postscript to the Panopticon* (1791), Bentham adds dark inspection galleries painted in black around the inspector's lodge, each making it possible to observe two storeys of cells.
4. In his first version of the *Panopticon*, Bentham had also imagined an acoustic surveillance, operated by means of pipes leading from the cells to the central tower. In the *Postscript* he abandoned the idea, perhaps because he could not introduce into it the principle of dissymmetry and prevent the prisoners from hearing the inspector as well as the inspector hearing them. Julius tried to develop a system of dissymmetrical listening (N.H. Julius, *Leçons sur les prisons*, vol. I (1831), p. 18).
5. G. Loisel, *Histoire des ménageries*, vol. II (Paris, 1912), pp. 104–7.
6. Imagining this continuous flow of visitors entering the central tower by an underground passage and then observing the circular landscape of the Panopticon, was Bentham aware of the Panoramas that Barker was constructing at exactly the same period (the first seems to have dated from 1787) and in which the visitors, occupying the central place, saw unfolding around them a landscape, a city or a battle? The visitors occupied exactly the place of the sovereign gaze.

9. NORMAN BRYSON, 'SEMIOLOGY AND VISUAL INTERPRETATION'
(From *Visual Theory: Painting and Interpretation*, ed. Norman Bryson, Michael Ann Holly and Keith Moxey (Cambridge, 1991), pp. 61–73.)

Summary

Norman Bryson appropriates semiology, a theory that identifies culture and its practices as a system of signs, for the analysis of paintings. His argument is based on the assumption that art, like any other sign-system, is a site of power which is historically constituted and constituting. This position, according to Bryson, has been occluded in traditional theories of art, which have either seen perception as a private, sensory experience, removed from social setting, or employed a reductive Marxist model of base and superstructure that allows for a certain idea of historical context but fails to identify art as a powerful, signifying practice that interacts with other institutions and ideologies. For Bryson, painting is semiological and discursive, the product of cultural codes and the mechanism by which these codes are shaped and defined. In the concluding section of the essay the very notion of interpretation is problematised, leading to a questioning of the extent to which a work's original context can be located and the suggestion that any view of history is dependent on one's own historical circumstances. It is here, Bryson argues, that semiology again proves important: as a self-reflexive tool for reading visual images, it does not so much delimit modes of interpretation as describe their processes.

Notes

1. John Ruskin, *Modern Painters* (London, 1856), vol. 4, pp. 26–31.
2. Adolf Hildebrand, *Das Problem der Form in der bildenen Kunst* (1893), 3rd edn (Strasbourg, 1901); Heinrich Wölfflin, *Kunstgeschlichtliche Grundbegriffe: Das Problem der Stilentwicklung in der neueren Kunst* (Munich, 1915); Alois Riegl, *Spätromiche Kunstindustrie* (1901) (Vienna, 1927); Erwin Panofsky, Introductory

chapter to *Studies in Iconology: Humanistic Themes in the Art of the Renaissance* (1939) (reprinted New York, 1962).
3. E. H. Gombrich, *Art and Illusion: A Study in the Psychology of Pictorial Representation*, 2nd edn (Princeton, NJ, 1961).
4. On the examples of understanding a mathematical formula and learning to read, see Ludwig Wittgenstein, *Philosophical Investigations*, 3rd edn, trans. G. E. M. Anscombe (New York, 1953), esp. paras 186–90, 156–71.
5. Jan Mukarovsky, 'Art as Semiological Fact', in *Calligram: Essays in New Art History from France*, ed. N. Bryson (Cambridge, 1988); Svetlana Alpers, *The Art of Describing: Dutch Art in the Seventeenth Century* (Chicago, 1983); Michael Baxandall, *Painting and Experience in Fifteenth Century Italy* (Oxford, 1972).
6. Keith Moxey, 'Panofsky's Concept of "Iconology" and the Problem of Interpretation in the History of Art', *New Literary History*, 17 (Winter 1986), 271.
7. W. K. Wimsatt and Monroe Beardsley, 'The Intentional Fallacy', in *Literary Intention*, ed. David Newton-De Molina (Edinburgh, 1976), pp. 1–13; Roland Barthes, *Critique et vérité* (Paris, 1966); Jacques Derrida, *Of Grammatology*, trans. Gayatri Spivak (Baltimore, MD, 1976).

10. TERESA DE LAURETIS, 'IMAGING'

(From *Alice Doesn't: Feminism, Semiotics, Cinema* (London, 1984), pp. 37–9, 53–8.)

Summary

In this extract Teresa de Lauretis traces the intersection between feminism and 'imaging' (the production and perception/interpretation of images in the cinema). She argues that the focus on positive and negative images of women found in some film criticism is reductive since both cinema and feminism challenge such hierarchical oppositions. In particular, feminism undermines the distinction between the subjective and the social because the personal is also ideological, inscribed in the world: the female subject is a cultural and political construct. Lauretis's analysis of the process of seeing leads her to locate a traversal of similar oppositions in the cinema, where the subjective/social binarism is translated into the critical distinction between perception and signification (or semiology). Using examples from both spheres, Lauretis contends that neither fully explains the process of imaging, which relies on an interaction between the two: images are both biologically motivated and socially determined. The word used to signify this bridging of diverse theoretical approaches is 'mapping', a concept that emphasises the relation between feminism and cinema and inaugurates a critical practice that takes account of the connection between the social and subjective.

Notes

1. A compact and fully articulated formulation of these concepts with regard to cinema may be found in Stephen Heath, *Questions of Cinema* (Bloomington, IN, 1981), especially ch. 1, 'On Screen, In Frame: Film and Ideology', and ch. 10, 'The Cinematic Apparatus: Technology as Historical and Cultural Form'. On the notion of signifying practice, see also Julia Kristeva, 'Signifying Practice and Mode of Production', *Edinburgh '76 Magazine* (London, 1976), pp. 64–76.

2. While some works assume that cinema and film make up and circulate certain images of women, and accordingly examine and classify them, others start from the premise that cinema and film construct woman as image, and take as their task the understanding of that process in relation to, or as it affects, female spectators. As even a basic list of bibliographical references would be too extensive, only a few will be cited. In the first category, see Marjorie Rosen, *Popcorn Venus: Women, Movies and the American Dream* (New York, 1973); Joan Mellen, *Women and Their Sexuality in the New Film* (New York, 1974); Molly Haskell, *From Reverence to Rape: The Treatment of Women in the Movies* (New York, 1974). The notion of images of women is critically discussed in the following: Claire Johnston, 'Feminist Politics and Film History', *Screen* 16, no. 3 (Autumn 1975), 115–24; Griselda Pollock, 'What's Wrong with Images of Women', *Screen Education*, no. 23 (Summer 1977), 25–33; Elizabeth Cowie, 'Women, Representation and the Image', *Screen Education*, no. 23 (Summer 1977), 15–23. As for the second category, which I refer to as the feminist critique of representation, the following are general and/or survey works which provide additional and specific references: Claire Johnston (ed.), *Notes on Women's Cinema* (London, 1974); Julia Lesage, 'Feminist Film Criticism: Theory and Practice', *Women and Film*, no. 5/6 (1974), 12–14; 'Feminism and Film: Critical Approaches', editorial, *Camera Obscura*, no. 1 (Fall 1976), 3–10; Karyn Kay and Gerald Peary (eds), *Women and Cinema: A Critical Anthology* (New York, 1977); Christine Gledhill, 'Recent Developments in Feminist Criticism', *Quarterly Review of Film Studies* 3, no. 4 (1978), 457–93; Laura Mulvey, 'Feminism, Film and the Avant-Garde', *Framework*, no. 10 (1979), 3–10; Annette Kuhn, *Women's Pictures* (London, 1982); E. Ann Kaplan, *Women and Film: Both Sides of the Camera* (London and New York, 1983).
3. Basic works in these areas, with regard to cinema, include Teresa de Lauretis and Stephen Heath (eds), *The Cinematic Apparatus* (London and New York, 1980); Christian Metz, *Film Language: A Semiotics of the Cinema*, trans. Michael Taylor (New York, 1974), *Language and Cinema* (The Hague and Paris, 1974), and *The Imaginary Signifier* (Bloomington, IN, 1981); *Screen Reader 1* (London, 1980) and *Screen Reader 2* (London, 1981); Bill Nichols, *Ideology and the Image* (Bloomington, IN, 1981).
4. Colin Blakemore, 'The Baffled Brain,' in *Illusion in Nature and Art*, ed. R. L. Gregory and E. H. Gombrich (New York, 1973), p. 26. All further page references in the text are to this edition.
5. Cf. Hermann von Helmholtz, *Handbook of Physiological Optics*, trans. and ed. J. P. Southhall (London and New York, 1963).
6. R. L. Gregory, 'The Confounded Eye', in *Illusion in Nature and Art*, p. 61.
7. Umberto Eco, *A Theory of Semiotics* (Bloomington, IN, 1976), p. 245.
8. For example, the word/cinema/: in linguistic terms, when one utters the word/cinema/ one merely reproduces it from the language; one does not invent it, one cannot be creative by changing the phonemes or the morphological aspects of the word. See Eco, *A Theory of Semiotics*, pp. 182–3.
9. The critique of cinema, of course, is not limited to critical discourses on cinema but includes, and to some extent depends on, feminist film practices. A short list of film-makers whose work has been important to the feminist critique of representation would include Chantal Akerman, Dorothy Arzner, Liliana Cavani, Michelle Citron, Marguerite Duras, Valie Export, Bette Gordon, Bonnie Klein, Babette Mangolte, Laura Mulvey, Ulrike Ottinger, Sally Potter, Yvonne Rainer, Jackie Raynal, Helke Sander.

11. JACKIE STACEY, 'DESPERATELY SEEKING DIFFERENCE: JACKIE STACEY CONSIDERS DESIRE BETWEEN WOMEN IN NARRATIVE CINEMA'
(From _Screen_, 28, 1 (Winter 1987), 48–61.)

Summary

Jackie Stacey analyses the ways in which spectatorial roles in the cinema are problematised by female viewers. She argues that women do not necessarily adopt a masculine way of looking, nor do they fully identify with the images that they see on screen. Rather, their viewing position is often defined by the very differences between women. To emphasise this point, Stacey analyses how female characters view each other on screen and contends that their ways of seeing parallel those adopted by the spectators of the film. Her discussion of _Desperately Seeking Susan_ and _All About Eve_ suggests a potentially liberating role for the female viewer because the women are not only image-objects but desiring (and gazing) subjects.

Notes

1. Laura Mulvey, 'Visual Pleasure and Narrative Cinema', _Screen_, 16, no. 3 (Autumn 1975), 6–18.
2. Ibid., p. 13.
3. Ibid., p. 10.
4. Ibid.
5. There have been several attempts to fill this theoretical gap and provide analyses of masculinity as sexual spectacle: see Richard Dyer, 'Don't Look Now – The Male Pin-Up', _Screen_, 23, nos 3–4 (September–October 1982); Steve Neale, 'Masculinity as Spectacle', _Screen_, 24, no. 6 (November–December 1983); and Andy Medhurst, 'Can Chaps Be Pin-Ups?', _Ten_, 8, no 17 (1985).
6. David Rodowick, 'The Difficulty of Difference', _Wide Angle_, 5, no 1 (1982), 8.
7. Mary Ann Doane, 'Film and the Masquerade: Theorising the Female Spectator', _Screen_, 23, nos 3–4 (September–October 1982), 74–87.
8. Constance Penley, 'Feminism, Film Theory and the Bachelor Machines', _m/f_, no 10 (1985), 39–56.
9. _Enunciator_: 'the term ... marks both the person who possesses the right to speak within the film, and the source (instance) towards which the series of representations is logically channelled back', Raymond Bellour, 'Hitchcock the Enunciator', _Camera Obscura_, no 2 (1977), 94.
10. Raymond Bellour, 'Psychosis, Neurosis, Perversion', _Camera Obscura_, nos 3–4 (1979), 97.
11. Janet Bergstrom, 'Enunciation and Sexual Difference', _Camera Obscura_, nos 3–4 (1979), 57. See also Janet Bergstrom, 'Alternation, Segmentation, Hypnosis: An Interview with Raymond Bellour', _Camera Obscura_, nos 3–4 (1979).
12. Doane, 'Film and the Masquerade', p. 78.
13. Ibid., p. 80.
14. Mary Ann Doane, Patricia Mellencamp and Linda Williams, 'Feminist Film Criticism: An Introduction', in Mary Ann Doane, Patricia Mellencamp and Linda Williams (eds), _Re-Vision_ (American Film Institute, Frederick, MD, 1984), p. 9.
15. Mulvey, 'visual Pleasure'.

16. Bellour, 'Psychosis, Neurosis, Perversion'.
17. Doane, 'Film and the Masquerade'.
18. Doane et al., *Re-Vision*, p. 14.
19. Laura Mulvey, 'Afterthoughts on "Visual Pleasure and Narrative Cinema" ... Inspired by "Duel in the Sun" ', *Framework*, nos 15–17 (1981), 12–15.
20. Ibid., p. 15.
21. Mary Ann Doane citing Julia Kristeva, *About Chinese Women*, in 'Caught and Rebecca: The Inscription of Femininity as Absence', *Enclitic*, 5, no 2, 6, no 1 (Fall 1981, Spring 1982), 77.
22. For a discussion of films which might be included under this category, see Caroline Sheldon, 'Lesbians and Film; Some Thoughts' in Richard Dyer (ed.), *Gays and Film* (New York, revised edn, 1984).
23. Teresa de Lauretis, *Alice Doesn't: Feminism, Semiotics and the Cinema* (London, 1984), pp. 113, 119.
24. Ibid., p. 121.
25. See, for example, Sigmund Freud, 'Some Psychical Consequences of the Anatomical Distinction Between the Sexes' (1925) in *On Sexuality*, Pelican Freud Library vol. 7 (Harmondsworth, 1977), pp. 331–43.
26. See Jacques Lacan, 'The Mirror Stage as Formative of the Function of the I as Revealed in Psychoanalytic Experience', *Ecrits* trans. Alan Sheridan (London, 1977), pp. 1–7.

12.   BELL HOOKS, 'THE OPPOSITIONAL GAZE: BLACK FEMALE SPECTATORS'

(From *Black Looks: Race and Representation* (Boston, MA, 1992), pp. 115–31.)

Summary

bell hooks asserts that how one sees and what one sees is determined by race as well as gender. Black women spectators, then, have been doubly marginalised in mainstream Hollywood cinema, where a lack of representation or stereotypical construction means that they are unable to identify with the images on screen. In some ways, however, this exclusion has positive as well as negative implications. Drawing on Michel Foucault's notion that the power relations formulated by seeing always already contain the possibility of subversion, hooks contends that the black female viewer's distance from the image means that she can either choose not to look, or opt to look 'critically' or 'oppositionally', with a gaze that brings with it the pleasure of interrogation. hooks's essay is as much a criticism of existing feminist film theory as it is of the cinema. She argues that such theory is complicit with the assumptions of films because it categorises all women as white and fails to recognise that sexual difference is not the only determinant in a politics of vision.

13.   JACQUES LACAN, 'OF THE GAZE AS *OBJET PETIT A*'

(From *The Four Fundamental Concepts of Psycho-Analysis*, ed. Jacques-Alain Miller, trans. Alan Sheridan (Harmondsworth, 1994), pp. 80–90. *The Four Fundamental Concepts of Psycho-Analysis* was originally published as *Le Séminaire de Jacques Lacan, Livre XI*, '*Les quatre concepts fondamentaux de la psychanalyse*' (Paris, 1973).)

Summary

In this extract Jacques Lacan distinguishes between the act of seeing (associated with the biological organ, the eye) and the gaze. Seeing is associated with a subject who is unified and autonomous, who takes possession of the things seen, or can annihilate them by choosing not to look. The gaze, on the other hand, exposes the fact that this idea of subjectivity is an illusion, for, according to Lacan, the subject is not the omnipotent origin of sight but the effect of it, situated in a condition of seeingness that precedes it and that it cannot control. The subject's lack is precipitated by his or her entry into the symbolic order (the system of language and law) and leads to the birth of desire, which is repressed in the inaccessible realm of the unconscious. The '*objet a*' is the cause of unconscious desire, the lack that motivates it, a role adopted in the specular order by the gaze: the condition, and limitations, of looking and being looked at. Lacan takes Holbein's anamorphic skull in *The Ambassadors* as an example of the *object a* because it exposes the incompleteness and fragmentation of the gaze and motivates unconscious desire. Like the divorced realms of the conscious and unconscious, the painting and skull can only be viewed separately and at the cost of obliterating the other field of vision. The skull is the reminder that desire can never be satisfied and that the subject cannot recover direct access to the real, except in death.

14.   SLAVOJ ŽIŽEK, 'PORNOGRAPHY, NOSTALGIA, MONTAGE: A TRIAD OF THE GAZE'

(From *Looking Awry: An Introduction to Jacques Lacan through Popular Culture* (Cambridge, MA, 1991), pp. 109–19.)

Summary

Why is the pornographic film such an anticlimax? Where lies the power of the nostalgic movie? And what makes Hitchcock's films so 'uncanny'? Slavoj Žižek accounts for these diverse effects in terms of the Lacanian split between the eye and the gaze. In pornography, for example, the characters on screen do not expose the conditions of seeingness associated with the gaze. On the contrary, by showing too much they 'miss' desire. Nostalgia also elides the gaze but in different ways, evoking a spectatorial fascination and identification with the vision of the characters that conceals the split between the eye and the gaze and creates the illusion of 'seeing oneself seeing' that Lacan associates with a Cartesian subjectivity. The gaze and its concomitant feelings of desire and anxiety is elicited in montage, and particularly in the filmic cuts and camera shots associated with Alfred Hitchcock. Here one becomes aware of a look that is always already there and that sees others from a point at which it cannot itself be seen.

Notes

1. Jacques Lacan, *The Four Fundamental Concepts of Psycho-Analysis* (London, 1977), p. 109.
2. It is precisely because in pornography, the picture does *not* gaze back at us, because it is 'flat', without any mysterious 'spot' needing to be looked at 'awry' in order to assume distinct form, that the fundamental prohibition determining the direction of the gaze of actors on the screen is suspended: in a pornographic movie, the actor – as a rule, the woman – in the moment of intense sexual pleasure looks directly into the camera, addressing us, the spectators.
3. This paradox of 'impossible knowledge' that is inscribed in the way persons react on screen is far more interesting than it appears at first sight; for example, it offers us a way of explaining the logic of the *cameo appearances* of Hitchcock in his own films. What is his worst film? *Topaz*. In it, Hitchcock appears in a wheelchair in an airport lounge, as if wishing to inform us that his creative power is definitely crippled. In his last film, *Family Plot*, he appears as a shadow on the windowpane of the registry office, as if wishing to inform us that he is already close to death. Every one of his cameo appearances reveals such an 'impossible knowledge', as if Hitchcock were capable of assuming for an instant a position of pure meta-language, of taking an 'objective look' at himself and locating himself in the picture.
4. Cf. Fredric Jameson, 'Postmodernism, or the Cultural Logic of Late Capitalism', in *New Left Review*, 146 (1984).
5. Lacan, *The Four Fundamental Concepts of Psycho-Analysis*, p. 74.
6. This problem was first articulated by Noël Burch in his theory of off-screen space, i.e., of a specific exterior implied, constituted by the very interplay of the shot and counter-shot; cf. Noël Burch, *The Theory of Film Practice* (New York, 1973).
7. Cf. Raymond Bellour, *L'analyse du film* (Paris, 1979).
8. It is no coincidence that in both cases, the object approached by the hero is a *house* – apropos of *Notorious*, Pascal Bonitzer developed a detailed theory of the house as the location of an incestuous secret in Hitchcock's work; cf. Pascal Bonitzer, 'Notorious', in *Cahiers du cinéma*, 358 (1980).
9. In his ironic, amiably sadistic teasing of the spectator, Hitchcock takes into account precisely this gap between the formal procedure and the content to which it is applied, i.e., the fact that anxiety results from a purely formal procedure. First, by means of formal manipulation, he bestows upon an everyday, trivial object an aura of mystery and anxiety; it then becomes manifest that this object effectively *is* just an everyday object. The best-known case of this is found in the second version of *The Man Who Knew Too Much*. On a suburban London street, James Stewart approaches a lonely stranger. Silently, they exchange glances as an atmosphere of tension and anxiety is created; it seems that the stranger is threatening Stewart. But we soon discover that Stewart's suspicion is entirely unfounded – the stranger is just an accidental passerby.
10. Lacan, *The Four Fundamental Concepts of Psycho-Analysis*, pp. 95–6.

15. JULIA KRISTEVA, 'MOTHERHOOD ACCORDING TO GIOVANNI BELLINI'

(From *Desire in Language: A Semiotic Approach to Literature and Art*, ed. Leon S. Roudiez, trans. Thomas Gora, Alice Jardine and Leon S. Roudiez (Oxford, 1981), pp. 237–50, 266–9. 'Motherhood According to Giovanni Bellini' was originally published in French in *Peinture* (December 1975).)

Summary

Julia Kristeva juxtaposes psychoanalysis, biography and art history to analyse images of maternity in the paintings of Leonardo da Vinci and Giovanni Bellini. According to Kristeva, motherhood is the site of tension between the social and biological, the world of language (the symbolic) and the semiotic (a pre-linguistic system of movements and sounds that have not been fixed as signifiers by language). The mother is situated in the symbolic, where she is a subject, but she also embodies biological and instinctual drives that elude social relations and representation. After locating this tension in art as well as maternity, Kristeva argues that, while da Vinci depicts the mother in terms of the symbolic, the knowable and representable, Bellini's paintings, like maternity itself, are on the threshold between the symbolic and semiotic. In their use of colour and volume they suggest what is beyond figuration and identity, evoking a joy and ecstasy that Kristeva calls 'jouissance'.

Notes

1. 'Dormition' refers to the period of the Virgin Mary's death, which is viewed merely as a period of sleep, before she was carried to heaven (Assumption). The word originated in the *Transitus Maria*, a fifth-century Byzantine apocrypha. [Leon S. Roudiez]
2. The French word 'enceinte' has been kept as the only way to preserve the pun: 'enceinte' is a protective wall around a town; 'femme enceinte' is a pregnant woman. [Leon S. Roudiez]
3. Cf. G. Fiocco, *Giovanni Bellini* (Milan 1960); R. Longhi, *Viatico per cinque secoli di Pittura veneziana* (Florence, 1946); L. Coletti, *Pittura veneta del quattro cento* (Novara, 1953); and others.
4. Dante, *Paradisio*, xxi, 58–63.

16. JACQUES DERRIDA, 'WHY PETER EISENMAN WRITES SUCH GOOD BOOKS'

(Extract trans. Sarah Whiting. From *Architecture and Urbanism*, August 1988 (Extra Edition), pp. 113–24. Reprinted in Jacques Derrida and Peter Eisenman, *Chora L Works*, ed. Jeffrey Kipnis and Thomas Leeser (New York, 1997), pp. 95–101.)

Summary

In this essay Jacques Derrida describes his interdisciplinary collaboration with Peter Eisenman on a design project for the Parc de la Villette in Paris, which takes its impetus from literature, music and choreography. Derrida argues that Eisenman's work destabilises the desire for origin and presence and is therefore linked to his own deconstructive enterprise. Eisenman's architecture is a kind of writing that undermines the seemingly fixed distinction between the visual and textual, inaugurating a dissolution of boundaries that is intensified in this particular project: Derrida, the author, draws the sketches, and Eisenman, the artist, invents the title. Eisenman's architecture is informed by the play and deferral of meanings; it is a space where hierarchies and oppositions are subverted. Indeed, this is suggested as much in the plural and playful language of the essay itself as in *Choral Work* which, in its very title, defies any search for truth or origin.

Notes

1. Desmond Lee, trans., Plato, *Timeaus and Critias* (Harmondsworth and New York, 1971), p. 72.
2. *en abyme*: French expression meaning telescoping image, that is, an image which gets smaller in constant multiplication of itself (trans. note).
3. *L'aphorism a Contretemps*, in *Romeo et Juliette, le Livre* (Paris 1986; to be published in English).
4. 'So an endless play of readings: "find out house", "fine doubt house", "find either or", "end of where", "end of covering" (in the wealth of reading possibilities, two of an "inside" nature that have recently arisen might be interesting to indicate. "Fin d'Ou T" can also suggest the French *fin d'août*, the end of August, the period, in fact, when the work on the project was completed. In addition, an English reader affecting French might well mispronounce the same fragment as "fondu", a Swiss cooking technique (from the French *fondu* for melted, also a ballet term for bending at the knee) alluding to the presence of a Swiss-trained architect, Pieter Versteegh, as a principal design assistant!) etc., is provoked by regulated manipulations of the spaces – between letters, between languages, between image and writing – a manipulation that is in every way formal, in every way writing, yet blatantly independent of the manipulations that the foundations (of French or English) would permit.' Jeffrey Kipnis, *Architecture Unbound, Consequences of the recent work of Peter Eisenman*, in *Fin d'Ou T Hou S*, p. 19.
5. Or the book to a monument. Hugo, for example, in *Notre Dame de Paris*: 'The book will kill the edifice', but also 'The bible of stone and the bible of paper'...'the cathedral of Shakespeare...' 'the mosque of Byron...'

17.   MICHEL FOUCAULT, '*LAS MENINAS*'
(From *The Order of Things* (London, 1970), pp. 3–16. *The Order of Things* was originally published as *Les Mots et les choses* (Paris, 1966).)

Summary

Michel Foucault's close critical analysis of Velázquez's *Las Meninas*, a picture that 'shows' itself and 'looks back' at its observer, explores the relations established between inside and outside, spectator and spectacle. The viewer here is not simply in control, or able to 'read' and consume the image, but is positioned in certain ways and even as the model which the artist seems to be studying. Foucault argues that this painting is self-referential, illustrating, in the figure of the painter and the finished canvases that line the walls, the whole cycle of representation. The gaps in this artistic process are signified by the mirror which problematises the limits of pictoriality and attempts to show what lies outside the painting. It reflects the King and Queen, whose positions the spectator has usurped, and offers another central focus that competes with the little Infanta. Foucault also engages with the question of whether the visual and verbal are equivalents, whether one can speak about what one sees. His answer is a resounding 'no', and his essay can be read as an attempt to retain the differences between these forms, to expose their otherness, or, in his own words, the 'infinity' of their relation.

18.　JEAN BAUDRILLARD, 'AESTHETIC ILLUSION AND VIRTUAL REALITY'
(From *Art and Artefact*, ed. Nicholas Zurbrugg (London, 1997), pp. 19–27.)

Summary

What are the implications for human life in a visual culture? What is at stake in technological and media advancement? To answer these questions, Jean Baudrillard examines the permeation of the image in society and presages a future of 'virtual reality', where technology aims to build a perfect world, without defect. In a playful and disturbing premonition, he pictures a future obsessed with surface and appearance in which artificial intelligence and high fidelity sound have irrevocably changed human existence. It is a future, Baudrillard reassures the reader, that is ultimately impossible, but even in contemporary society the boundaries between reality and image have already been confused, with reality erased in favour of 'real time', in which an event or thought is immediately 'realised' on a television or computer screen. Our relation to visuality, Baudrillard contends, has been internalised to the extent that we no longer need a literal camera in order for what we see or do, and who we are, to be determined by images.

Glossary

Note: Words or phrases given in italics are also defined in their alphabetical place in the Glossary.

anamorphosis Especially popular in seventeenth-century painting, anamorphosis is an optical trick of *perspective* in which the image is laterally stretched so that when looked at from the front it makes no sense but is rectified when seen from a different angle.

Bentham, Jeremy Bentham (1748–1832) was an English philosopher and founder of utilitarianism. His concern with morals and law led to plans for a Panopticon, a building of correction, where prisoners were controlled by being watched (or thinking that they were) from a central tower. The Panopticon is discussed by Michel Foucault in 'Panopticism'.

castration complex For Freud, the castration complex takes place when the child discovers the anatomical differences between the sexes. It is, therefore, bound up in vision and appearance. The boy assumes that this genital difference is due to the female's penis having been cut off and, because of this threat of castration, renounces his desire for the mother. For the girl, the discovery leads to her resentment of the mother, whom she blames for castration, and the redirection of her desires to the father. Lacan modified these ideas of the castration complex, moving away from the idea that it is precipitated by the presence or absence of an actual penis to the significance of the 'phallus', which, as a signifier of the *symbolic order* and imaginary plenitude, is possessed by no one.

cogito The cogito is the formulation, 'I think therefore I am', devised by the philosopher René Descartes, which encapsulates Western ways of thinking about *subjectivity*. It implies a subject who is defined by consciousness and therefore unified, autonomous, and in control of its actions and meanings. This idea of the subject has been challenged by psychoanalysis and *poststructuralism*, where the subject is regarded as produced by, and an effect of, language and redoubled by the unconscious.

constancy Size constancy is a perceptual process that compensates for changes in the retinal image with viewing distance. It depends upon a knowledge of the size of objects and distance, which enables the viewer to see objects as the right size whether they are near or distant. For a discussion of constancy see Richard L. Gregory, *Eye and Brain: the Psychology of Seeing* (London, 1966), pp. 151–60.

deconstruction A term coined by Jacques Derrida to describe how the play of *difference* in language means that what seems singular and self-identical contains the trace of otherness. This allows for a subversion of hierarchical binary distinctions because each term relies on and contains the trace of its opposite.

desire As part of the *symbolic order*, the *subject* loses its illusory plenitude and autonomy and becomes the unstable effect of language and meaning. This loss

227

is the cause of desire. In the *specular order* the cause of desire, known as the *objet a*, is the *gaze*, which is the lost object in the inextricable *real*.

difference   Ferdinand de Saussure argued that language is a system of differences with no positive terms, that is, that signs only acquire their value in a negative relation: by being what all the other signs in the system are not. Jacques Derrida employed and modified this idea in his notion of 'differance' (spelt with an 'a'). See *poststructuralism*.

discourse   For Michel Foucault a discourse is a knowledge (such as science or law), which has its own distinct vocabulary. It can serve the interests of particular *ideologies* and institutions and is instrumental in constituting the *subject* through the positions and relations that it sets up.

Eisenman, Peter   An American architect, whose designs engage with *postmodern* and *poststructuralist* theories. In 1985 he collaborated with Jacques Derrida on a project for the Parc de la Villette in Paris.

eye   Jacques Lacan argues that there is a split between the eye and the *gaze*. This mirrors the subjective split itself because, while the eye is the organ of sight and on the side of the *subject*, the gaze is on the side of the object or other: it is the condition of looking. There is no coincidence between the eye and the gaze because we can never see from the position of the other.

fetishism   In Freud's theory fetishism is the dependence on an object for sexual excitement. It originates in the child's horror at female castration and the substitution of a fetish object for the missing penis. For Jacques Lacan, the fetish is not a substitute for the actual penis but for the imaginary phallus and the power and plenitude that it symbolises.

gaze   In French '*le regard*', the look. Jacques Lacan uses this term to describe the condition of seeingness in which the subject is inserted in the *specular order*. The gaze undermines the idea that the subject is in control of or the origin of sight because s/he is looked at, objectified, and unable to see from the position of the other. In Lacanian theory, the gaze is distinct from the *eye*. See *objet petit a*.

Gombrich, Ernst (Hans Josef)   An Austrian art historian, whose writings promote linguistic readings of art and deal with aspects of perception and the role of seeing in the interpretation of visual images.

ideology   The system of thoughts and beliefs that determine the *subject's* actions and behaviour. Karl Marx saw ideologies as abstract ideas that stemmed from the economic base and were internalised by the individual, using the metaphor of the *camera obscura* to describe this false consciousness. The French structuralist Marxist Louis Althusser developed these ideas and argued that ideologies can be both demonstrated and produced in institutions and material practices themselves. Thus, visual images and even vision can embody and constitute ideologies.

imaginary   This is the realm of images and identification described by Jacques Lacan. According to Lacan, images constitute *subjectivity* but do so in a deceptive and illusory way (thus the meaning of the word 'imaginary' as fictional or delusive), giving the subject a false impression of its mastery, autonomy and plenitude. The hypnotic effect of the imaginary is described in Lacan's account of the 'mirror stage'. See 'The Mirror Stage as Formative of the Function of the I as Revealed in Psychoanalytic Experience', *Ecrits: A Selection*, trans. Alan Sheridan (London, 1977), pp. 1–7.

jouissance   Enjoyment, or a sexual/orgasmic pleasure, that also involves pain. Jacques Lacan used this term but it is developed in the work of Julia Kristeva.

look   see *gaze*

Marxism Critical ideas of Karl Marx and his followers in which the history of humanity is seen to depend on its changing mode of material production, that is, on its economic base. See *ideology*.

mimesis Widespread idea that the aim of art is to imitate or mirror the external world.

modernism Term often used to identify the distinctive features of the late nineteenth and early twentieth centuries when literature and art broke with traditional Western concepts concerning not only literary and artistic forms but also ideas of social organisation and subjectivity. The philosopher Walter Benjamin is a modernist critic. See *postmodernism*.

objet petit a This is the lost object in the *real*, which is the cause of desire. In the *specular order* the *objet a* is the *gaze*, the condition of seeingness, which the *subject* is inserted into but over which it has no control.

oculocentrism The primacy that Western culture attributes to looking and the visual.

perspective The method of representing distance and the relative position and size of objects in space, known as 'perspective', was instigated in the Renaissance and culminated in the invention of photography. It depicts objects along pyramidal lines that converge towards a vanishing point. In order for perspective to be effective it depends on a depiction of what would be seen by a single eye rather than on binocular vision.

phallocentrism A belief in the primacy of masculine sexuality predicated on the centrality of the phallus (see *castration complex*), which relegates woman to a position of subordination and lack.

postmodernism This marks a development and break from *modernism* rather than a distinct or definable historical period. Postmodernism transforms the social, political and aesthetic, so that art is no longer regarded as self-sufficient or separate from the world but bound up in it, even to the extent that there is no distinction between art and life. Jean Baudrillard argues that the image has actually taken priority over reality. Postmodernism also emphasises the unstable nature of language, where 'difference' constitutes the world in a way that refuses the possibility of any full or secure meaning. See Jean-François Lyotard, *The Postmodern Condition: A Report on Knowledge*, trans. Geoff Bennington and Brian Massumi (Manchester, 1984).

poststructuralism Poststructuralist criticism, which includes the later work of Roland Barthes as well as that of Jacques Derrida, employs Saussurean linguistics but stresses that meanings are never as fixed as *structuralism* seems to imply. Derrida uses the term 'differance' (spelt with an 'a' to distinguish it from *difference*) to describe the play of language, in which meanings are not only defined according to their negative difference from everything else in the system but are constantly deferred or postponed, referring to other absent meanings in a way that makes closure or a full intelligibility an impossibility.

power/knowledge For Michel Foucault power is a series of shifting relations that constitute the *subject* and are exercised in discourses and institutions. Central to Foucault's thesis is the idea that discipline and control can be achieved through relations of looking and the knowledge and power that vision allows over what is seen.

real The real is defined by Jacques Lacan as part of the triad of the real, the *imaginary* and the *symbolic*. It refers to a world of full and present things that precede the *subject* but that the subject has no access to because, in its very position as subject, it is already inserted into a system of language which names these things and, in so doing, takes their place.

referent   The object in the world that the signifier points to.

scopic drive   The drive or instinct to look. See also *scopophilia* and *voyeurism*.

scopophilia   The sexual pleasure involved in the act of looking. See *voyeurism*.

semiotic   Term used by Julia Kristeva to describe the system of instinctual and biological drives that precede, allow for, and are in opposition to, the *symbolic*. The semiotic 'chora', a word that Kristeva takes from Plato, is bound up in maternity and the way in which primary processes and family structures are mediated through the body of the mother. The chora can erupt in literature, music and art, where it consists of colours, movements, sounds, or even silences, that have not been fixed as *signifiers* by language.

semiotics   The science of *signs*. Also called semiology. This theory stems from *structuralism* and analyses how signs function at all levels of human experience. See Roland Barthes, *Mythologies*, trans. Annette Lavers (London, 1972).

signifier, signified, sign   The basic components of language as outlined by Ferdinand de Saussure. A signifier is the 'word-image', that is, a sound or visual manifestation. A signified is the concept or meaning attached to the signifier. According to Saussure, we rarely separate the signifier from the signified: when we say a word we automatically think of what it means, and the unit that the two components form is known as the sign. Such ideas are complicated in *poststructuralist* theory. Jacques Derrida uses the term 'signifier' rather than 'sign' because he contends that there is no simple meaning secured to a word. Rather, the meaning, or the possibility of a full and secure meaning, is constantly deferred in an endless play of language.

specular order   The specular order is the realm of vision and visuality and the relations and identifications that it precipitates. In Lacanian theory it mirrors the *symbolic order*. See *imaginary*.

structuralism   The Swiss linguist Ferdinand de Saussure argues that language is a self-contained structure, made up of a system of arbitrary and differential *signs* which do not name or reflect thoughts or concepts that pre-exist it but actually construct them. *Semiotics* developed out of this theory. See also *poststructuralism*.

studium   Roland Barthes uses this Latin word to describe a culturally determined reaction to a photograph. The *studium* is a trained or conventional reading that relies on the human interest that the image evokes. This interpretation is threatened by the 'punctum', a detail or object in the photograph that disturbs or shocks the viewer.

subject   The subject is an effect of language, a being that speaks and says 'I'. As such, it is never autonomous or fully present to itself but unfixed and in process. Just as the subject is inserted into a linguistic system over which it has no control, it also takes its place in a *specular order* in which it is constituted according to its relation to the image. See *imaginary*.

symbolic order   A Lacanian term for the system of language and law that constitutes the *subject* and *difference*. The *unconscious*, which, Lacan argues, is 'structured like a language' belongs to the symbolic.

uncanny   The uncanny is a feeling produced when one confronts a double, ghosts or spirits. It is also a word that shows the play of language and differance (see *poststructuralism*) because, according to Freud, the meaning of *'heimlich'* ('homely or canny') slip into those of its opposite, *'unheimlich'* (or 'uncanny'). See Sigmund Freud, 'The "Uncanny"', trans. James Strachey, Penguin Freud Library, vol. 14, ed. Albert Dickson (Harmondsworth, 1985), pp. 335–76.

unconscious   Psychoanalysis undermines the Cartesian *cogito* by drawing attention to the unconscious, the location of repressed desires and wishes, to which the subject has no access. Jacques Lacan complicated Freud's notion of the unconscious by linking it with the ideas of *structuralism* and arguing that it is 'structured like a language'.

voyeurism   This is a sexual perversion in which the subject gains pleasure from spying on the activities of others.

Suggestions for Further Reading

Adler, Kathleen and Marcia Pointon (eds), *The Body Imaged: The Human Form and Visual Culture Since the Renaissance* (Cambridge, 1993).

Barthes, Roland, *Image–Music–Text*, ed. and trans. Stephen Heath (London, 1977).

——, *Mythologies*, trans. Annette Lavers (London, 1972).

Baudrillard, Jean, *The Evil Demon of Images* (Australia, 1994).

Berger, John, *Ways of Seeing* (London, 1972).

Brennan, Teresa and Martin Jay (eds), *Vision in Context: Historical and Contemporary Perspectives on Sight* (London and New York, 1996).

Bryson, Norman, *Looking at the Overlooked: Four Essays on Still Life Painting* (London, 1990).

——, *Vision and Painting: The Logic of the Gaze* (London, 1983).

Burgin, Victor, *In/Different Spaces: Place and Memory in Visual Culture* (Berkeley, CA, 1996).

Burston, Paul and Colin Richardson (eds), *A Queer Romance: Lesbians, Gay Men and Popular Culture* (London and New York, 1995).

Crary, Jonathan, *Techniques of the Observer: On Vision and Modernity in the Nineteenth Century* (Cambridge, MA and London, 1990).

Debord, Guy, *The Society of the Spectacle* (New York, 1994).

Denzin, Norman K., *The Cinematic Society: The Voyeur's Gaze* (London, 1995).

Derrida, Jacques, *The Truth in Painting*, trans. Geoff Bennington and Ian McLeod (Chicago and London, 1987).

——, *Memoirs of the Blind: the Self-Portrait and Other Ruins*, trans. Pascale-Anne Brault and Michael Naas (Chicago and London, 1993).

Diawara, Manthia, *African Cinema: Politics and Culture* (Bloomington, IN, 1992).

Dixon, Wheeler Winston, *It Looks at You: The Returned Gaze of Cinema* (New York, 1995).

Doane, Mary Ann, *Femmes Fatales: Feminism, Film Theory, Psychoanalysis* (London and New York, 1991).

Dyer, Richard, *Now You See It: Studies on Lesbian and Gay Film* (New York and London, 1990).

Foster, Hal (ed.), *Vision and Visuality* (Seattle, 1988).

Foucault, Michael, *This Is Not A Pipe*, ed. and trans. James Harkness (Berkeley, CA and London, 1983).

Fried, Michael, *Realism, Writing, Disfiguration: On Thomas Eakins and Stephen Crane* (Chicago and London, 1987).

Friedberg, Anne, *Window Shopping: Cinema and the Postmodern* (Berkeley, CA and Oxford, 1993).

Gamman, Lorraine and Margaret Marshment (eds), *The Female Gaze: Women as Viewers of Popular Culture* (London, 1988).

Golden, Thelma (ed.), *Black Male: Representations of Masculinity in Contemporary American Art* (New York, 1995).

Gregory, Richard, L., *Mirrors in Mind* (New York, 1997).

Hall, Stuart (ed.), *Representation: Cultural Representations and Signifying Practices* (London, 1997).

Haraway, Donna J., 'Situated Knowledges: The Science Question in Feminism and the Privilege of Partial Perspective', *Simians, Cyborgs, and Women: The Reinvention of Nature* (London, 1991), pp. 183–201.

hooks, bell, *Reel to Real: Race, Sex, and Class at the Movies* (New York and London, 1996).

Horne, Peter and Reina Lewis (eds), *Outlooks: Lesbian and Gay Sexualities and Visual Cultures* (London and New York, 1996).

Irigaray, Luce, *Speculum of the Other Woman*, trans. Gillian C. Gill (Ithaca, NY, 1985).

Jay, Martin, *Downcast Eyes: The Denigration of Vision in Twentieth-Century French Thought* (Berkeley, CA and London, 1993).

Jenks, Chris (ed.), *Visual Culture* (London and New York, 1995).

Kaplan, E. Ann, *Looking for the Other: Feminism, Film, and the Imperial Gaze* (New York and London, 1997).

Kemp, Martin, *The Science of Art: Optical Themes in Western Art from Brunelleschi to Seurat* (New Haven, CT and London, 1990).

Lacan, Jacques, 'The Mirror Stage as formative of the function of the I as revealed in psychoanalytic experience', *Ecrits: A Selection*, trans. Alan Sheridan (London, 1977), pp. 1–7.

Lauretis, Teresa de, *Technologies of Gender: Essays on Theory, Film and Fiction* (London, 1989).

Lindberg, David C., *Theories of Vision from Al-kindi to Kepler* (Chicago, 1976).

Marling, Karal Ann, *As Seen on TV: the Visual Culture of Everyday Life in the 1950s* (Cambridge, MA and London, 1994).

Mayne, Judith, *Cinema and Spectatorship* (London and New York, 1993).

Melville, Stephen and Bill Readings (eds), *Vision and Textuality* (London, 1995).

Mercer, Kobena, *Mirage: Enigmas of Race, Difference and Desire* (London, 1995).

Mirzoeff, Nicholas (ed.), *The Visual Culture Reader* (London and New York, 1998).

Mitchell, W. J. T., *Iconology: Image, Text, Ideology* (Chicago and London, 1987).

Morrison, Toni and Claudia Brodsky Lacour (eds), *Birth of a Nation'hood: Gaze, Script and Spectacle in the O. J. Simpson Case* (London, 1997).

Mulvey, Laura, *Visual and Other Pleasures* (London, 1989).

Nead, Lynda, *The Female Nude: Art, Obscenity and Sexuality* (London and New York, 1992).

Perchuk, Andrew and Helaine Posner (eds), *The Masculine Masquerade: Masculinity and Representation* (Cambridge, MA and London, 1995)

Pollock, Griselda, *Vision and Difference: Femininity, Feminism and the Histories of Art* (London and New York, 1988).

Rabaté, Jean-Michel (ed.), *Writing the Image after Roland Barthes* (Philadelphia, 1997)

Robins, Kevin, *Into the Image: Culture and Politics in the Field of Vision* (London and New York, 1996).

Rose, Jacqueline, *Sexuality in the Field of Vision* (London, 1986).

Salecl, Renata and Slavoj Žižek (eds), *Gaze and Voice as Love Objects* (Durham, NC, 1996).

Stacey, Jackie, *Star-Gazing: Hollywood Cinema and Female Spectatorship* (London and New York, 1994).

Stafford, Barbara, *Good-looking: Essays on the Virtue of Images* (Cambridge, MA, 1996).

Taylor, Mark C. and Esa Saarinen, *Imagologies: Media Philosophy* (London and New York, 1994).

Tschumi, Bernard, *Architecture and Disjunction* (Cambridge, MA, and London, 1996).

Virilio, Paul, *The Vision Machine* (Bloomington, IN, 1994).

Žižek, Slavoj, *Enjoy Your Symptom! Jacques Lacan in Hollywood and Out* (London and New York, 1992).

Notes on Contributors

Roland Barthes (1915–80) was an influential French literary critic and semiotician. From 1976 he was Professor of Semiology at the Collège de France. His publications include *Mythologies* (1957), *Elements of Semiology* (1964), *S/Z* (1970), and *Camera Lucida* (1980).

Jean Baudrillard is best known as a theorist of the postmodern. He has written extensively on the visual arts as well as exhibiting his own photographic works. His books include *Simulations* (1981), *The Anti-Aesthetic: Essays on Postmodern Culture* (1983), *Seduction* (1991), *Simulacra and Simulation* (1995), and *Andy Warhol: Paintings 1960–1986* (1996).

Walter Benjamin (1892–1940) was born in Berlin and greatly influenced by Marxism. He wrote many essays and reviews and his books include *The Concept of Art Criticism in German Romanticism* (1920), *The Origin of German Tragedy* (1928) and *One-Way Street* (1928). Other major texts such as *A Berlin Childhood Around 1900* and *Charles Baudelaire: a Lyric Poet in the Era of High Capitalism* were published posthumously.

Norman Bryson is a professor in the Department of History of Art and Architecture at Harvard University. He edited *Calligram: Essays in New Art History from France* (1988), and is the author of *Word and Image: French Painting of the Ancien Régime* (1981), *Vision and Painting: The Logic of the Gaze* (1983) and *Looking at the Overlooked: Four Essays on Still Life Painting* (1990).

Rosalind Coward is a Senior Research Fellow at Nene College, Northampton. As well as writing a column for the *Guardian*, she is author of *Language and Materialism* (with John Ellis, 1977), *Patriarchal Precedents* (1983), *Female Desire* (1984), *Our Treacherous Hearts: Why Women Let Men Get Their Way* (1992), and *Sacred Cows: is Feminism Relevant to the New Millenium?* (1999).

Jacques Derrida is the French philosopher who formulated deconstruction. Among his many publications are *Of Grammatology* (1967), *The Truth in Painting* (1978), *The Post Card: From Socrates to Freud and Beyond* (1980), *Memoirs of the Blind: The Self-Portrait and Other Ruins* (1990), and *Specters of Marx* (1994).

Michel Foucault (1926–84) was a French philosopher and historian of ideas, who taught at the Collège de France. He is author of *Madness and Civilisation* (1961), *The Order of Things* (1966), *The Archaeology of Knowledge* (1969), *Discipline and Punish: The Birth of the Prison* (1975), and *The History of Sexuality* (vols 1, 2 and 3, 1976 and 1984).

Richard L. Gregory is a professor in the Department of Psychology, Bristol University. He is editor of several books on the psychology of seeing and author of *Eye and Brain* (1966), *Odd Perceptions* (1986), *Even Odder Perceptions* (1994), and *Mirrors in Mind* (1997).

bell hooks is a prolific writer and teaches at City College, New York, where she is Distinguished Professor of English. Her publications include *Ain't I a Woman: Black Women and Feminism* (1982), *Black Looks: Race and Representation* (1992), *Reel to Real: Race, Sex, and Class at the Movies* (1996), and *Bone Black: Memories of Girlhood* (1997).

Julia Kristeva is a practising psychoanalyst and teaches at the University of Paris VII. Many of her books have been translated into English, including *Desire in Language: A Semiotic Approach to Literature and Art* (1980), *Powers of Horror: An Essay on Abjection* (1982), *Revolution in Poetic Language* (1984), *Tales of Love* (1987), *Strangers to Ourselves* (1991), and *New Maladies of the Soul* (1995).

Jacques Lacan (1901–81) was a French psychoanalyst. His seminars, which began in 1953, were influential for many philosophers and critics, and attended by Barthes, Derrida and Kristeva. He is author of *The Four Fundamental Concepts of Psycho-Analysis* (1973), along with over 20 volumes that include the seminars themselves. A variety of Lacan's essays are collected in *Ecrits: A Selection* (trans. Alan Sheridan, 1977) and *Feminine Sexuality: Jacques Lacan and the Ecole Freudienne* (ed. Juliet Mitchell and Jacqueline Rose, trans. Jacqueline Rose, 1982).

Teresa de Lauretis is Professor of History of Consciousness at the University of California, Santa Cruz. She is co-editor (with Stephen Heath) of *The Cinematic Apparatus* (1980), and author of *Alice Doesn't: Feminism, Semiotics, Cinema* (1984), *Technologies of Gender: Essays on Theory, Film and Fiction* (1987), and *The Practice of Love: Lesbian Sexuality and Perverse Desire* (1994).

Kobena Mercer is Visiting Professor on the African Studies Program at New York University. He lectures and has written on African diasporic visual arts, and his books include *Black Film, British Cinema* (1988), *Welcome to the Jungle: New Positions in Black Cultural Studies* (1994), and *Mirage: Enigmas of Race, Difference and Desire* (1995).

Susan Sontag is a well-known American novelist, essayist and playwright. She has also written and directed four feature-length films. Her most recent books are *The Volcano Lover* (1992), a novel; *Alice in Bed* (1993), a play; and *In America* (1999), a novel. Among her non-fiction books are *On Photography* (1977), *Illness as Metaphor* (1978), and *Under the Sign of Saturn* (1980).

Jackie Stacey teaches sociology and contributes to the MA in Visual Culture at the Institute for Cultural Research at Lancaster University. She is author of *Star-Gazing: Hollywood Cinema and Female Spectatorship* (1994) and *Teratologies: A Cultural Study of Cancer* (1997). Stacey is an editor of *Screen* and co-edited *Screen Histories* with Annette Kuhn (1998).

Julia Thomas is a lecturer at the Centre for Critical and Cultural Theory, Cardiff University. She has published articles on painting and illustration and is author of *Victorian Narrative Painting* (2000). She is currently working on the relation between text, image and ideology in mid-nineteenth-century art.

Slavoj Žižek is a Researcher in the Institute of Sociology at the University of Ljubljana and a leading intellectual in the social movements of Eastern Europe. His books include *Looking Awry: An Introduction to Jacques Lacan through Popular Culture* (1991), *Enjoy Your Symptom: Jacques Lacan in Hollywood and Out* (1992), *The Metastases of Enjoyment: Six Essays on Woman and Causality*, and *Gaze and Voice as Love Objects* (1996), which he co-edited with Renata Salecl.

Index

237